FLOWERS AND REVOLUTION

A COLLECTION OF WRITINGS ON JEAN GENET

He is free who is unaware of his origin.
He is free who is born of an egg dropped in the woods.
He is free who is spat out from the sky and touches
the earth without a pang of gratitude.

Milan Kundera, *Life is Elsewhere*

The Jean Genie lives on his back
The Jean Genie loves chimney stacks
He's outrageous, he screams and he bawls
Jean Genie let yourself go!

David Bowie, 'The Jean Genie'

For Michael

FLOWERS AND REVOLUTION

A COLLECTION OF WRITINGS ON JEAN GENET

Fond Wishes

Jeremy

Edited by Barbara Read

with Ian Birchall

MIDDLESEX UNIVERSITY PRESS

First published in 1997 by Middlesex University Press.
Middlesex University Press is an imprint of Middlesex University Services Limited,
Bounds Green Road, London N11 2NQ, UK.

© 1997 Middlesex University Press (Middlesex University Services Limited)

A CIP record for this book is available from the British Library.

ISBN 1 898253 07 2

Cover illustration by Emily Booth
Design by Tim McPhee
Production in association with Book Production Consultants plc,
25–27 High Street, Chesterton, Cambridge CB4 IND, UK.
Typeset by Cambridge Photosetting Services

Typeset in Sabon
Printed and bound by Hillman Printers (Frome) Ltd

Contents

Acknowledgements

The editor would like to thank the following for their help in preparing this book: John Annette and Marion Locke of Middlesex University Press for their encouragement and enthusiasm for the project; Tracy Gardner and Guthrie Walker for help with the esoteric world of the word-processor; Patrick Riordan for office space; Ian Birchall, the assistant editor, for translations, transcribing the interviews, helping to compile the bibliography of Genet's texts and for compiling the index; Neil Bartlett, Jean-Paul Davidson, Nuria Moreno and Edmund White for taking time out from busy schedules to give interviews; and Stephen Barber, David Bradby and Albert Dichy in particular for their advice and support.

The editor and publishers are grateful for permission to use the following material:

Milan Kundera's *Life is Elsewhere* (by kind permission of Faber and Faber and the author).

'The Jean Genie' by David Bowie ©1973 Tintoretto Music/Chrysalis Music Ltd/ Mainman Music. All rights for Tintoretto Music administered for the World (ex USA and Canada) by RZO Music Ltd of 72 Marylebone Lane, London, W1M 5FF. All rights for Chrysalis Music Ltd administered for the World by Chrysalis Music Ltd. All rights for Mainman Music administered for the World by EMI Music Publishing Ltd. Lyrics used by kind permission of the publishers and David Bowie.

BBC 'Arena' interview with Jean Genet ©1991 the Estate of Jean Genet, c/o Rosica Colin Ltd (with thanks to Jean-Paul Davidson, Nigel Williams and Joanna Marston). This interview is published in French by Éditions Gallimard in Albert Dichy (ed.), *L'Ennemi déclaré: textes et entretiens* in Jean Genet, *Œuvres Complètes VI*, Paris 1991.

Neil Bartlett's 'The Uses of Monotony', the 1994 William Matthews Lecture © 1995 Birkbeck College, University of London (by kind permission of Neil Bartlett and Birkbeck College).

Allen Ginsberg's preface to Jean Genet's *May Day Speech* © 1970 City Lights Books (by kind permission of the late Allen Ginsberg and Peter Hale).

Jean Genet's letter to Allen Ginsberg © 1986 Bill Morgan and Bob Rosenthal (by kind permission of the late Allen Ginsberg and Joanna Marston, the Estate of Jean Genet, c/o Rosica Colin Ltd).

Stephen Barber's 'Genet and Artaud: The crematorium and the slaughterhouse' (rights to publish this article in Britain and elsewhere jointly held by Stephen Barber and by his literary agent, Deborah Rogers, 20 Powis Mews, London W11 1JN) © 1995 Stephen Barber and Deborah Rogers.

Albert Dichy's 1993 *Le Monde* article 'Aventures éditoriales', translated and reproduced here as 'Publishing Adventures' (by kind permission of Albert Dichy).

Every effort has been made to contact owners of copyright and to ensure the accuracy of references.

Contributors

Stephen Barber is the leading authority on Antonin Artaud and author of the biography *Antonin Artaud: Blows and Bombs* (Faber). Other recent books include *X-Position* (Schwarzkopf) and *Fragments of a European City* (Reaktion). He is also a musician and film-maker, and is currently writing a filmscript, *The Children of the Slaughterhouse*. His recent book, *Weapons of Liberation* (Faber), explores the work of Artaud and Genet in post-war Paris. He is currently working on a study of the writer Edmund White.

Neil Bartlett is a novelist and Artistic Director of the Lyric Theatre, Hammersmith, where he staged the English-language première of Genet's *Splendid's* in his own translation in 1995. His latest novel *Mr Clive and Mr Page* (Serpent's Tail) was shortlisted for the Whitbread prize.

Ian Birchall was formerly Senior Lecturer in French and History of Ideas at Middlesex University; he is now an independent writer. He has published extensively on Sartre, and is completing a book on Babeuf.

David Bradby is Professor of Drama and Theatre Studies in the University of London, a post he has held at Royal Holloway since 1988. He is author of several studies of contemporary European theatre, including *Modern French Drama 1940–1990* (Cambridge University Press), *The Theater of Michel Vinaver* (Michigan University Press) and (with David Williams) *Directors' Theatre* (Macmillan). His active involvement in theatre includes translating plays by Vinaver (*The Television Programme*) and Koltès (*Return to the Desert*) and directing plays by many modern European playwrights, including the first English-language production of Pirandello's *The Mountain Giants* in 1990. He is on the board of directors of the Orange Tree Theatre, Richmond.

Sharon Cornford obtained her MA in Modern French Literature on Genet's and Beckett's theatre from the University of Hull in 1990. She was awarded her PhD, for a thesis entitled 'Responses to the Human Condition in the Prose Fiction of Jean Genet', in 1995. She qualified as a counsellor and social worker in 1996 and now works as a NHS counsellor in Hull.

Jean-Paul Davidson is a freelance film-maker who worked on the BBC's 'Arena' programme. He has made over forty films including documentaries on Eugène Ionesco, the Dalai Llama and Gore Vidal. His most recent film is *The Grotesque*, adapted from the novel by Patrick McGrath.

Albert Dichy was born in Beirut in 1952. He is the director of the Jean Genet archives at IMEC, Paris (see below, p. *xi*) and editor of Genet in Gallimard's prestigious *La Pléiade* collection. He is the foremost authority on Genet, and is the author of books, articles and films on Genet but he has also found time to write on French Middle Eastern writers, his studies mainly focusing on philosophy, literature and ethnology.

Allen Ginsberg, American beat poet and friend of Jack Kerouac, William Burroughs, Neil Cassidy and others. His first book was *Howl and Other Poems* (1956). Other collections include *Kaddish and Other Poems* (1961), *The Gates of Wrath: Rhymed Poems, 1948–52* and *First Blues: Rags and Harmonium Songs 1971–74* (1975). He has won numerous awards and honours and his *Journals* were published in 1977. He knew Genet during Genet's visits to the United States from 1968 to 1970.

Mairéad Hanrahan lectures in French at University College Dublin and has published articles on Genet, Djuna Barnes and Hélène Cixous. Her book on Genet, *Lire Genet: une poétique de la différence*, will shortly be published by Presses de l'Université de Montréal.

Barbara Read has a background in European literature and culture. She is preparing a work on Lindsay Kemp and his company, as well as a study of the English 1960s folk revival and its influence on popular culture.

Jeremy Reed has published over forty books of poetry, fiction and non-fiction, and is noted for the visual dynamics of his poetry readings. Among his recent books are a novel about Antonin Artaud, *Chasing Black Rainbows* (Peter Owen), a study of the singer Marc Almond, *The Last Star* (Creation), and a new collection of poems, *Sweet Sister Lyric* (Enitharmon).

Angeliki Rosi holds an MA in Drama from the University of Essex and a PhD from the University of London. Her doctoral research demonstrated the development of a personal and subversive *parole* in the work of Genet, Adamov and Ionesco, using concepts drawn from Lacanian psychoanalysis. She lives in Greece and has a teaching assistantship at the University of Patras Drama Department.

Grace Russo Bullaro is attached to the English Department at the City University of New York, Lehman College where she teaches courses on gender in film and literature as well as composition; in the Foreign Language Department at Nassau Community College she teaches French and Italian. She has written and published on gender issues in the novels of DH Lawrence, on gender and politics in the films of Lina Wertmuller and, of course, on Jean Genet. She is at present working on a book on Wertmuller's major films of the 1970s.

Philip Thody is Emeritus Professor at the University of Leeds. In 1968 he published the first book in English on Genet, *Jean Genet: A Study of his Novels and Plays* (Hamish Hamilton), which was published simultaneously with Richard Coe's *The Vision of Jean Genet* (Peter Owen). Both these works remain important texts for all Genet scholars. He maintains he is intensely ordinary, lives in a semi-detached house, is married, plays golf, votes Conservative, dresses and looks like a suburban bank manager, and is a grandfatherly figure. In fact, the opposite in every way to the people about whom he has written, who include Sartre, Camus and Anouilh.

Edmund White is the author of the definitive biography *Genet* (Chatto and Windus, 1993) and is a distinguished writer and critic. His other titles include *A Boy's Own Story* (Picador, 1983) and *The Beautiful Room is Empty* (Picador, 1988). He lives in Paris, where he has recently completed his latest novel, *The Farewell Symphony* (Chatto and Windus).

The Genet Archive at the Institut Mémoires de l'Édition Contemporaine (IMEC)

With the support of the publisher Marc Barbezat, and benefiting from contributions and items on loan from many of those who were close to Genet, the Genet archive at IMEC provides direct access to extensive documentation about the writer: first editions of his works, new and foreign editions, articles in journals, audio and visual recordings, press cuttings, thematic and iconographic collections, critical works, university theses, etc.

The archive also contains a large number of manuscripts, unpublished texts (notably the various versions of all Genet's film scripts) and correspondence, which can be consulted only with prior permission in accordance with current legislation.

A policy of actively encouraging research based on the archive has allowed IMEC to publish two key texts on the author (*Jean Genet, essai de chronologie* and *La Bataille des Paravents*), to organise several conferences, notably those held at Parma and at the Odéon theatre in Paris, and to hold a major exhibition (in October 1992 at the Institut du Monde Arabe in Paris) tracing Jean Genet's literary and political journey.

Institut Mémoires de l'Édition Contemporaine

IMEC was established in 1988 and holds, in addition to the Genet collection, the archives of Albert Camus, Louis-Ferdinand Céline, Marguerite Duras, Hervé Guibert, Pierre Guyotat, Bernard-Marie Koltès and the Jérôme Linden (director, Éditions Minuit) Samuel Beckett archives which constitute all of Beckett's correspondence with publishers worldwide. It also houses the archives of the main French publishers Hachette, Flamarion, Gallimard, La Table Ronde and Jean Paulhan, together with those of John Calder and archives of press dossiers and the history of literary publishing in the twentieth century. In all it holds about 150 archives of writers and publishers.

IMEC contains only archives belonging to private estates, its purpose being to make these archives available to the public. It is the first institution of its kind in the world; an institute based on the IMEC model is due to open in Germany.

IMEC's president is Christian Bourgois, one of France's leading publishers, whose archives are also held at the institute. Its administrative director is Olivier Corpet and Albert Dichy is academic director.

After the Bibliothèque Nationale, IMEC is the most important library for French literature in France. A large annexe is currently being set up in an abbey near Caen in Normandy. When this annexe opens in 1999, it will become one of the major cultural centres in France.

(Institut Mémoires de l'Édition Contemporaine, 25, rue de Lille, 75007 Paris)

Editor's Note

In this book Genet's works are referred to by both their French and English titles. To avoid confusion a list of his principal works is given here with both their original titles and the titles of the standard English translations. Publication details are given in the bibliography on pp. 201–205.

NOVELS
Journal du Voleur (The Thief's Journal)
Miracle de la Rose (Miracle of the Rose)
Notre-Dame-des-Fleurs (Our Lady of the Flowers)
Pompes funèbres (Funeral Rites)
Querelle de Brest (Querelle of Brest)

PLAYS
Le Balcon (The Balcony)
Les Bonnes (The Maids)
Haute surveillance (Deathwatch)
Les Nègres (The Blacks)
Les Paravents (The Screens)
Splendid's

FILM
Un Chant d'Amour (A Song of Love)

POEMS
Un Chant d'Amour (A Song of Love)
Le Condamné à Mort (The Man Condemned to Death)
L'Enfant criminel (The Criminal Child)
Le Pêcheur du Suquet (The Fisherman of Suquet)

OTHER WORKS
'Adame Miroir (ballet)
L'Atelier d'Alberto Giacometti (The Studio of Alberto Giacometti)
Un Captif amoureux (Prisoner of Love)
Ce qui est resté d'un Rembrandt déchiré en petits carrés ... (What remains of a Rembrandt torn into little squares ...)
L'Ennemi déclaré: textes et entretiens (The Declared Enemy: texts and interviews)
L'Étrange mot d' ... (The Strange Word 'Urb')
Fragments ... et autres textes (Fragments ... and other texts)
Le Funambule (The High-Wire Artist)
Lettres à Roger Blin (Letters to Roger Blin)
May Day Speech
Quatre Heures à Chatila (Four Hours in Shatila)

Most of Genet's unpublished letters, film scripts, plays, poems and other texts are held in the Genet archive at IMEC.

CHAPTER 1

Introduction

Barbara Read

'JEAN GENET'S EYE embarrasses and disturbs you. He's right and the rest of the world is wrong. But what's to be done?' So wrote Cocteau after reading the manuscript of *Our Lady of the Flowers*.[1] Jean Genet's eye is an astonishing eye looking out of the air (to paraphrase one of the American poet Kenneth Patchen's titles),[2] challenging our outworn modes of seeing and daring us to transgress the social mechanisms that control our perception and values. He has constantly railed against society in an effort to make it see through its own deceptions. And he has done this consistently throughout all the phases of his work.

This is the first anthology in English on Jean Genet since the 1979 *Twentieth Century Views* collection edited by Peter Brooks and Joseph Halpern.[3] Much has changed in our understanding of Genet since that time, largely due to the efforts of Albert Dichy, Genet's archivist, who has spent many years researching, collecting and documenting Genet's work at the Institut Mémoires de l'Édition Contemporaine in Paris, and also those of Edmund White, who published the definitive biography of Genet in 1993,[4] a watershed in Genet scholarship and a work which will now serve as a reference point for all subsequent writing on Genet. Due to the work of these two men, the traditional – if one can ever use such a term in relation to Genet – view of Genet as scandalous, shocking, deviant and petulantly subversive has had to be challenged. Not that such a view does not contain elements of truth, but it needs to be placed within a much wider perspective, a perspective that will show Genet as more politically aware and committed than had commonly been thought, and will also highlight the inter-disciplinary and cross-cultural elements of his work.

This collection addresses both the unity and immense diversity of Genet's work and interests and indicates how his concerns traverse the boundaries of many key issues taken up by contemporary theoretical debates. Genet, in his work and through his own experience, interrogated both institutions and socio-cultural discourses such as the penal system, gender and homosexuality, language and aesthetics, race and post-colonialism; all these concerns are absorbed within a central unifying theme focusing on the need to challenge and subvert conventional ways of apprehending and negotiating society and our experience within it.

Appearing a decade after the death of Genet, this book points up his continuing legacy across several cultural genres: drama, the novel, poetry, political writing and criticism. It also illustrates how the areas of sexuality, aesthetics and politics are all interrelated in Genet's work and how he encountered and was taken up by a number of important twentieth-century writers such as Artaud, Ginsberg and Sartre, as well as inspiring icons of popular culture, David Bowie and Patti Smith, and theatrical innovator Lindsay Kemp. The collection benefits from contributions by important writers and thinkers in the field and also includes the first English publication of the BBC 'Arena' interview with Genet, which was originally broadcast in November 1985, just months before he died.

The question of being and identity in Genet's work

Any discussion of Genet's work inevitably interrogates the territory of being and identity. In other words (and flying in the face of the problematic relationship between biography and narrative voice) we nevertheless find ourselves puzzling over the question: 'Who *was* Jean Genet, the writer and the man?' At one point during the BBC 'Arena' interview,[5] the following exchange takes place between Nigel Williams and Genet:

> **NW:** Let's suppose we meet the writer Jean Genet himself. Is it the real Genet we are meeting?
>
> **JG:** Is there a false one going around? Is there a false Genet at large? Am I the real one? You ask me if I am the real one. So where is the false one?
>
> **NW:** Yes, I understand.
>
> **JG:** Perhaps after all I am an impostor who has never written a book. Perhaps I am a false Genet, as you say.

Genet was ever determined to play the impostor of himself, and engaged in a continual process of self-mythologisation whilst constantly subverting the basis upon which any notion of self or identity might be built. He created a multitude of vanishing and reappearing 'selves' like the characters in some of his plays, and as a biographical subject he is as slippery as quicksilver. Nevertheless the 'truth' of Genet's life is more fascinating than any of the myths. He was orphaned at seven months and grew up in a foster-family in the Morvan region of France. He received no formal education beyond the age of thirteen and yet grew up to be one of France's most elegant twentieth-century writers. Much of his youth and adulthood was spent travelling through the countries of Europe, the Middle East and North Africa and spending frequent, though brief, periods in European prisons. It was in prison that he began to write, initially in secret and without any readership in mind, and these early, furtive explorations of his imagination resulted in *Our Lady of the Flowers*, his first novel, published in 1943. Writing also led to Genet eventually receiving a state pardon for a life sentence in 1949 from President Vincent Auriol when a petition was raised by a number of writers led by Sartre and Cocteau, insisting that this pardon be granted on the grounds that Genet was a gifted writer. I will not recount any more details of Genet's life here, not least because these have been set down at length by Edmund White in his biography, *Genet*; rather I will address some of the more interesting philosophical questions that Genet raises. Like Antonin Artaud, Genet interrogates at the margins of philosophy (and it is no coincidence that both these writers have been the subject of some of the most notable philosophers of this century).[6]

Truth, language, aesthetics and the wound

To begin with the problematic term 'truth'. Truth for Genet is a quality synonymous with beauty. Speaking of his account of the Sabra and Shatila massacres of September 1982, 'Four Hours in Shatila', he said that his text was beautiful because it was true and that what is true is always beautiful. But beauty for Genet is not only synonymous with truth but also with the idea of the 'wound'. In his essay 'The Studio of Alberto Giacometti'[7] (Genet was a subject for Giacometti, 1954–5)[8] and in a language that is almost mystical in its tone, he is explicit about this relationship between beauty, the wound and the necessity of exposing this secret wound in order that its possessor may become more fully aware of his or her being:

> Beauty has no other origin than the singular wound, different in every case, hidden or visible, which each man bears within himself, which he preserves, and into which he withdraws when he would quit the world for a temporary but authentic solitude … Giacometti's art seems to me determined to discover this secret wound in each being and even in each thing, in order for it to illuminate them.[9]

This project which Genet attributes to Giacometti's art – and which has resonances with some of the chief aims of Antonin Artaud's Theatre of Cruelty – may also be seen as Genet's own project. In the earlier works this project functions chiefly in relation to himself, and in the later works in relation to society. In this latter sense the question of beauty and the wound is most noticeably present in his two main essays on the Palestinians and in *Prisoner of Love*, all of which focus on the 'wounds' of a dispossessed people engaged in a struggle to establish an identity and a homeland and celebrate the beauty of a revolution that aims at freedom – at the rediscovery of a lost freedom.[10]

Genet is also concerned with the relationship between language and truth. Indeed, Genet has a very special relationship to language, a fact brought out in a number of pieces in this collection (most notably by Mairéad Hanrahan and Neil Bartlett). Language for Genet is something that is more than just a symbolic system acting as a mediating and representational code. It is also a linguistic *material* and has as much substance as the paint, plaster and bronze employed by Giacometti. Thus as a *writer* Genet is concerned with language as a symbolic system but as a *poet* (and in keeping with Sartre's assertion that for the poet words are 'natural things which sprout naturally upon the earth like grass and trees'[11]) he is concerned with its materiality, with its potential to create new worlds from symbols and images. (For more on Genet's use of poetic language see Jeremy Reed's essay, Chapter 9 of this collection, 'Gender in Genet's Poetry'.) As the wound which gives birth to beauty must be uncovered by the artist, so the poet must use words, images and symbols which take on the power of a magical incantation, to reveal the ideological underpinning of a society and culture in order to confront and subvert it. Words are imbued with power for Genet, they have the potential of a real force for change and revolution by bringing about a renewal in our conscious apprehension of and orientation towards the world at social, cultural and political levels.

In his essay 'The Palestinians' Genet warns of the power of language to delude and advocates a revolution that will free language from lies, deceptions and a contaminating morality that uses words to express condemnations. He writes that

> language becomes more beautiful to the extent that there is an exact correspondence between facts on the one hand and the expression of those facts on the other.[12]

Naturally there is a difficulty here since it could be argued that no exact equation exists between truth and facts; in other words, could a fact ever have the potential to reflect a singular and transparent truth? And there is a second difficulty in that language is deficient as a means of expressing reality. I draw particular attention to these philosophical problems because they are in some ways central to Genet's project and remain pertinent throughout all his phases as a writer. Truth, falsity, pretext, language and reading (as in the most meaningful orientation towards a work), these are as much the main concerns of Genet's work as are the themes of power and submission, violence and oppression, revolution and freedom, ritual and transformation, reality and dream.

Reading, writing fiction, and life as legend

Reading and writing became a central motif for Genet early on his life. As Edmund White tells us, Genet received no formal education beyond the age of thirteen and for many years was unable to string a sentence together without the aid of a dictionary and a grammar. However, he developed into a writer of such grace, fluency and skill that Cocteau described him as 'the greatest writer of the modern era'.

Life for Genet is the pretext for reading, for language and for poetry. In *The Thief's Journal* he tells us:

> My life must be a legend, in other words, legible, and the reading of it must give birth to a certain new emotion which I call poetry. I am no longer anything, only a pretext.[13]

Here Genet employs a subtle play on words, 'legend' deriving from the Latin *legere* meaning 'to read', a meaning which he signals in his subsequent use of the adjective 'legible' (also having its origin in the Latin term *legere*). Thus Genet's life, by his own prescription, is a life to be written and read, a life which must engender poetry. And the 'truth' of this life will of necessity be a poetic one. It will also be bound up with relations of power, acting as a resistance to existing power structures while using its own power to subvert them. Michel Foucault, in his own analysis of truth and power, drew the conclusion that truth could/should not be separated from power, but rather inhabit it. And in this project truth will employ fictions to further its aims.

> It seems plausible to me to make fictions operate within truth, to introduce truth-effects within a fictional discourse, and in some way to make discourse arouse, 'fabricate' something which does not yet exist, thus to fiction something. One 'fictions' history starting from a political reality that renders it true, one 'fictions' a politics that does not yet exist starting from a historical truth.[14]

Power enters into the space where something 'does not yet exist' and provides the impetus for generation.

This fragile boundary between truth and fiction is pointed up by Jung:

> Thus it is that I have now undertaken ... to tell my personal myth. I can only ... 'tell stories'. Whether or not the stories are 'true' is not the problem. The only question is whether what I tell is *my* fable, *my* truth.[15]

In the same way, Genet's writing, indeed his whole *œuvre*, is a poetic transcription of *his* fable, *his* truth.[16]

In any case, no text or author can be approached from the standpoint of expecting a yield of objective truths and facts, either in relation to the work or the life. As Hans-Georg Gadamer asserts in his philosophical hermeneutics,[17] it is impossible to construct a coherent theoretical explanation or absolute meaning in relation to either an author or a text. So, ultimately, any questions concerning truth and authenticity in relation to a writer's life, even their work, are essentially meaningless. Every phenomenon is conditioned and constrained by its relative historical and cultural condition. Thus we can only ever employ relative conceptual frameworks with which to assess writers, texts, things in the world, experiences, even ourselves.

With the above in mind, all that can be said of Genet is delimited by our own specific cultural and historical perspective. And this is as true of what I write here as it is of the other contributions in this collection. However, this does not mean that we are unable to arrive at more or less proximate truths and it is hoped that such a project will be achieved with this anthology.

Truth as solitude, speech as the lie

Genet maintained that he could only be completely truthful when he was alone. Even writing called forth the lie and he said on a number of occasions[18] that everything he wrote was 'against himself'. This writing 'against himself' occurs whenever 'poetry fails to penetrate' the writing.[19] If we use the equation poetry equals beauty equals truth, then the writing 'against himself' is a writing which lacks truth, the truth of Jean Genet.[20] In his interview with Hubert Fichte in *The New Review* he says:

> Truth has nothing to do with confessions, nothing to do with dialogues, I'm talking about my truth … I can say nothing to anyone except lies. If I'm alone I may speak a little truth. If I'm with someone, what I say is never completely accurate, I lie.[21]

And when questioned further about this statement in a later interview with Rüdiger Wischenbart, Genet replied:

> To an extent I was joking, but at a deeper level it's what I feel. I am true only with myself. As soon as I speak, I am betrayed by the situation, I am betrayed by the person who is listening to me, simply as a function of communication. *I am betrayed by my choice of words.*[22]

Genet struggles with the limitations implied by choosing words – *this* word and not *that* or *those* words. He also suffers here from the betrayal of mystery that framing thoughts, feeling states and experiences within language inevitably implies. Truth, as in rational truth, is somehow superficial and instead of revealing experience can actually lie about it. Susan Sontag, in her 1963 essay on Simone Weil (which makes reference to Genet and in the less specific sections of the text could just as easily relate to him as to Weil), echoes this theme when she writes:

> In the respect we pay to such lives we acknowledge the presence of mystery in the world – and mystery is just what a secure possession of the truth, an objective truth, denies.[23]

Betrayal and revolt as assertion of identity

The question of betrayal looms large in Genet's work, in discussions about the work and, inevitably and almost routinely, about the man himself. Edward Said, in his insightful essay 'On Jean Genet's Late Works', locates this need to betray, not only as a revengeful response to a society which had treated him as a pariah, but more importantly within a more encompassing and urgent need to maintain an unstable, creative identity:

> For Genet, to betray is to assert that 'exceptional' identity foisted unjustly on him by a society that has found him to be a guilty criminal, but it is also to assert his power to elude any attempts to rehabilitate or reclaim him. Better the destabilising effects of a permanent will to betray, always keeping him one step out of everyone's reach, than a permanent identity as a crook who can be punished or forgiven by others.[24]

To betray enables Genet to retain an exceptional identity and also facilitates his poetic sensibility. Further, as Said also points out, Genet's status as an outcast, which his acts of betrayal both reflect and guarantee, is that of the individual who refuses to be confined by everyday social values and norms, thus is not simply the status of someone who has been cast out but of someone who has fashioned his own identity, set of values, codes of practice. And those whose causes he championed – most notably the Black Panthers and the Palestinians – likewise had to create their own identities and assert their own cultural and social values against a world which held these values and identities to be inferior. They had to carry out a necessary revolt. In the interview with Rüdiger Wischenbart, Genet insisted that 'the revolt of each man is necessary'[25] because as Said asserts

> identity is the process by which the stronger culture, and the more developed society, imposes itself violently upon those who, by the same identity process, are decreed to be a lesser people.[26]

Oppression is achieved by the aggressor through the assertion of images which deprive individuals of their freedom.[27] Thus these images must be challenged by acts of revolt.[28]

In his solidarity with the oppressed and criminalised identities cast out by Western society, Genet made the reverse step to the imperialist as 'he traversed the space from the metropolitan centre to the colony'.[29]

However, Genet's interest in the Palestinians may be based on more than just the fact that they exemplified his concern for a people colonised and dispossessed. Given Genet's deep interest in culture and its potential as an indicator of identity, of heritage and also as a means to recreate and rediscover identity, the Palestinians would particularly appeal to him since they are located in a geographical area that, as Edward Said comments, 'is more saturated in religious, historical and cultural significance than any place on earth'.[30]

From power to freedom through revolution

There are two main trajectories in Genet's œuvre; the first is a slow and determined progression from a focus on games of power and submission to a celebration of beauty and freedom (and within this trajectory is also included the trajectory from crime/imprisonment to writing/freedom),[31] the latter precluding the need for power. As he wrote of the *fedayeen* in 'Four Hours in Shatila', 'they didn't want power; they had freedom'.[32]

But this must be a freedom that remains a freedom which is realised through *acts* and not through institutions. Genet said in the aforementioned interview with Rüdiger Wischenbart that he did not know if he could support a Palestine that was institutionally and territorially satisfied.[33] For the Palestinians, as for most people in a state of revolt, existence is affirmed through rebellion. They exist without a nation, without a territory but they continue to exist through their *acts*. Even though their ultimate goal is the establishment of a national territory, what is important is that in pursuing this aim 'they continue to have the freedom to exist precisely through their acts'. And it is this freedom with all its potential for creativity that Genet values and celebrates rather than the attainment of the goals of the revolution. In the same way there is a paradoxical sense in which prison for Genet also represented a form of freedom – a freedom to dream – and the attainment of freedom from prison also entailed a *loss* of the freedom to dream. The period leading from his release from prison up to his support of the revolutionary movements of the Black Panthers and the Palestinians was a kind of limbo for Genet. The world of the prison represents the world of the dream with all its potential for freedom, and the world of the revolutionaries enables Genet to find himself in the real world, a world which has its own special discipline; but the world in-between is a kind of twilight world that has neither the reality of the dream nor the impact of the real world. Further, the movement from the dream to the real necessitates an acceptance of limitation and a movement away from writing towards action:

Dreams are part of reality. But we also know that one can act on dreams in a practically unlimited fashion. One can not act on the real in an unlimited fashion. A different discipline is needed, which is not a grammatical discipline.[34]

The word as violence

This action may be associated with violence, with what Antonin Artaud referred to when he asserted that 'everything that acts is a cruelty'.[35] For Genet, as for Artaud, there is an important distinction between brutality and violence.[36] Brutality involves gratuitously hurting another for fun or for the sake of a whim, whereas violence involves restraining another/others for the sake of a greater good, and to allow for a change in the accepted – but outworn – order to take place. In 'The Palestinians', Genet wrote:

> Violence is essential. By violence I mean effort aimed at achieving a rupture with a pattern of withdrawal that prevents living: the bursting open of buds is violence; the growth of grains of wheat when their shoots pierce the surface of the earth is also violence. If the press ... are against violence, it is because ... they deliberately confuse it with coarseness. But coarseness is in fact inconsistent with violence in the sense that it derives from an action, or a group of actions, restricted to themselves, whereas violence is the search – easy or otherwise – undertaken by a new generation.[37]

This question of violence in relation to necessary social and political change has never been more important than in these last ten years following Genet's death. This last decade has seen extreme nationalistic violence in Eastern Europe, Africa and elsewhere, fundamentalist violence in Algeria and imperialist violence in the Gulf. There is also the long history of violence in Northern Ireland and the continuing brutal occupation of Tibet and the exile of its religious and cultural leaders and their followers. Some positive changes have occurred, as in South Africa, but many conflicts are still in need of resolution as nations seek the means to establish a stronger national and cultural identity according to their own standards and definitions, and not those of the Western superpowers.

Violence is also related to language, as language constitutes the gap between thought and being, subject and object, self and other. And within this gap a potential for transgression and disruption as well as the more deceiving and less creative process of naming and codifying, occurs. As Edward Said writes:

> Genet always wants to transform [language] from a force for identity and statement into a transgressive, disruptive, and perhaps even consciously evil mode of betrayal.[38]

Perhaps all language involves a betrayal of some kind and perhaps the gap constituted by language can only be bridged by love or *agape* as a potential dissolver of difference. One could just as easily oppose Hegel's assertion that 'every consciousness seeks the death of the other' with the less brutal and less devouring assertion, 'every consciousness seeks unity/union with the other/s'.

From eros *to* agape

This brings me to the second trajectory in Genet's work, which might be seen as a movement from *eros* to *agape*, from a desiring of the other which inevitably involves a mutually destructive power-play of the two parties to a genuine compassion and love for another/others.

This trajectory begins with *Our Lady of the Flowers* and ends with *Prisoner of Love*. The title 'Our Lady of the Flowers' may be read as a signifier for both Genet himself (his feminised self) and for his mother. *Genet* is both the French for 'broomflower' and the name of Genet's mother.[39] Thus we have an association between the name of the mother, the feminised Genet, prison and homosexuality (through the setting and theme of the novel) and a lack of completion of mourning – as one version of homosexuality may originate in the unmourned relationship with the mother. Thus we may read *Our Lady of the Flowers* as a novel inspired by Genet's unrequited love for his mother and his unmourned loss of his mother. Further we might perceive the ghost of Genet's unknown mother hanging over all his novels (and most of the drama) of failed relationships with their obligatory ingredients of betrayal, power-play, deception, narcissism/ onanism and, consequent upon all this, lack of consummation.

Yet in the last two of Genet's major plays, *The Blacks* and *The Screens*, we have the image of the unity of the couple. At the end of the former the two main protagonists are searching for their own language to express their love for one another, and the latter ends with the reconciliation between Saïd and his mother in the realm of nothingness. Finally, in *Prisoner of Love* we find again the reunion of the mother and son (Hamza) but this time in life, not in death. The spiritual quality of the love between Hamza and his mother is brought out by Edmund White in his introduction to the English translation of *Prisoner of Love*:

> In *Prisoner of Love* the tension between the Romantic cult of the unique individual and the Christian faith in spiritual equality is reconciled in the central quest of the book ... In Genet's mind the mother and son become reworked as emblems of the pietà.[40]

In his story of the search for Hamza, as Leila Shahid points out, Genet is finally able to come full circle, pick up the missing threads from his early life and exorcise the need for revenge against a world (and more importantly, a mother) who had abandoned him to orphanhood. Because in writing about Hamza and his mother, as he himself is facing death, he can now finally 'understand what the absence of a mother had meant for him'.[41]

Writing for Genet had always been linked to childhood, as is clear from his comments in the Wischenbart interview:

> The act of writing is always to speak of one's childhood. It's always nostalgic. In any case, it's true of my writing, and modern writing, principally.[42]

Hence to a man for whom writing had been dominated by ghosts from childhood, it is writing itself that finally facilitates the means to exorcise those ghosts and also enables the birth of transparency and truth in an act of love; for, as Leila Shahid makes clear in her interview with Jérôme Hankins, *Prisoner of Love* is Genet's gift to his readers:

> As he faced death, at the moment when the circle was completed, he suddenly wanted to share with the only people he loved, his readers. He was prepared to share the truth with them and to say everything he had been hiding for seventy years. And all this he tells us as he weaves his life.[43]

Genet's legacy

It is now more than ten years since Genet's death and his legacy and his power to influence remain as strong as ever. Genet is one of the few twentieth-century European writers to have a wide-ranging and continuous influence; this is due partly to the fact that he worked across a range of media, including poetry, prose, theatre, cinema, criticism and political commentary, and also because, like Artaud, he has inspired writers, artists and thinkers across multiplicitous cultural discourses, all of which are still in currency today.[44]

Genet has inspired a number of important figures in post-war France, most notably Sartre, whose introduction to Genet's collected works became the monumental *Saint Genet, Actor and Martyr*, and Genet had said that Derrida's *Glas* was the only critical text that had really added anything to his work.[45] Jacques Lacan wrote on the case of the Papin sisters,[46] whose act of murder formed the basis for Genet's play *The Maids*. Genet has also prompted debates around the issues of gender and sexuality,[47] penal reform[48] and post-colonial discourse.[49]

In the art world he was a great inspiration to the Swiss-born sculptor Alberto Giacometti and Genet's essay *The Studio of Alberto Giacometti*[50] remained the sculptor's preferred commentary on his work.

In cinema Genet wrote and directed *Un Chant d'Amour* (1950), produced by Nico Papatakis, and has exercised a far-reaching influence on other film-makers,[51] including Rainer Werner Fassbinder who directed the adaptation of *Querelle* in 1982. Genetian elements are evident in contemporary cinema, in the work of John Maybury, one of Britain's foremost experimental film-makers, and of Cerith Wyn Evans, Derek Jarman and Todd Haynes.

Genet has also been cited as an inspiration for several notable popular cultural icons, not least Patti Smith and David Bowie, and the extraordinary director, mime artist and theatrical innovator Lindsay Kemp. Bowie was first introduced to Genet's work during a period when he was involved with Kemp's mime company in the early 1970s, and his song 'The Jean Genie' was partly inspired by Genet.[52]

Lindsay Kemp not only engaged with Genet, but also has probably been most responsible for introducing him to a wider audience, particularly through his revolutionary mime *Flowers ... a pantomime for Jean Genet*, which was based on *Our Lady of the Flowers* and received widespread critical acclaim. After seeing its opening performance in 1974 at the Regent Theatre, London, *The Times*' critic Harold Hobson was prompted to describe Kemp as the only director and performer who truly understood Genet.

One of the finest works to have been inspired by Genet, *Flowers* is a masterpiece in its own right and has had in turn a tremendous effect on many people. Derek Jarman, for instance, testified to the lasting impact that seeing this piece was to have on his own work:

> I first saw Lindsay Kemp in the early seventies giving a performance of *Flowers*. It had quite an effect on me at the time ... The main thing that I took away with me ... was these extremely strong visual images which are still with me today. There quite clearly is Lindsay twirling and swirling around and around like a magical dervish.[53]

Genet's blurring of the boundaries between fantasy and reality, between the dream and lived experience, between the theatre and life all find echoes in Kemp's work and the life of his company.

The same dislocation of reality that is found in Genet's work (Irma, for example, at the close of *The Balcony*, tells the audience that they must now 'go home, where everything ... will be falser than here'[54]) is one of the hallmarks of Kemp's theatre – a theatre of dream, spectacle, magical incantation and voluptuous imagery and gesture. One leaves these performances wondering whether the world of the imagination is not more truly vital than the mundane world outside, which seems to be in need of the animation of the dream to yield its full store of possibilities. This animation is one of the forces which drive Kemp's company, where life and the theatre have no boundaries; the company is held together by bonds of mutual inspiration. And also by the omnipotent presence of Kemp himself.[55]

Elements of the religious and the profane, the theatre as the place wherein the religious rite takes place – notable features of Genet's theatrical enterprise[56] – are also present in Kemp's theatre. The actor in Kemp's company is a hierophant who reveals to the spectator the hidden depths which lie behind reality:

> In the indelible fact of the performer's own flesh and blood and the necessary precision of his physical control he will always have one foot in the 'real' world, but with his ability to transform himself and *become* the image he represents he may draw the spectator into the magical position of existing in two worlds …[57]

If Genet was seen as the *enfant terrible* of twentieth-century French literature, Lindsay Kemp has been cast in a similar role by the British theatrical establishment, and, while he is celebrated on the continent as a 'maestro', has yet to receive in Britain the status his unquestionable contribution to theatre and performance deserves.

The American singer, poet and icon for the punk generation Patti Smith has always been drawn to the symbolism of French poets and writers and has been much affected by Genet, as well as Artaud and Rimbaud. The sleeve of her 1979 album *Wave* carries the lines from Genet's poem *The Man Condemned to Death*:

> Oh go through the walls; if you must, walk on the ledges
> Of roofs, of oceans; cover yourself with light;
> Use menace, use prayer …
>
> My sleepers will flee toward another America[58]

In a recent interview with the *Evening Standard*[59] about her involvement in the Institute of Contemporary Arts' conference 'Incarcerated with Artaud and Genet',[60] Smith cites Genet as one of her 'main inspirations and guides'. She had read him as a teenager and thought his language 'beautiful and intoxicating'. Although she is better known for her work as a rock singer and musician, Patti Smith has been publishing collections of writings since the early 1970s (and has written a number of unpublished poems specifically influenced by Genet), and it was in fact poetry that led her to the world of rock'n'roll.[61]

Commenting on her collection *Babel*, which is characterised by a merging of rock'n'roll and poetry, Jonathan Cott wrote in the *New York Times Book Review*:

> By adopting a paradoxical theatrical stance – one that confuses male and female roles and combines the acoustic magic of Rimbaud and the Ronettes – Patti Smith has been able to develop, explore and create a certain shamanistic presence that has eluded many aspiring rock-and-roll seers and heroes … Out of the 'realm of dreams and of fever' and in the 'forbidden cinema' of her naturally hallucinating mind, Patti Smith has also given us some wonderful passages.[62]

Her first substantial collection after *Babel* was *Woolgathering* (1992), a finely
honed collection of autobiographical prose poems that reflect on significant
childhood scenes and experiences through the filter of the consciousness of a
mature, adult artist. More recently she has published *The Coral Sea*, sixteen
prose poems dedicated to the memory of her friend and one-time collaborator,
the photographer Robert Mapplethorpe. All these texts show Patti Smith to be
a mature poet deserving of critical attention.

Speaking on Genet at the ICA conference,[63] Patti Smith insisted that the
internal pressure that produced a writer like Genet had much less to do with
environment and circumstance and much more to do with the mysteries of
inspiration, which are ultimately beyond analysis and explication:

> Genet was obviously a man who was so gifted and born with a certain calling. We
> don't know who his father was, we don't know, genetically, where his gifts came
> from; we know very little about his mother, and so we can't trace certain things.
> So they came from within him ...
> ... And the thing with Genet that tormented him most was that he never really
> knew where his gifts came from. One day he's writing a letter on this beautiful
> sheet of paper, and instead of just writing 'I'm in prison in Spain; wish you were
> here', he starts elaborating about the texture of this white paper, and all of a
> sudden he's really writing, and he realises he knows how to write.[64]

This concern with the imagery produced by textures is something Smith shares
with Genet, and the merging of the sensuous and the imaginary, which she has
now refined to a high degree, is what constitutes the main impact of her art. As
in her trenchantly powerful rock performances, her written work frequently
involves a juxtaposition of opposing elements: vulnerability and strength,
innocence and knowing, mysticism and realism, viscerality and romanticism.
The objects of her imagination are described with such vividness that they can
become almost tactile to her readers. Here we have romanticism at the raw edge.
Sometimes she is the poet-warrior who hurls images at her reader and forces him
or her to adopt a completely new framework of perception. At other times she
is the seductress who beckons from a world of raw and fragile beauty. Hers is a
fierce heart and she refuses to make concessions to literary fashions or critical
sensibilities, allowing her to retain an honesty and purity of vision which refuses
to be compromised by literary 'standards'.

In the works of all these creative figures, Genet's legacy lives on and troubles
all cultural boundaries and limits.

* * *

The contributions in this collection fall into five main categories (some of which overlap): life and criminality; gender and sexuality; language and aesthetics; politics and intertextuality. In relation to Genet's life and criminality, there are pieces from Albert Dichy,[65] Philip Thody, the short interview with Edmund White about his biography and the renewed interest it has evoked in Genet's work, the BBC 'Arena' interview[66] and the interview with one of its producers, Jean-Paul Davidson. Mairéad Hanrahan examines gender in *Miracle of the Rose* and Grace Russo Bullaro has located her discussion of Genet's work and criminality within the wider framework of the politics of homosexuality. Jeremy Reed's discussion of gender and aesthetics focuses on Genet's poem *The Man Condemned to Death* and the symbolism contained in it. Genet's use of and preoccupation with language is taken up by Sharon Cornford and Angeliki Rosi in their respective examinations of *Funeral Rites* and *The Strange Word 'Urb'*, and is a subject also considered in Mairéad Hanrahan's chapter. Neil Bartlett's 1994 William Matthews Lecture 'The Uses of Monotony' is reprinted here and draws particular attention to the rhythms of Genet's language; and in his interview Bartlett points out how Genet's language derives from the gay slang he encountered amongst the Montmartre queens.[67] Genet's politics is represented in the essay by David Bradby, 'Genet, the Theatre and the Algerian War', Allen Ginsberg's preface to Genet's *May Day Speech* and Ian Birchall's 'The Politics of *Saint Genet*'. Genet's encounter with other thinkers also finds expression in this latter essay, which mainly examines Sartre's political reading of Genet's evolution as a writer; and Stephen Barber draws attention to some of the important links between Genet and Antonin Artaud, in terms of thematic preoccupations, dramatic intention and the figures of Roger Blin and Paule Thévenin. Genet's theatre is examined by David Bradby, both in his essay and in his review of Neil Bartlett's translation and production of *Splendid's*. David Bradby considers Neil Bartlett to be one of the finest interpreters of Genet working in the theatre, so it is to be hoped that Bartlett might eventually stage productions of Genet's three major plays. Finally, Albert Dichy has given permission to reprint his 1993 *Le Monde* article, 'Publishing Adventures', which offers much insight into the early publishing history of Genet's novels.

This book presents some of the best contemporary writing on Genet, with the result that this anthology is the first significant text on Genet since Edmund White's biography.

NOTES

1 See Edmund White, *Genet* (London, 1993), p. 228.

2 Kenneth Patchen, *An Astonished Eye Looks Out of the Air* (Waldport, Oregon, 1945).

3 Peter Brooks and Joseph Halpern (eds), *Genet: A Collection of Critical Essays* (New Jersey, 1979). Apart from this, the only comprehensive critical studies in English on Genet to emerge in recent years are Jeanette L Savona, *Jean Genet* (New York, 1983) and Gene A Plunka, *The Rites of Passage of Jean Genet: The Art and Aesthetics of Risk Taking* (London and Toronto, 1992).

4 Edmund White, *Genet* (London, 1993).

5 First broadcast 12 November 1985. See also the translation by Ian Birchall of this interview in Chapter 6 of this book.

6 Artaud has been the subject of Gilles Deleuze (*A Thousand Plateaux*), Jacques Derrida ('La Parole soufflée' and 'Le Théâtre de la Cruauté et la clôture de la représentation' in the collection *Writing and Difference*), Julia Kristeva ('The Subject on Trial' in *Polylogue*), Michel Foucault (*Madness and Civilisation*) and Susan Sontag ('Approaching Artaud' in *Under the Sign of Saturn*). Genet has been the subject of Sartre (*Saint Genet, comédien et martyr*), Derrida (*Glas*) and Hélène Cixous (*Souffles*).

7 See Jean Genet, 'The Studio of Alberto Giacometti', translated by Richard Howard in Edmund White (ed.), *The Selected Writings of Jean Genet* (New Jersey, 1993), p. 310. 'L'Atelier d'Alberto Giacometti' was first published by Marc Barbezat, L'Arbalète, in 1958. This essay was considered by Giacometti to be the most insightful account of his work.

8 Giacometti produced a number of drawings and paintings of Genet between 1954 and 1957. One portrait hangs in the Pompidou Centre, Paris, and a second in the Tate Gallery, London. For more details see 'The Studio of Alberto Giacometti' in Edmund White (ed.), *The Selected Writings of Jean Genet* (New Jersey, 1993), pp. 309–29.

9 Edmund White (ed.) *The Selected Writings of Jean Genet* (New Jersey, 1993), p. 310.

10 See 'Jean Genet, Affirmation of Existence Through Rebellion', interview with Jean Genet and Leila Shahid Barrada by Rüdiger Wischenbart in *Journal of Palestine Studies*, Winter 1987, Vol. XVI, No. 2, Issue 62, p. 68. This interview was given over 6–7 December, 1983 and first appeared in the autumn 1986 issue of *Revue d'études palestiniennes*.

11 Jean-Paul Sartre, *What is Literature?*, translated by Bernard Frechtman (London, 1987), p. 5.

12 Jean Genet, 'The Palestinians' in *Journal of Palestine Studies*, 3, 1 (1973), p. 18.

13 Jean Genet, *The Thief's Journal*, translated by Bernard Frechtman (London, 1982 edition), p. 98.

14 Interview with Lucette Finas, in M Morris and P Patton (eds), *Michel Foucault: Power, Truth, Strategy* (Sydney, 1979), p. 75.

15 Carl Gustav Jung, *Memories, Dreams, Reflections*, recorded and edited by Aniela Jaffé (London, 1983).

16 In the interview with Hubert Fichte in *The New Review*, Vol. 4, No. 37, April 1977, translated by Patrick McCarthy, Genet says at the very end: 'Discover the truth that lies within [lies]. Discover what I wanted to hide when I told you some of these things' (p. 21). This interview was originally published in German in *Die Zeit*, 13 February 1976.

17 Hans-Georg Gadamer, *Truth and Method* (London, 1975).

18 The most notable of these is in a letter to Roger Blin, the first director of *The Screens*, in Jean Genet, *Reflections on the Theatre and other writings,* translated by Richard Seaver (London, 1972), p. 52.

19 Jean Genet, *Reflections on the Theatre and other writings*, translated by Richard Seaver (London, 1972), p. 52.

20 Edward Said, in his essay 'On Jean Genet's Late Works' in J Ellen Gainor (ed.), *Imperialism and Theatre* (London, 1995), pp. 230–242, testifies to the fact that when he met Genet in 1972, 'he seemed totally unlike anything of his that I had read' (p. 233).

21 Interview with Hubert Fichte in *The New Review*, Vol. 4, No. 37, April 1977, translated by Patrick McCarthy, p. 21.

22 'Jean Genet, Affirmation of Existence Through Rebellion', interview with Jean Genet and Leila Shahid Barrada by Rüdiger Wischenbart in *Journal of Palestine Studies*, Winter 1987, Vol. XVI, No. 2, Issue 62, p. 78 (emphasis my own – Ed.).

23 Susan Sontag, *Against interpretation and other essays* (London, 1967), p. 51.

24 Edward Said, 'On Jean Genet's Late Works' in J Ellen Gainor (ed.), *Imperialism and Theatre* (London, 1995), p. 234.

25 'Jean Genet, Affirmation of Existence Through Rebellion', interview with Jean Genet and Leila Shahid Barrada by Rüdiger Wischenbart in *Journal of Palestine Studies*, Winter 1987, Vol. XVI, No. 2, Issue 62, p. 76.

26 Edward Said, 'On Jean Genet's Late Works' in J Ellen Gainor (ed.), *Imperialism and Theatre* (London, 1995), p. 238.

27 This idea receives fictional representation in Genet's three great plays, *The Balcony*, *The Blacks* and *The Screens*. Theatre may be likened to revolt, in that it offers the possibility to break free of these constricting images.

28 In this observation that it is through language that oppression can be resisted, by resisting the images and concepts which reinforce its dominant ideology, there is a parallel with the views Genet puts forward in *Fragments ... and other texts* (Paris, 1990). As Edmund White points out in *Genet* (London, 1993), pp. 447–8, in this text Genet maintains that homosexuals can only have a certain kind of relationship to language, and that is one of mockery. This is because Genet considers that homosexuals, by virtue of their homosexuality, are, in White's words, 'cut ... off from the world – even from the world of other pederasts', and are unable to participate in a common shared humanity. Because language is based on this shared common humanity, homosexuals 'can do nothing more than mock language – "alter it, parody it, dissolve it". Pederasty does constitute a "civilisation", though one that isolates rather than unites its citizens.'

29 Edmund White, *Genet* (London, 1993), p. 239.

30 Edward Said, 'Cry Palestine' in *New Statesman and Society*, 10 November 1995, p. 27.

31 The granting of Genet's state pardon in August 1949 (by President Vincent Auriol), on the basis that he was a gifted writer, has echoes of the Benefit of Clergy in English law which was finally abolished in 1827. This was the privilege, initiated in the twelfth century, that allowed the clergy to only be tried in ecclesiastical courts. From the fourteenth century this pardon was granted to all those who were literate; a man could claim Benefit of Clergy and therefore save his neck by reading Psalm 51.1 (the 'neck verse'), thus proving he could read Latin.

32 Jean Genet, 'Four Hours in Shatila' in *Journal of Palestine Studies*, 6, 1 (1983), p. 22.

[33] 'Jean Genet, Affirmation of Existence Through Rebellion', interview with Jean Genet and Leila Shahid Barrada by Rüdiger Wischenbart in *Journal of Palestine Studies*, Winter 1987, Vol. XVI, No. 2, Issue 62, p. 82. See also p. 77: 'Listen. The day the Palestinians become institutionalised, I will no longer be on their side. The day the Palestinians become a nation like other nations, I will no longer be there.'

[34] 'Jean Genet, Affirmation of Existence Through Rebellion', interview with Jean Genet and Leila Shahid Barrada by Rüdiger Wischenbart in *Journal of Palestine Studies*, Winter 1987, Vol. XVI, No. 2, Issue 62, p. 72.

[35] For Artaud cruelty is an 'implacable necessity ... that pain apart from whose ineluctable necessity life could not continue; good is desired, it is the consequence of an act; evil is permanent,' Antonin Artaud, letter to Jean Paulhan, Paris, 14 November 1932, in *The Theatre and its Double*, translated by Mary Caroline Richards (New York, 1958), p. 102. I would also like to make clear that the distinction between violence and brutality which I am focusing on here is not at all supported by the distinction which Genet makes in his introduction to the French translation of the writings of the Baader-Meinhof, published by Éditions Maspero. Titled 'Violence et brutalité', it first appeared in *Le Monde* in the form of an article on 2 September 1977. It is republished in *L'Ennemi déclaré* as 'Violence et brutalité, Préface Textes des prisonniers de la "Faction Armée Rouge" et dernières lettres d'Ulrike Meinhof', with notes accompanying this text appearing on pp. 384–92 of the same volume. Edmund White discusses the controversy the essay aroused in *Genet* (London, 1993), pp. 686–9. Since the Baader-Meinhof perpetrated indiscriminate and random acts of violence and were not members of an oppressed group fighting for their freedom, I would perceive their actions to be examples of brutality and not violence in the very specific sense in which I use the term here.

[36] Artaud wrote: 'As soon as I have said 'cruelty', everybody will at once take it to mean "blood." But 'theatre of cruelty' means a theatre difficult and cruel for myself first of all. And ... it is not the cruelty we can exercise upon each other by hacking at each other's bodies, carving up our personal anatomies ... but the much more terrible and necessary cruelty which things can exercise against us. We are not free. And the sky can still fall on our heads. And the theatre has been created to teach us that first of all.' ('No More Masterpieces' in *The Theatre and its Double*, translated by Mary Caroline Richards (New York, 1958), p. 79.)

[37] Jean Genet, 'The Palestinians' in *Journal of Palestine Studies*, 3, 1 (1973).

[38] Edward Said, 'On Jean Genet's Late Works' in J Ellen Gainor (ed.), *Imperialism and Theatre* (London, 1995), p. 237.

[39] It is also interesting to note in relation to the name 'Genet' that the French *gêner* has amongst its meanings 'to hinder', 'to be in someone's way' or 'to *embarrass*'. The latter was something Genet did frequently to his readers. Jean Cocteau after receiving the manuscript of *Our Lady of the Flowers* wrote in his journal, 'Jean Genet's eye embarrasses and disturbs you. He's right and the rest of the world is wrong. But what's to be done?' Quoted in Edmund White, *Genet* (London, 1993), p. 228.

Further, the French *gêner* derives from the Biblical *Gehenna*, a place of torment; this was originally a placename in Palestine. The term Gehenna in English used to mean prison. (I am grateful to Ian Birchall for this reference – Ed.)

40 Edmund White's introduction to *Prisoner of Love*, translated by Barbara Bray (London, 1989), p. xvii.

41 Leila Shahid, interview with Jérôme Hankins in *Genet à Chatila* (Paris, 1992), p. 63: '...de comprendre enfin ce que cela aussi avait signifié pour lui, l'absence d'une mère.'

42 'Jean Genet, Affirmation of Existence Through Rebellion', interview with Jean Genet and Leila Shahid Barrada by Rüdiger Wischenbart in *Journal of Palestine Studies*, Winter 1987, Vo. XVI, No. 2, Issue 62, p. 72.

43 Leila Shahid, interview with Jérôme Hankins in *Genet à Chatila* (Paris, 1992), p. 61: 'Et face à la mort, au moment où la boucle est bouclée, il a soudain eu envie de partager avec les seuls qu'il aimait, ses lecteurs. Avec ceux-là il était prêt à partager la vérité et à dire tout ce qu'il cachait depuis soixante-dix ans. Et il nous raconte tout cela en nous tissant sa vie.'

44 For a detailed account of Artaud's influence on contemporary culture see Stephen Barber, *Weapons of Liberation* (London, 1996).

45 Leila Shahid, interview with Jérôme Hankins in *Genet à Chatila* (Paris, 1992), p. 62.

46 Jacques Lacan, 'Motifs du crime paranoïaque; le crime des sœurs Papin', first published in the review *Le Minotaure*, No. 3, December 1933.

47 See Kate Millett, *Sexual Politics* (New York, 1969), in which she refers to *Our Lady of the Flowers* as a feminist text because it portrays femininity as a social role, not a biological given, which may be inhabited by both men and women. See also Hélène Cixous, 'The School of Roots' in *Three Steps on the Ladder of Writing*, translated by Sarah Cornell and Susan Sellers (New York, 1993), pp. 109–62.

48 See Michel Foucault, *Discipline and Punish*, translated by Alan Sheridan (London, 1979).

49 See particularly Edward Said, 'On Jean Genet's Late Works' in J Ellen Gainor (ed.), *Imperialism and Theatre* (London, 1995).

50 In Edmund White (ed.), *The Selected Writings of Jean Genet* (New Jersey, 1993), pp. 310–29.

51 For a full account of Genet's involvement with cinema, see Jane Giles, *The Cinema of Jean Genet* (London, 1991).

52 Edmund White also describes a brief meeting between David Bowie and Genet, when they had agreed to meet at a London restaurant to discuss the possibility of Bowie starring as Divine in a film version of *Our Lady of the Flowers*. Genet noticed an attractive woman sitting alone at a table, went up to 'her' and declared, 'Mr Bowie, I presume.' He was correct. See Edmund White, *Genet* (London, 1993), p. 572.

53 Derek Jarman's preface in Anno Wilms, *Lindsay Kemp and his Company* (London, 1987), p. 5.

54 Jean Genet, *The Balcony*, translated by Bernard Frechtman (London, 1984 edition), p. 96.

55 Nuria Moreno, who has been with Kemp's company since 1981, says quite emphatically: 'Lindsay is a magician. He will make you feel that you have so much more than you think you have. In his workshops he has this ability to give performers and students alike the confidence to tap potentials of which they are unaware. Lindsay puts a spell on people. He makes all those he works with and his students feel they can achieve anything. He changes the colours of things, the colours of life around you.' (Conversation with the author.) David Bowie, who was a member of Kemp's company in the early 1970s and for whom Lindsay Kemp created the Ziggy Stardust concerts at the Rainbow Theatre, has also

testified to the importance of Kemp's work for his own sensibility and artistic development. (Conversation with the author.)

[56] Bernard Frechtman, Genet's English translator, admonished Peter Zadek after the world première of *The Balcony* at the Arts Theatre Club in April 1957, saying that the brothel scenes 'should be presented with the solemnity of a Mass in a most beautiful cathedral'. Quoted in Martin Esslin, *The Theatre of the Absurd* (Harmondsworth, 1970 edition), p. 210.

[57] David Haughton, 'Between Worlds' in Anno Wilms, *Lindsay Kemp and his Company* (London, 1987), pp. 14–15.

[58] Jean Genet, *Le Condamné à Mort* (L'Arbalète, 1948, first published in 1942):

> O traverse les murs; s'il le faut marche au bord
> Des toits, des océans; couvre-toi de lumière,
> Use de la menace, use de la prière ...

And the last line of this long poem:

> Mes dormeurs vont s'enfuir vers une autre Amérique.

(I am indebted to Albert Dichy and Ian Magedera for providing the source of the original lines – Ed.)

[59] 'Hot Tickets' in the *Evening Standard*, 31 May 1996.

[60] Organised by Stephen Barber and myself to commemorate the centenary of Artaud's birth and the tenth anniversary of Genet's death, this took place from 31 May to 2 June 1996, and also included a three-week season of films by, about and inspired by Artaud and Genet.

[61] Patti Smith has published several collections of poetry and prose, the most recent being *Woolgathering* (New York and Madras, 1992), *Early Work, 1970–1979* (New York and London, 1994) and *The Coral Sea* (New York and London, 1996), a series of meditations on the photographer, Robert Mapplethorpe, describing his journey to the Southern Cross, a voyage of self-discovery and transformation as he struggles with illness and mortality.

[62] Jonathan Cott, 'Rock and Rimbaud' in *New York Times Book Review*, 19 February 1978, pp. 9 and 29.

[63] See Note 60 above.

[64] Patti Smith in conversation with Michael Bracewell at the ICA, Friday 31 May 1996, transcribed in *The Guardian*, 22 June 1996.

[65] The English translations in this book of the two pieces by Albert Dichy, 'Jean Genet: Portrait of the artist as a warrior' and 'Publishing Adventures', as well as that of the BBC 'Arena' interview with Genet, are by Ian Birchall.

[66] This was first published in French in Albert Dichy (ed.), *L'Ennemi déclaré: textes et entretiens* in Jean Genet, *Œuvres Complètes VI* (Paris, 1991).

[67] This insight makes absolute sense once it has been pointed out, yet Neil Bartlett provides one of the first in-depth discussions of this important origin of Genet's language.

CHAPTER 2

Jean Genet: Portrait of the artist as a warrior

Albert Dichy

IF GENET'S APPROACH throughout his life as a writer had to be summed up in a single word, perhaps 'war' would be the most apt. Genet's entire work is one long declaration of war. From the outset, with one word used like a bullet, the opening sentence of his first novel, *Notre-Dame-des-Fleurs*, indicates the enemy and marks him out in peremptory fashion:

> Weidmann appeared to you in a five o'clock edition, his head swathed in white bandages, a nun and yet still a wounded aviator, fallen into the fields of rye on a September day ...

The enemy is not, as one might think, Weidmann, the 'seductive murderer', killer of six women, who was guillotined in public in Paris in 1939, and under whose protection Genet puts his book as though under the blessing of a saint. The enemy is exposed in the sentence by the indicative quality of one word, by the 'you' [*vous*], a discordant pronoun which, in the very first edition of *Notre-Dame-des-Fleurs*, the proof-reader wanted to replace with a more conventional 'us' [*nous*]. Who is addressed by this 'you'? You and I, everybody, the whole of society, and first and foremost, the reader. At the very moment when he invites the complicity of the reader, Genet betrays it. Between the work and the reader runs the line of fire.

In this way does the theatre of Jean Genet take its initial form, 'absolute oppositionist' in the words of Jean-Paul Sartre. There are two sides, two camps: on the one hand, the world; on the other, Genet himself. The prison where Genet drafted his first writings provides the whole of his work with its chief *site of enunciation*. Whether imprisoned or not, Genet always speaks from the other side of a wall, always separated from the person he is speaking to; it is as though this separation constituted the very space of his speech. When the boundary is marked out and the roles allocated, the dramaturgy of war is in place: it will be deployed on the territory of language for a full forty years, without any weakening, drawing on all the resources of the military art: decoys and deceptions, attacks and withdrawals, stratagems and infiltration, alliances and betrayals.

Regulated like a series of strategic operations, passing through and overturning the various literary drawing-rooms – poetry, novel, theatre, essay, memoirs – Genet's war develops in three phases and using three different tactics.

Frontal attack or the period of the novels

Genet's first literary tactic, and doubtless the most brilliant one, extends from *Le Condamné à Mort* to *Journal du Voleur*. It records the (illegal) entrance of the delinquent, the prisoner, the thief onto the stage of literature. It is a skilful attack, sometimes surreptitious, sometimes brutal, but always *frontal*: it brings into opposition, as we have just seen, 'I', Jean Genet, author and character, and 'you', readers, free men, upright people. An attack carried out in Genet's own name, but also in the name of those he calls the 'convicts of his breed' – thieves, transvestites, murderers, the [Vichy] militia, traitors – in the name of all those who have chosen the obverse side of the world and whom society has made responsible for the evil which it secretes. A despairing attack, but one which draws from that very despair its hidden strength and its brilliance.

This first period comes to an end around 1949, that is, the very year in which Genet received from the then president of the French Republic, Vincent Auriol, a pardon covering the years of jail he still had to serve. And in that same year he began to experience the first signs of literary recognition. In a sense it was this double catastrophe of success and pardon which led Genet into such deep depression that he considered, at the age of around forty, putting an end to his life; the violence of Genet's writings paralleled the risks he was running. The walls of the prison that overshadowed his writing were, in a way, the guarantee of his authenticity. 'Once free, I was lost,' Genet was to say much later on, in an interview. Lost, reduced to being no more than an artist like any other, appeased, tamed by society, defeated by his own victory.

The oblique manoeuvre or the period of the theatre

Genet was to spend six years finding his way out of the dead-end. It was only in 1954 that he was to find a means of escape from the trap in which he had imprisoned himself. And essentially it was the theatre which was to offer him this escape. Of course by this time Genet had already written three plays (not only *Haute surveillance* and *Les Bonnes*, but also *Splendid's*, which was written in 1948 and stands on the borderline between the two phases), but he had not yet systematically exploited the resources of dramatic technique which hitherto he had used intuitively.

With *Le Balcon* Genet came to understand that the theatre allowed him a different angle of fire from the poem or the autobiographical novel. His work took a different direction: instead of directly attacking the social order, Genet attacked its representation. The aim of his threatre was now to dismantle and betray the image that society creates of itself. Genet thus discovered the possibility of a diagonal manoeuvre, of a style of fighting that would no longer be frontal, but *oblique*. Already operative in *Les Bonnes* and in *Splendid's*, this technique found its full development in Genet's three great plays, those which put him among the first rank of playwrights in the twentieth century: *Le Balcon*, *Les Nègres* and *Les Paravents*.

But, by attacking, as rust attacks metal, the very principle of representation, Genet slowly caused the disintegration of his own instrument. With *Les Paravents*, it was as though the playwright had blown up his own engine of war. The explosive charge of the play was so strong that it blew up the marksman along with his target. As if he had unknowingly reached an invisible limit, Genet – despite himself, despite the enormous but futile efforts he made to finish his next play, *Le Bagne* [*The Penal Colony*] (of which, after three years, he had only managed to draft three or four scenes) – stopped publishing. And this time his silence was to last twenty-five years.

The last festival or the phase of political fiction

It was politics which would supply his last bullets. With the Black Panthers in the USA, the North African immigrants in Europe and the Palestinian fighters, Genet discovered, around the 1970s, a third way, another means of continuing his personal war. If it was separation which uniquely enabled him to write (first of all the separation of prison, then the separation between actors and audience, the basis of theatrical representation), political struggle was to provide him with a new distance: geographical distance. At the age of sixty, from the Palestinian camps in Jordan to the black ghettos of America, Genet would again become what he had been at the beginning of his life: a vagabond. The poet of the most confined space in the world (the prison cell) became the chronicler of planetary wars.

Always in the company of those rejected by society, Genet also learned of something hitherto unknown to him: fraternity. For the first time he discovered that revolt can be collective, that it can be a festival. Written in the shadow of sickness and death, dedicated to the last revolutions of the century, his final work, *Un Captif amoureux*, is also the most joyous, the most transparent of his books. Genet died pen in hand, correcting the proofs of this book which would only appear a month after his death.

Perhaps Genet's greatness (if we dare use this word which hardly suits him) will derive from not laying down his arms, not resigning himself to his fame, not becoming well mannered, not turning into a respectable old rogue. He was a victor – one who had won 'by force of arms', as he wrote, at the age of thirty-seven, in *Journal du Voleur* – but one who did not rejoin the camp of the victors; he did not return to the family, he did not settle down. He remained until the very end, against the whole world – and above all against himself – in the place society had assigned to him from birth: *outside*.

CHAPTER 3

Sartre and White: Biographers of a contrary child

Philip Thody

THERE CAN BE few writers who have suffered more from their first and most famous admirers than Jean Genet. Not only did Sartre make a number of crucial and highly misleading mistakes in his presentation of Genet's childhood and early experiences, but he also used him so ruthlessly in order to express his own ideas about existentialist choice, the nature of evil, and the unspeakable wickedness of bourgeois society that it is even now very difficult to see Genet's most interesting works, *Notre-Dame-des-Fleurs* and *Le Balcon*, in any but Sartrean terms. Writing with only apparent irony about his own father's early death, Sartre claimed in *Les Mots*:

> If he had lived, my father would have lain down on me and crushed me. Fortunately, he died young; among the Aeneases each carrying his Anchises on his shoulders, I cross from one bank to the other alone, detesting those invisible fathers who ride piggy-back on their sons throughout their lives.[1]

In a way, Sartre performed the characteristically disastrous paternal function for Genet that his own father Jean-Baptiste was prevented, by fever contracted in Indochina, from performing for him, imposing an all-embracing reading on his works which Genet's other admirers, and perhaps even Genet himself, initially found as difficult to shake off as the pious Aeneas did the influence of the old Anchises or Sinbad the Sailor the Old Man of the Sea.

It was not until the publication, in 1988, of Albert Dichy's and Pascal Fouché's *Jean Genet: essai de chronolgie 1910–1944* that three of the main props on which Sartre had constructed his 1952 *Saint Genet, comédien et martyr* were shown to have been completely non-existent. Genet was not, as he himself claimed in *Journal du Voleur* and as Sartre repeated in his existentialist biography, entrusted to a peasant family in the Morvan when he was eight years old, but when he was seven months. This family was not one of brutal, brutalised and brutalising peasants, but of modest and well-meaning artisans. Although they did not have much money, they lived in one of the larger houses in the village, and one which had the advantage of being next door to the school.

As Edmund White points out in the 810-page biography which he published in 1993, Genet was much better treated than most of the other foster-children in the village of Alligny-en-Morvan, and the proximity of his foster-parents' house to the school meant that he learned to read and write. Indeed, it would appear that he was clever and hard-working enough to be something of a teacher's pet.

Genet may, as Sartre argues, have felt alienated from the property-owning society in which he was brought up by virtue of the fact that he had been a penniless orphan. He certainly did not have the opportunity, available to clever children living with their biological parents, to pursue his education beyond primary school. But his foster-father, Charles Regnier, was 'un menuisier', a carpenter-joiner, so it could have been perfectly possible for Genet to have learned from him the lesson which Sartre maintains could have come to him only if he had been placed with a family of proletarians: that people are also defined by what they do. And, most important of all, there is no evidence for the story of Genet being caught thieving and officially labelled a thief, on which Sartre based his vision of Genet making his 'existentialist choice of evil' as a reaction to the role forced upon him by society.

It is easy to see why Sartre was so tempted by the myth which he himself created and which Genet may have encouraged, stringing him along as the Rat Man finally confessed that he had done with Freud. It is when he is six that the Baudelaire of Sartre's 1946 essay undergoes the shock of his mother's remarriage, and makes his existentialist choice to be unhappy and different. It is when Sartre himself is six or seven that grandfather Schweitzer takes him on his knees and solemnly warns him of the dangers of following a literary profession, thus ensuring – if *Les Mots* is to be believed – the choice which the infant Sartre made to become a writer. And it is when Flaubert is six or seven that his father tries to teach him to read, discovers that he is not as bright as his elder brother, and behaves in such a way as to compel young Gustave to make his existentialist choice to be the fool of the family. Sartre wished to replace Freud's idea that our personality is determined by the way we fail to deal adequately with our unconscious impulses before we reach the age of four, with the view that we make our own mind up between six and eight. He was thus understandably delighted to find ammunition in as real a person as Genet for his campaign against Freudianism.

It is an interesting theory, and one which must have been curiously tempting to a writer brought up, albeit with considerable reluctance on his own part, in the Catholic culture of France. It is, after all, at about the age of six or seven that French children are deemed to have reached 'l'âge de raison', the age when they are able to distinguish between good and evil, and are therefore allowed to take their first communion.[2] The trouble is that there is even less evidence to support

Sartre's choice of around seven as the crucial age than there is for the Freudian hypothesis, and his presentation of Genet is a case in point. Indeed, if Genet's early life and subsequent career illustrate anything at all about how and why children develop as they do, it is by the very depressing contribution which they make to the debate about nature and nurture. For what emerges both from the researches of Dichy and Fouché and from White's biography, is that Genet was, from the beginning, what people used to call 'a throughly bad lot', and for reasons which it is tempting to attribute as much to a hereditary disposition to misbehave as to social pressures or existentialist choice.

We naturally know nothing about Genet's parentage, apart from the fact that his mother was almost certainly not a prostitute. She was, in all probability, a domestic servant who had been seduced and abandoned, and who had no choice but to give birth to her child in a public maternity ward and then give him up to the social services. Adoption remained for many years much more difficult in France than in England, so that the solution which would nowadays have been found of entrusting the child to parents who would have made it their own and loved it with the same or even greater passion than those who were biologically their own was not available. Instead, the state did the next best thing and placed Genet as a foster-child with a family who, as White points out, gave him as good an upbringing as they could. He was, he writes, 'doted on' and 'pampered' by his foster-mother, Eugénie Regnier, as well as his godmother, Lucie Wirtz, herself a foster-child sent by the authorities in Paris to the same area.

But although neither White nor Dichy and Fouché can find any trace of the ceremony in which Genet was publicly denounced as a thief, the interviews which all three biographers have managed to obtain with people who knew Genet as a child leave no doubt either about his thieving or about his incipient homosexuality. Like Proust, Genet sees the homosexual as the victim of a cruel biological joke whereby somebody who is sexually a woman is imprisoned in a male body, and there is no sense in which his work can be seen as a contribution to the gay liberation movement. He was, writes White, 'to reject the idea of homosexual literature as a plea for understanding or as a rational assignment of blame'.[3] Instead, he presents the homosexual as victim of a contradiction which it is impossible for him to resolve. Ideally, Proust and Genet both argue, the homosexual would like to be loved by a 'real man'. But since, in their view, the main characteristic of a 'real man' is to be attracted sexually only to women, this is something which can never happen. A 'real man' may do it for money, and Simon Raven's entertaining essay on the London homosexual world, reprinted in *Boys will be Boys*, not only describes how this happens, especially among members of some of the Household regiments, but also offers a partial corrective to Genet's and Proust's pessimism by pointing out how some heterosexuals become quite fond of the men who pay them to do it for money.[4]

But for Proust and Genet, a 'real man' who spontaneously enjoys sex with another man immediately forfeits his virile status, and becomes no more than another 'poofter' for whom no self-respecting queen can feel any real sexual enthusiasm.

Sartre himself underwrites this vision of homosexuality, which one would normally attribute only to the fairly robust queer-basher, when he dismisses the claim of Mignon-les-petits-pieds that 'a male that fucks another male is a double male' with the comment '[no]: he is a female without realising it'.[5] Like Genet, Sartre is not in this respect an enlightened rationalist reformer on the lines of Gide; he is a man of limited imagination and even narrower appreciation of how wide and catholic perfectly genuine sexual tastes can be.

White quotes an interview in which Genet stated, in 1950, that a homosexual was 'a man for whom, first of all, the entire female sex, half of humanity, does not exist', and where he claims that there is never any possibility of affection between men who are united sexually. As White shows, Genet did not order his relationships with his various lovers on this assertion. He either married them off to women and set them up in houses which he himself had bought and sometimes even designed, or, as was the case with one of the great loves of his life, the acrobat Abdallah, paid their medical bills with impeccable generosity.

In Genet's written work, however, there is no question of his presenting what Proust called 'the monstrosity of masculine loves' in any but a negative and depressing way, and there is a parallel to this in the support which White's biography unconsciously gives to the view that Genet was born a bad lot, was weak-willed to the point of idiocy, and brought far more unhappiness upon himself by incompetence than he ever did by any existentialist choice of evil or conscious defiance of bourgeois society. He was, it is true, a victim of society in not being allowed to go on from primary school, where he had been the prize pupil, to secondary school, and then perhaps even to university. But he was not, unlike most of the other foster-children sent to the Morvan, given no choice but to work in the fields. In 1924, he was sent as an apprentice typographer to the École d'Alembert in Paris. Printers, as indeed they still are nowadays, were among the best-paid members of the skilled artisan class, the aristocracy of labour from whom the political leaders of the working class were traditionally recruited.

Ten days after his arrival, Genet absconded and was arrested in Nice. But he was not sent to reform school; instead, he was placed with a blind composer, René de Buxeuil, from whom he proceeded to steal 180 francs (not that small a sum of money at the time) and waste it in entertaining himself in a fairground. He was placed under psychiatric observation, but twice ran away again. He was re-arrested, paroled, but absconded once again, leaving the authorities with little apparent choice but to commit him, for his own protection as well as for the sake of society, to some kind of penal institution. They sent him to Mettray (the setting for the 1946 *Miracle de la Rose*), where there is no doubt from the other witnesses whom White quotes that life was hell. But Genet was again given the choice of seeing how he fared outside what the authorities clearly recognised as the criminogenic world of juvenile institutions, and was sent to work on a farm. He ran away again, was caught, and sent back to Mettray. He escaped only by joining the army, where he served for six years, and reached the rank of corporal, re-enlisting twice, before deserting in June 1936 and beginning the nomadic life which he was later to describe in *Journal du Voleur*.

In this respect, Genet's life up to the discovery in 1942 that he could write highly original prose, and the consequent free pardon granted to him by Vincent Auriol in 1949, is strikingly like the one chronicled by Tony Parker in his first book *The Unknown Citizen*.[6] Like the fellow delinquents whom Parker met during his repeated spells in prison, Genet was a social inadequate who lacked the perseverance to do anything positive with his intelligence, and who could achieve some kind of stability only in the disciplined framework of the armed services. But if, as Sartre contends throughout *Saint Genet, comédien et martyr*, he was a man whom bourgeois society had chosen to elect as a scapegoat for its manifold sins and wickednesses, then bourgeois society had a funny way of showing it. Time and again, what Sartre calls 'notre abjecte société' leaned over backwards to avoid punishing him with the full rigour of the law, giving him instead every opportunity to encourage him to mend his ways. If he did not do so, his conduct offers a strong temptation to think that it was perhaps because he was, as Mr Hubble put it in reply to Uncle Pumblechook in *Great Expectations*, 'naterally wicious'.

This is at least as likely an explanation as Sartre's 'existentialist choice', and one for which there seems to be a certain amount of evidence. But although there is no means of proving whether it is true or not, it is an aspect of Genet's life which runs curiously parallel both to the portrayal of homosexuality in his work and to his depiction of crime and criminals. Nobody in his work, with the possible exception of the murderous Querelle in the first part of the novel *Querelle de Brest*, derives either pleasure or profit from his crimes. Genet's criminals all get caught and spend most of their time in prison. His homosexuals are incapable of loyalty and affection, and he himself devotes a long passage in *Miracle de la Rose* to challenging the romantic image of the convict as an irredeemable member of society. If ever an author offered through his life and works a set of compelling and irrefutable arguments in favour of keeping to the social as well as to the sexual straight and narrow, it was Jean Genet.

It is true that if Genet had benefited from the successful adoption which would have probably been his fate if he had been born in post-war England, we should never have heard of him. This would have been a pity, since we should not be able to read the splendid account of the world of homosexuality in *Notre-Dame-des-Fleurs* and see the even more entertaining account of kinky sex in *Le Balcon*. What individuals can do in a private context – it is not unusual, for example, for homosexual friends of conventionally married men to make comments, to their face, which are as devastating in their accuracy as they are disturbing in their humour and perceptivity – Genet the playwright does in a public one with *Le Balcon*. It is perhaps because Genet's own sexual life was so disturbing a mixture of splendid dreams and tawdry reality that his portrait of Madame Irma's establishment hits the nail so accurately on the head, and brings out the extent to which men in search of unorthodox sex are led so consistently to make fools of themselves.

Once Genet was established as a writer, bourgeois society took every advantage of the opportunity to lavish its tolerance and generosity on one of its most declared enemies. Already, as I have suggested in my summary of Genet's innumerable brushes with the law, it had done everything it could to help a man apparently determined to reject every opportunity offered to him to stop making such a nuisance of himself and lead a sensible and law-abiding life. Neither in White's biography nor in Dichy and Fouché's *Jean Genet: essai de chronolgie* is there any reference to the legend of Genet writing *Notre-Dame-des-Fleurs* in his cell at Fresnes on the brown paper that he was supposed to turn into carrier bags. But as soon as it had appeared, even in clandestine form, Genet had begun to benefit from the same kind of preferential treatment which had enabled André Malraux to escape a long prison sentence when he was caught stealing statues in Cambodia in 1927.

According to a harsh but perhaps predictable article in the criminal code, Genet became liable in May 1943 to being sent to prison for life. There are, after all, limits to the extent to which the law can give up its task of protecting the law-abiding citizen against the inconvenience of having his property stolen, and Genet was by that time a compulsive thief whose approach the booksellers of Paris must have watched with dread. But Jean Cocteau, of whom White rightly observes that he never wrote a bad line or a good book, procured for Genet a skilled lawyer who made good use of psychiatric evidence to claim that he was 'in the category of people whose will and moral sense is weak', and Genet was sent to prison for only three months. He stole more books in September 1943, and again was sentenced to only four months for an offence for which a petty thief not blessed with literary talent could have expected to be put away for a great deal longer; one incidental truth which emerges from White's biography is that the idea of the equality of all men before the law disappears in France if you can prove yourself to be a good writer.

Once Genet was established as a writer, and earning enough money to buy himself a house in the south of France, he proceeded to involve himself in a series of political activities which all had two features in common: they were all violently opposed to Western, capitalist society, and none of them achieved their aims. White makes the interesting suggestion that Genet's enthusiasm for Arabs in general and for the Palestine Liberation Organisation (PLO) in particular stemmed at least in part from the fact that the system in Mettray provided the option for inmates who had completed training on the farm to settle in Algeria: Genet's understandable dislike of the régime to which he had been subjected between the ages of seventeen and nineteen made him immediately sympathetic to the Arabs whose lands, since the nineteenth century, had been confiscated to allow Frenchmen to practise European-style farming. A continuity can be seen here between the consequences of his delinquent childhood and the performance of *Les Paravents* in 1966 – wanting to drive the nails firmly home in the coffin of 'Algérie française', de Gaulle was happy to sanction the performance at the state-subsidised Comédie Française of a play which depicted 130 years of French presence in Algeria as a farce in bad taste.

White gives a graphic account of Genet's involvement with the Black Panthers and of the publication in *Le Monde* on 2 September 1977 of 'Violence et brutalité' which was subsequently adopted as the preface to a collection of writings by members of the Red Army Faction and the Baader-Meinhof movement. Here again, as with *Les Nègres* in 1959, there is a strong similarity with positions taken by Sartre, although the two men differed on the subject of PLO support. For Sartre, who in this respect if in no other remained faithful to the traditions of European liberalism, Israel had a right to exist (the PLO, at the time, consistently refused to acknowledge any such right). Genet, not surprisingly for a man whose attitude to existence had never been marked by a quest for intellectual consistency, never made his position clear on this particular issue, preferring to argue that, for the West, the Arab had become the new Jew, with anti-Arab prejudices taking the place of the anti-Semitism of the past.

As with Genet's own career and literary production, the first half of White's book is more interesting than the closing chapters. He chronicles the various attempts which Genet made to give up writing, though without noting how similar his attitude had become to that of Sartre in that respect as well. Both men, from this point of view, came to represent a disillusionment with literature which stemmed in all probability from their growing realisation that literature would not change society, and that if the causes with which they had identified themselves were going to win, it would not be in the ways that they had desired. It was, after all, an ageing, outwardly cynical, conservatively-minded Catholic general who gave Algeria its independence, not the French intellectual left. Capitalist society, in turn, having made both Sartre and Genet very rich, seems as invulnerable to revolutionary change as it was when Genet was born into the very different world of the France of 1910. Where it has changed is in its attitude to children and the even greater tolerance it extends to those who would like to see it abolished, but it would not appear that either Genet or Sartre was greatly influential in bringing about either of these changes.

NOTES

1 Jean-Paul Sartre, *Words*, translated by Irene Clephane (Harmondsworth, 1985), pp. 14–15.

2 There is a misleading mistake in the translation of Sartre's title for the first volume of *Les Chemins de la liberté* as *The Age of Reason*. Unlike the English expression, the French term does not evoke the reasonableness of the Enlightenment or 'le siècle des lumières', but rather what is known in the Anglican Communion as the 'years of discretion'. With what is perhaps a greater realism in its awareness of when children become capable of moral choice, the Church of England places this at thirteen or fourteen. Had *L'Âge de raison* been translated as *The Years of Discretion* the irony of the title would have been as obvious to Sartre's English-speaking admirers as it was to his French readers. Mathieu has not reached 'l'âge de raison', since he can still not make any kind of informed moral choice – something amply illustrated by the plot of the novel.

There is a more clumsy if less misleading mistake in the translation of the 1952 essay *Les Communistes et la paix* as *The Communists and the Peace*, and a lack of appreciation, too, of cultural parallels in the translation of *L'Idiot de la famille* as *The Family Idiot*. In England it was traditionally the 'fool' of the family who was sent into the church, and this is very much Sartre's thesis as far as Flaubert is concerned. A verbatim translation of the title does not highlight this cultural association, the term 'idiot' carrying a harsher connotation in English.

3 Edmund White, *Genet* (London, 1993), p. 199.

4 Simon Raven, 'Boys will be Boys' in Simon Raven, *Boys will be Boys* (London, 1963).

5 Jean-Paul Sartre, *Saint Genet, Actor and Martyr*, translated by Bernard Frechtman (New York, 1963), p. 131.

6 Tony Parker, *The Unknown Citizen* (Harmondsworth, 1959).

CHAPTER 4

Interview with Edmund White

Stephen Barber

Editor's note: This interview took place on 1 October 1995 at Edmund White's flat in Paris. Stephen Barber and Edmund White have known one another for some years, and the interview was conducted during one of the periods Stephen Barber spent in Paris doing research for his forthcoming book on Edmund White.

Stephen Barber: It's over two years now since your biography of Genet came out, Ed. I wonder how you see it, looking back over the process of writing the biography. Does it seem something that is distanced now, or does it still seem that day-to-day intimate process of something alive?

Edmund White: I think [Genet] seems quite distant to me now. And I sometimes wonder how I ever managed to do it. I look at the book and I don't even recognise whole chapters of it. But even when I finished the book, at the moment I finished it, I realised I didn't really have a complete mastery of all the information in the book. And so I thought, books are really very curious things, especially full-scale biographies, because they are these compendia of all this information, that no-one, not even the author, ever masters. Certainly not the subject. Because Genet was very wrong about all the dates and the events and the sequence of events in his life, as one is. Usually the biographer knows more than the subject about the subject's life. But even the biographer can't keep it all in his head at any one moment. So there's something finally very elusive about a life, I would say, if for no other reason than just because of the sheer quantity of facts.

SB: Do you think that there's been any change in the level of interest in Genet in France since the book came out? I see that the German production of *Splendid's* is on at the Odéon at the moment, and they're having the autumn festival at La Villette.

EW: I do think that Genet is definitely someone who is awakening a lot of interest in France now, especially as we can judge from the people who come into IMEC [Institut Mémoires de l'Édition Contemporaine] to do research for doctoral theses. There are many more dissertations being done on Genet than ever before, and I think there's especially a renewed interest in his fiction, which didn't exist before. As best I can see, there are conferences being organised everywhere. Recently Philippe Sollers had a conference in Stockholm with a number of French people, and he presented two *inédits* of Genet that nobody knew about until then. (I think they had been discovered by a young researcher called Hérold.) I talked to Sollers this last summer and his interest in Genet certainly continues to grow, is very sustained. As you say, the theatre piece *Splendid's* has been performed in London with Neil Bartlett, and in Germany, and soon in America. A theatre magazine in America approached me and asked me to write a piece about Genet, which I did recently. So it seems to me that both on the level of fiction and on the level of theatre there is considerable interest. I published a book in the United States with Ecco Press of selected writings by Genet, a sort of Genet anthology, which did quite well. The biography is coming out soon in Italy and in Japan, so that should be of some interest. It was very, very widely reviewed in Germany, and it got a full-page review in *Die Zeit* by Fritz Raddatz, who's a leading novelist and critic; he used to be the editor of *Die Zeit*'s literary page. I was very pleased by that.

SB: It does seem to me, certainly from my perspective in Britain, there's an accumulating interest in Genet's work, especially from young novelists and young film makers in London. I think certainly your book has helped to crystallise a lot of their thoughts and the way in which they're working with Genet's texts.

EW: I think the book is a little too long to be entirely a popular success. I think if I had written a shorter, more interpretative or romanticised biography of Genet, it might have done more for his legend, and for mine. But it wasn't the kind of book I wanted to write. I think that if you are a novelist, you don't want to write a *biographie romancée*, you want to do something entirely different. The only reason to write in different genres is to explore their uniqueness, not just to blur them all one into the other.

CHAPTER 5

Interview with Jean-Paul Davidson

Barbara Read

Editor's note: Jean-Paul Davidson was the co-interviewer with Nigel Williams, for the BBC 'Arena' documentary on Jean Genet (November 1986). This interview took place on the evening of 12 May 1995 at the Union Club, 50 Greek Street, London W1.

Barbara Read: Whose idea was it to have the [BBC 'Arena' programme] interview [with Genet]?

Jean-Paul Davidson: Genet's. We got called up; I wasn't involved directly in that. It was very quick. We got a call from Joanna [Marston]. And we'd been trying for Genet for ages, because he was the sort of person that you want to interview. And suddenly the call came through that, yes, he would do an interview. And he'd be in London for two days, here was the fee, which was quite expensive for what it was, but he would do the interview, and it was to be in about ten days time, so it was, like, immediately. And then there was: 'Who's going to do it? Who knows anything about Genet?' And Nigel [Williams], obviously, because he knew about Genet. And I got called in the next day to see whether I would help out, because I knew the dramatic works quite well and spoke French – and they needed somebody to speak French. So we split it up so that Nigel would do the novels and I would do the plays.

BR: But you never actually appear as the interviewer.

J-PD: No, we shot it, in fact, with everyone, but then it seemed more confusing to have two people. So at the last minute we re-cut it so there would just be one person seeming to interview Genet, but in fact we split it up between the two of us.

BR: But when you originally filmed it, it was both of you interviewing him, wasn't it?

J-PD: Well, when we originally filmed it we didn't have any of us in it because the convention is that you don't actually see the interviewer. We were just by the camera and we exchanged questions. And then once we started cutting it, we realised, actually, it was so interesting, the dynamic that had gone on in the interview and so symptomatic of all his work, and so we would make a point of it; so we went back and shot all those cutaways – the reverses of Nigel, myself and the group – two months later. And then cut me and everyone else out.

BR: But it's quite interesting that he was the one who requested to be interviewed, because the way it comes over is almost as though it was the BBC who really wanted to interview him.

J-PD: Well we did. We'd been trying for ages. But why he suddenly decided that he would give the interview a bit out of the blue, I don't know. There were two conjectures that we had. One that he needed the money – I don't know what his financial circumstances were. Second, he had throat cancer, which was fairly advanced at the time, so maybe he needed to pay for that, or to provide money for his friends in Tunisia and Algeria, his various extended family. Or that he wanted to make a last testament and the BBC had a sort of grudging respect for it. They needed someone like Genet to do it.

BR: But yet there's one point in the interview where he says that he is annoyed with himself for having agreed to be interviewed. And yet he initiated it.

J-PD: He certainly initiated it in the sense of agreeing to do it. I don't think he phoned up and said, 'Oh, let's do an interview with the BBC now, I'm about to die.'

BR: Did you know he was about to die?

J-PD: No.

BR: You didn't? So none of the production crew knew?

J-PD: No. We knew that he had cancer, his throat cancer, but didn't know how advanced it was. And he was actually in very good form. What surprised me was (a), how well he had aged – he was a very handsome man, even aged seventy or whatever – and (b), he seemed in very good spirits as well. Cheeky as hell.

BR: Yes, there are moments where he's very lively. But in the beginning he looks very cagey.

J-PD: Yes, well he's not someone you can charm. It wasn't like you could get your way round him easily. I think the significant thing is – and maybe that was because we didn't even think about it – the interview style. You do an interview like you do, you have him on one chair, and then there are ten people on the other side; because there's camera, sound, lights, PA, Nigel and myself. And so it was interrogatory. And it is. That's when interviews work the best, when you have all that energy focused on one person, and then it's sort of confessional. And I think he responded to that, both in a positive and a negative way. He actually revealed quite a lot about himself, and then got irritated by the fact that he was. He thought he could con us, and you can't really because whatever you say is revealing.

BR: Yes, in a way I suppose that whole interview situation highlights the way in which you can't completely stand outside the norm and agree to participate in the ordinary, familiar environment.

J-PD: Yes, in that sense he'd taken part in lit. crit. He said one thing that's interesting – I can't remember if it's in the film or not. I asked him why he had never become a member of the French establishment. They would have given him a *chevalier de la légion d'honneur*, or made him like Sartre if he had wanted to, and he had no truck with it at all. He never did. He was never tempted by that. And I had a tremendous respect for that. That he was not to be bought out. I suppose his feeling of slight sulliedness with the interview was that he'd accepted this bit of filthy lucre but then had to play the game, and didn't like playing the game.

BR: One of the things that I noticed in the interview is that he says very little (and neither does he seem to have been asked, at least in the interview as broadcast) about his association with other writers like Cocteau and Sartre, or his time in America and knowing Allen Ginsberg.

J-PD: No, he didn't talk very much about other writers. You got the sense that he rather despised other writers. But then most writers don't talk about other writers.

BR: But you never asked him about them?

J-PD: We certainly asked about Sartre, he didn't have a lot to say about Sartre. And he didn't talk much about Ginsberg. The thing to do would be to get the original transcript for that and have a look what else is in there. Because there is a lot of editing, obviously, that goes on. I remember being very interested in the Black Panthers and his whole involvement with them. Is that in the film, or not?

BR: No, it's not.

J-PD: Because we did talk about that, I know.

BR: And the other thing that isn't in the film, that is perhaps quite surprising, is his involvement with the Palestinians.

J-PD: That's all in there, it's certainly in the interview.

BR: But not as broadcast.

I-PD: No, I know, but that's what I'm saying, there's probably ten times as much material. We did get into all that political thing. But, of course, in the end, because it's an arts programme, it broadly did the life, the biopic, and less of the politics.

BR: I know people who said after they watched the interview when it was first broadcast that they felt that more interesting questions could have been asked.

J-PD: Yes, well, I hope so! It's always a premier problem; what you include and what you exclude. He was quite evasive about the Palestinians. I can't remember but if I try and guess what he said, I have some vague memories that that was a period of his life, he got involved with the Palestinians – end of story.

BR: But it wasn't really, because at the time that he conducted the interview he was actually writing his last book, *Prisoner of Love*.

J-PD: Did he talk about that in the interview?

BR: He didn't, no. And I also wondered whether the crew was aware that he was writing this work, or whether he kept very secret about it.

J-PD: I don't remember it at all, him mentioning that, that he was writing. He didn't really want to talk about his literature at all. But that's not uncommon. We're doing a film at the moment, the biography of Gore Vidal; he hates to talk about his own work. And he's the most loquacious, brilliant person at talking. But, it's one of those things that's slightly embarrassing to talk about. Genet said he'd never really read one of his books. Once it's done, it's done, it's forgotten, it's history, out the way. And it's kind of like you had to remind him that he'd written these things. Like *The Balcony* and what happened in it.

BR: I remember when Nigel Williams says to him in the interview, 'I studied Genet at university', he says, 'Oh, no!' and then he says that he's slightly flattered, but he's also rather annoyed about it, which is curious.

J-PD: Well, he'd be more annoyed if he was ignored! That's the point. I should look at it again – as I say I haven't watched it for ten years – to see what comes over from him. I sensed particularly a man who really didn't want to compromise his life. I had tremendous respect for him for that. He said what he thought. He still played the games, that was the sparkle that was there. That was great, because it was exactly like you would imagine him to be.

BR: When he turned the tables on Nigel Williams, which he did several times in the interview, was there a feeling of playfulness about it, or was there a feeling of contrariness?

J-PD: No. It was more contrariness and it was more aggressive than playful; he was genuinely irritated by the probing. And he said at one point I remember, it's like being back in the police-cell being interrogated. No, he didn't like that. And he got irritated with some of the questions.

BR: At the outset when Nigel Williams introduces the interview [a voice-over prior to the actual interview and therefore not included in the transcript], he says that Genet didn't want to be interviewed in France, he wanted to be interviewed in England and he stayed with a member of the crew in south London.

J-PD: We did the interview at Nigel's house – I can't remember if he was staying there. He came into Nigel's house, which is in Putney, and looked round and said, 'Ah, oui, c'est très Miss Marple!' I thought it was lovely. He liked Nigel's son a lot as well, who was at that time about three years old. He was very sweet with him, with Harry. Apart from the difficult bits in the interview, he was very affable. We broke and had lunch and he chatted.

BR: So he was quite different in an informal situation?

J-PD: Not that he was warm. I think he slightly despised the whole environment of middle-class intellectuals talking about his work. But he certainly wasn't offensive. He was very polite and perfectly affable.

BR: How did Nigel Williams actually feel during the interview situation?

J-PD: I think Nigel was more nervous than I was, because I liked poking fun at [Genet], and I think you have to with someone like that, because there's a sort of conceit there. Because I think the conceit is, if you agree to be interviewed, then you have to expect that. And I think he got more irritated with me than with Nigel during the interview. I just thought it was being slightly childish. Interesting, but it was a bit childish. You get paid ten thousand pounds, or whatever, to be interviewed and that's what you do. You don't then say, 'Oh, well, let's interview the cameramen instead.'

BR: Were you surprised when he did that?

J-PD: No, not at all. No, because the night before I'd been re-reading all his plays, it actually made complete sense. And I thought, 'This is rather brilliant because he's doing exactly what happens in his plays – turns the tables, and it's about power structures.' So it was actually very revealing.

BR: And also actually plays with the form of the interview.

J-PD: So it seemed very good, but completely unpremeditated.

BR: So it was spontaneous when it happened?

J-PD: Absolutely. No, that wasn't contrived at all. The only thing that we contrived was to do it as if we had two cameras running on it, so we could do the reverses of the rest of us the other side of the camera, which we did at a later stage.

BR: It seems a pity that you weren't actually included in the interview as broadcast.

J-PD: I don't know. It was just for simplicity really. Because you don't normally have two people interviewing someone. And so it might have been a bit confusing. We cut a lot of it out in fact. The interchanges between our side and him. It didn't bother me. But it maybe would have been more interesting. If you have two cameras then it's fine, but if you always have to come back and do all those questions, it's never quite as spontaneous as when you're doing it for real. If we'd have known that that was going to happen, it would have been actually better to have two cameras running on it.

BR: When he turned the tables?

J-PD: Yes, rather than try and reconstruct what we had said. Because what you have to do then is film our interchanges as they really· happened again, and we're not as good actors as we should be.

BR: There's one point right towards the end of the interview where he says to Nigel Williams, 'Now you're trying to turn me into a myth,' but at the same time you get the feeling that he was actually trying to mythologise himself. Early on in the interview he presents himself as not having had a secure childhood. He says that the family is the first prison cell. But in the light of Edmund White's biography it doesn't appear to have been a particularly unhappy childhood. He was fostered from the age of seven months, rather than six years as Sartre maintains in *Saint Genet*. And apparently, according to Edmund White's biography, his foster-mother absolutely doted on him and favoured him above her own children.

J-PD: Really? That was the nature of the person wasn't it? I just think, the way he lived was his own mythology. He obviously had a ken for that. Having been lauded as this great wonderful creature, the way the French do, when they decide that you're one of their stars, you're there for life. You can't lose it. It happens with Johnny Hallyday. You're there for ever – whereas here they'd be ditched. And he could have been that, a celebrity ex-con who became a great writer. Perfect material. But I think he didn't want that, that wasn't the myth that he wanted.

BR: But he was still that in a lot of ways. He's considered to be one of their great twentieth-century writers, I think even by themselves.

J-PD: Yes, I saw a fantastic performance of *The Screens*. They are doing Genet a lot today and particularly because of the homosexual side of it, and there are so many gay people in the theatre. So there's obviously an attraction there with Genet's work. He is, no doubt, one of the greats, but he didn't become a member of their little coterie of intellectuals. He didn't want that.

BR: No, but even so, during say the forties and fifties he was embraced by that culture, wasn't he?

J-PD: Yes. And I think the forties and fifties was fine; that was his coming out and being sought after. But what he could have done as he got older in the sixties and seventies and eighties was actually become a sort of doyen, in the way that Marcuse and any of the people who were radical became part of the establishment. And that's what I think he didn't want. He was unforgiving in that sense.

BR: And he always lived in hotel rooms.

J-PD: Yes, he never had a house.

BR: He bought houses for other people but never for himself.

J-PD: He was obviously very generous with his friends as well. You did get a sense of that generosity.

BR: And Edmund White testifies to that in his biography, that with his friends he was very generous. And it also comes out in a relatively short piece, Mohammed Choukri's *Jean Genet in Tangier*. He says the same thing.

J-PD: I got the feeling, I'm sure, the money was for people in Tangier. I definitely got that impression, that there was a need for some liquid cash. I don't know about the estate. He probably didn't have a huge amount of money coming in.

BR: He would get royalties.

J-PD: He would get royalties but Genet does not sell brilliantly. OK, it'd be very interesting to find out – find out what his income was.

BR: There's an interview with Hubert Fichte in *Die Zeit* [13 February 1976] where he talks about leaving Gallimard with wads of money and didn't care whether somebody robbed him or not. That was all part of the game.

J-PD: But he definitely wanted this money. There was definitely a sense that there was a need for it. Maybe he was paying their hospital bills or something like that. (Talk to Joanna, ask her. She was the one who actually put it together.) It was a lot of money, to cover his coming over from Paris with two other people. Ten thousand pounds. Compare ten thousand pounds now, ten years later. But obviously what you're paying for is an exclusivity there, and the fact that he hasn't done it before. But it wasn't a particularly expensive film overall because it was just the interview and some clips and that. I don't think Genet sells hugely well, you don't make a huge fortune with Genet worldwide. But it was very well appreciated by festivals and that. Just because you haven't done

Genet before. The audience wasn't particularly big because, again, who knows about Genet here? A very small number of people.

BR: And now, I think, with Edmund White's biography he has his exposure.

J-PD: Yes, but you see his plays aren't done, they haven't been done for ages.

BR: Not in a major sense, but just very recently there's been a production of *Deathwatch* at a small theatre down in Baron's Court.

J-PD: But I'm talking of the National or the RSC.

BR: The RSC did a series – at the Barbican, in 1987. That was the Trevor Hands series of productions. They did *The Balcony*, *The Maids* and *Deathwatch* – those three. And that ran for about a couple of months.

J-PD: But it's phases, isn't it? In the seventies he was performed everywhere.

BR: There seem to be quite a few people who've been influenced by Genet. Kathy Acker is a great admirer of him, and maybe to some extent she's been influenced by him. She cites him and Pierre Guyotat as being two writers she very much admires, and she's also to some extent influenced by Marguerite Duras. He's influenced a number of younger playwrights, particularly Bernard-Marie Koltès.[1]

J-PD: The person that I phoned about a week before was my old tutor at Bristol, Ted Bourne, saying 'I'm going to interview Genet'. I did a course on Genet at Bristol in the Drama department. It was certainly a very good course at the time, in the mid-seventies, when Genet was extremely popular. He was the man of the moment really. And it was strange to be successful in both spheres, in the novel and the theatre. I mean there are not many who manage that.

BR: No, Sartre to some extent, but then Sartre was more of a philosopher than anything else.

J-PD: Yes, neither the plays nor novels are brilliant. Whereas, I think people would admit that with Genet the best of his plays and the best of his novels are brilliant, and incredibly original and inspired texts.

BR: Although, apparently, he felt very insecure about them and worried about the quality of his writing and whether or not he was a good writer.

J-PD: I haven't seen the 'Arena' film for about ten years.

BR: I've watched it a few times because I've used it in teaching, and I also watched it a few times just after it came out. It was re-broadcast on 3 May 1986 about three weeks after he died.

J-PD: But it hasn't been broadcast again since. It's good that it has an academic life. Because I definitely felt at the time that there was something historic there, because he hadn't done any TV interviews before. So it was an opportunity to try and get something as a record.

BR: I certainly think it's seen as very valuable.

J-PD: I don't think he really found it that unpleasant an experience. There's the vanity of the writer who actually quite appreciates people who have read all of his books. And although they pretend not to be, I think secretly they are quite pleased that people have taken the trouble to read them and study them. He was quite headmasterish in a way. He'd sometimes say, 'That's quite a good question', or 'That's a stupid question.'

BR: But that's rather curious, because one would think that he wouldn't approve of such condescension. He certainly wouldn't like to be spoken to in that way himself, would he?

J-PD: Not at all.

BR: One of the interesting aspects of Genet, which I don't think came out too clearly in the interview as broadcast, is that, even though he did have an education, had more of an education than had previously been thought, he nevertheless finished his education when he was fourteen. He never went to university and yet went on to become one of France's greatest contemporary writers. Was that at all discussed?

J-PD: But I don't find that surprising. If you learn to read, then you can teach yourself all that. My father left school at fourteen and he was one of the most widely read and, in that sense, intellectual people that I've met. If you have access to books you can do it. I think that's part of the myth that we've got with university life now, that you have to have a university education to do it; whereas [Genet] was there with people, and he had a fantastic group of people in Paris at that time who took him up. And he was obviously incredibly curious about everything. And that's what's exciting about his life, that he remained curious, and went off with the Black Panthers or the Palestinians. I should have asked him about [Paul] Bowles – whether he knew Bowles, I don't know if he did.

BR: He was in Tangier. It might be worth asking Edmund White.[2]

J-PD: Bowles wrote his autobiography a couple of years ago. I must find it out. I should ask Gore [Vidal] about it, about Genet. He knows everything. He was a bit younger than Genet, but would obviously have been very excited by him, to have this very openly homosexual writer writing extravagant stuff.

BR: It seems from Edmund White's biography that Cocteau was actually quite jealous of Genet, because he was so open about his homosexuality in his works.

J-PD: He was quite lyrical about it as well. What was nice is it didn't come over as any type of perversion. It was just like his love affairs. And that's why *Un Chant d'Amour* – which I loved – is such a beautiful little film.

BR: Yes, it has a very strong aesthetic quality, even though at the time it was seen as pornography and was banned when it first came out. It was very difficult to show it – and the same with the books, they were sold under the counter but yet to our standards now they wouldn't be considered pornography.

J-PD: No, rather romantic and lyrical, very beautiful. I remember when we were doing the Genet course at Bristol; they got the film for us to view and I was quite amazed, because it was so graphic, even in the mid-seventies. Well it would be pornographic, because you're not allowed to have erect penises, are you? That's what it really amounts to, there's a curious bit of Anglo-Saxon law there.

BR: Is that only Anglo-Saxon?

J-PD: I don't know about other countries. I know certainly here you can have anything, basically, so long as there's not an erect willy there.

BR: But in Genet's case one wonders whether he was trying to be pornographic or just trying to be shocking?

J-PD: At the time he must have been wanting to shock. But also why it works is because it's truthful, isn't it? That's what you imagine prisoners do. And the whole thing of blowing smoke through the hole has a truthfulness about it.

BR: But yet you wouldn't think of it as being truthful until you actually see it, and you recognise it then. That is probably what happens.

J-PD: It seems very personal to me. That he would have experienced that sort of thing.

BR: In the interview, very early on, when Nigel Williams says to him, 'Wasn't there one special person in your life? One special love?', he replies, 'Oh no! There were two hundred!' But you wonder whether that's him exaggerating for the sake of effect.

J-PD: I don't think there was a particular person in his life.

BR: When he was very young?

J-PD: Well, throughout his life. There's not a constant companion who travelled through it.

BR: There wasn't one constant companion but there were a few very strong relationships.

J-PD: You don't get the sense as, say with Edmund White and Hubert [Sorin], that there's a 'love of his life', with Genet.

BR: In the biography Edmund White writes about one man, Decimo C, an Italian, who was homosexual and who Genet thought was dying of tuberculosis. And Edmund White wrote about this lover as being the love of Genet's life, but it was a disappointing love and Genet was very heartbroken. It didn't come to what he'd hoped it would.

J-PD: I remember he was quite cheeky. It was rather sweet because he kept teasing me about my pronunciation of certain words, I was asking him about love and *l'amour*.

BR: Oh, it was you! I think most people who've seen that interview, would have thought it was Nigel Williams asking that, and that he was pulling up Nigel Williams about his pronunciation.

J-PD: He was very cheeky about that, because he knew exactly what I meant. He was saying, '*L'amour* or *la mort*?'

BR: But that was done in play?

J-PD: Yes it was. But his playfulness always had a certain sort of barbedness to it. It wasn't completely banal. It had an edge.

BR: When Nigel Williams talks about the human need to be close to people and says something like, 'Do you never feel that with a special lover you want intimacy?', he actually says, 'No, what would worry me is if there were no space between me and you!'

J-PD: All the personal questions were my ones, I remember.

BR: What I noticed in watching the interview again recently is that when he answers the personal questions he's very defensive, and that's when he turns the tables.

J-PD: He doesn't like it. When he was talking generally about things, or even explaining things, then he was quite happy, and I was probing him all the time, and about death; I think I asked him about death quite a bit, as well.

BR: That doesn't really come out, only at the end of the interview he says: 'Oh, you're asking me about how I spend my time. I suppose I would say with Saint Augustine, I'm waiting for death.' But in the light of the fact that he had throat cancer, that doesn't have as poetic a ring as it had when one watched it not knowing.

J-PD: You should get hold of the longer transcripts definitely. It would be interesting because then you can see what his evasions are. Sometimes they're interesting, but sometimes they're just annoying. It's quite rare to have that amount of concentrated interview with someone. I do remember that we spent two days, literally ten o'clock till five o'clock, with a break for lunch. And that mode is very intense.

BR: It was through watching the interview that I myself really became fascinated by Genet. I was interested in his work before that, but watching the interview really inspired me, even though he was difficult and defensive. I remember some of the drama staff at Middlesex [University] saying, 'Oh, he was just awful, he came over as a really cantankerous old man.' And then other people who watched it said that they thought he came over as being really quite appealing. My initial impression of it was that he was very enchanting, whereas if I watch it now I can see how some of his responses were rather irritating. They seem to be purposefully obstructive to the interviewer.

J-PD: He was, he was. I can only compare them to those of someone like Ionesco, of the same age and ilk, equally famous in his own right, of a particular time, who was completely charming and you'd go out to dinner with him and he'd want to really talk and talk about his work. And almost embarrasingly so. Whereas Genet didn't really want to talk about himself or his work.

BR: Well, what did he want to talk about?

J-PD: He didn't. There was a sense that he was always on the point of saying, 'I've had enough; I've given what I came to give.'

BR: Albert Dichy met Genet in the Lebanon for about fifteen minutes at a political gathering and he said Genet would not talk about his work at all, he couldn't get him to talk about his work. He was only interested in discussing politics.

J-PD: No. I do remember that very distinctly, he really wasn't interested in his own work. That was a different life for him. Which is a bit annoying when you've paid somebody a whole bunch of money to talk about their work, and they say, 'Oh, that was irrelevant. That's not what's important now.'

BR: And when he talks about the plays he says, 'Oh, they were thirty years ago.' And the kind of impression he gives in the interview is that he doesn't have anything to do with writing and whiles away his time in Morocco, which in fact wasn't true because he was writing a book.

J-PD: I don't think he talked about that at all. I really don't. I think we would have had it in the interview if it had been there.

BR: And it was so important to him. Towards the end of his life (Albert Dichy told me this) he was given medication for the pain of the throat cancer; and he actually stopped taking his medication because it made him sleepy, just in order to finish the book. So it was important to him.

J-PD: Yes. There was a sort of con there with him, wasn't there? That, if you're a writer, you're a writer. You can't just say, 'That doesn't exist for me, it's not important.' And it's not like he then became a complete revolutionary. He didn't abandon his literary credentials to become a Black Panther or a member of the PLO; he was too much of an intellectual to do that.

BR: He didn't, but he had a very significant contact with the PLO. He was a good friend of Leila Shahid Barrada, who is now the French representative of the PLO. And he was in the Lebanon at the time of the Sabra and Shatila massacres and wrote about them very movingly. And he's had essays published in the *Journal of Palestine Studies.*

J-PD: Yes, he was very involved with that. That was his life, really, from the early seventies, wasn't it? He took that on and it became his home, the Arab world and the dispossessed. He could obviously identify with that notion. They were also terribly friendly and so hospitable. I can imagine him actually being very happy there.

You *know* when you meet extraordinary people, there are a few: and Genet, the Dalai Lama, Gore Vidal and Lech Wałesa are certainly the four I remember the most distinctly from those interview situations. You just *know* that they've done something extraordinary with their lives.

BR: And they have a certain charisma.

J-PD: Definitely. It's because they know who they are. They're so definite.

BR: It's interesting you should say that because in many ways Genet doesn't seem to know who he is; he's constantly struggling and playing with different personae and you get the sense of a great uncertainty about who he really is behind all of that.

J-PD: It may be true if you take away the onion layers, you know, 'Who's there?' But he has a very definite presence. When he came in you were aware that there was somebody who had a sparkling intellect and also there was a danger. A lack of compromise. They would play a game, but it was their game. And they might just suddenly say, 'Right! That's it!'

BR: So, he was completely in control?

J-PD: Yes.

BR: Almost like the crew were puppets?

J-PD: Well, I don't think we really got the better of him in any of that. He probably allowed us to get what he wanted. Which is true of the skilful ones like that, they tell you what they want. I think there was a sense you got with Genet, that he actually thought about each question before he answered.

BR: To try to get to the core of the truth.

J-PD: Exactly. Whereas other people, you ask them ...

BR: ... and they just speak off the top of their head.

J-PD: Yes, or they've done it so many times that they just do it. They have a felicity with language which enables them to just yabber, yabber, yabber. Whereas with Genet, I think you did sense that he was thinking about it. And that's what caused him pain. He wasn't a natural with the PR machinery. You couldn't wheel him out and say, 'You've got a new book Jean; go and sell it.' He wasn't prepared to play that game.

BR: I suppose he's that sort of writer, isn't he? Say if you'd interviewed Sartre, he would have been quite different.

J-PD: Yes, I think he would have played the game much more, because he was used to that, as well. It was the idea that [Genet] didn't become part of the establishment. Whether it was a literary establishment or a sort of cultural establishment.

BR: But did you sense he was happy being apart? Or maybe 'happy' isn't the right word.

J-PD: I don't know. 'Happy', it's a difficult concept, isn't it? But he didn't seem a miserable person at all. You sensed that. It's the old twinkle in the eye.

BR: Yes, that comes over – his eyes were really sparkling at times.

J-PD: It's the mischief in him. He didn't lose his mischief.

BR: Yes and I think it was that mischievous side that saved him from being really difficult and irritating.

J-PD: And pompous. He's not pompous. No, they were a hard couple of days because you had to concentrate. He kept you on your toes. You couldn't relax and, say, shoot the breeze with him. He was demanding in that sense. And I actually do think he was truly surprised that we'd read all his books and knew about them, because he couldn't remember them. And that doesn't surprise me.

BR: Somebody said to me quite recently that the Nembutal he was taking (because he couldn't sleep) had an effect on his memory. And that there were whole areas of his early life that he simply couldn't remember. Whether that was a convenience ... ?

J-PD: It might have been.

BR: And I understand that Nembutal only affects short-term memory but not long-term memory.

J-PD: So, elective memory loss. Very convenient. It's about the age as well, isn't it? You do lose memory at seventy. He could have remembered much more about his early years, I'm sure, if he'd wanted to. So I think that was a sort of elective 'I don't want to know', 'I don't want to go back to that'. And whether he'd convinced himself that it was unhappy, or it was truly unhappy, we'll never know.

NOTES

1 See Chapter 15 of this book, 'Genet, the Theatre and the Algerian War'.
2 White (Edmund White, *Genet* (London, 1993), pp. 574 and 593) says that Bowles never sought out Genet and that the two avoided each other, Genet thinking that Bowles had something of an 'orientalist' approach to the Arabs because of his recording of Moroccan music and his transcription and translation of oral accounts of Moroccan life (Ed.).

CHAPTER 6

BBC 'Arena' Interview with Jean Genet

Nigel Williams

Editor's note: This interview with Jean Genet was broadcast on BBC2 television, 12 November 1985. Although Nigel Williams is cited here and in *L'Ennemi déclaré* as the sole interviewer, and in the television programme itself only he is seen interviewing Genet, this interview was in fact conducted by both Nigel Williams and Jean-Paul Davidson. For more on this, see the interview with Jean-Paul Davidson, Chapter 5.

Jean Genet: On my police record, I think there are fourteen convictions for theft. What that means is that I was really a very poor thief, since I kept getting caught.

I was in prison, locked up, as I told you yesterday [the filming of the interview took place over two days], and on trial facing transportation for life. I wasn't going to get out of prison ever again. So I was certain that nobody would ever read my book. I could say whatever I liked, since there would be no readers. But it turned out that there were some readers.

* * *

Nigel Williams: Monsieur Genet, you were born in 1910. Is that right?

JG: Yes.

NW: In Paris?

JG: Yes.

NW: But you didn't know your parents, I believe.

JG: At that time? No. And I still don't.

NW: So you weren't brought up in a family?

JG: Yes I was, but not in my own family.

NW: Was it hard for you to live in a family which was not your own?

JG: You're asking me to talk to you about my feelings as a child. To do that properly, which would need a sort of archeological excavation of my life, is absolutely impossible. All I can tell you is that as I remember it, it was certainly a difficult period. But by escaping the family, I escaped the feelings I might have had for the family and the feelings which the family might have had for me. So I am completely – and this dates back to a very early age – completely cut off from any family feeling. It is in fact one of the good features of the French Child Welfare system which brings up kids pretty well by preventing them from getting attached to a family. In my opinion, the family is probably the first criminal cell, and the most criminal. If now, at my age, you want to envisage the child that I used to be, I can see him, but I see him surrounded by other children who were just kids like me; and all their struggles, all their humiliations, or all their courage, all that seems a bit trivial, a bit remote.

* * *

JG: It's true I had stolen previously, but I wasn't sent to Mettray for theft. I was sent to Mettray because I took a train without buying a ticket. I rode on the train from Meaux to Paris without a ticket. And I was sentenced to three months in jail and to the Mettray Penal Colony until the age of twenty.

NW: Do you think that if you had paid for that train ticket your life would have been completely different?

JG: Listen ... Do you believe in God?

NW: Sometimes.

JG: Then ask Him! Ask Him if my life would have been different. I've no idea.

* * *

JG: I think that the goings-on between the 'older brother'[1] (who had a position of authority) and the boys in the Colony like me (who were in a subordinate position) gave the warders a show they greatly enjoyed. If you like, the warders were in the front row of the audience, and we were the actors. And they took great delight in watching us.

NW: Was the discipline at Mettray tough?

JG: Ah! the discipline was very, very strict. It was, I suppose, military discipline. Does Mettray interest you?

NW: Very much.

JG: Mettray, you see, was set up in 1840, that is, under Louis-Philippe. It was when the French began to spread out all over the world. The French Empire – which you must certainly have heard of – France still had a navy of sailing ships and Mettray was a training centre for sailors. In the courtyard of the Colony at Mettray there was a huge sailing-ship and we learnt how to handle boats on dry land, at least how to handle sails and oars. So the discipline wasn't even military discipline, it was naval discipline. For example, we slept in hammocks; the youngsters of my age, all those being punished, had to sleep in hammocks. The language we used among ourselves was Navy language, naval slang.

* * *

NW: In your books, you have written about love in the Colony. For you, did love begin with a boy?

JG: Did you say love [*l'amour*]? I though you said death [*la mort*]!

NW: Love, I meant to ask about love, not death!

JG: All right. What was the question?

NW: For you, love began not in the family, but with a boy, I think …

JG: No! Not with *a* boy, with two hundred! What are you saying!

NW: With two hundred?

JG: One after the other, of course …

NW: But wasn't there a favourite, one special one?

JG: Oh! favourites, special ones, you know, there were so many of them!

NW: Did you make a politics of homosexuality?

JG: But is there a politics of homosexuality? How do you expect that when I was still a kid – let's say I experienced my first sexual feelings at around the age of thirteen or fourteen – how do you think that at that age I could have decided to make a political issue of homosexuality?

NW: Yes, yes, I understand that. But now, at the present time, it has become a political issue. Because you were one of the first to talk about it ...

JG: What are you on about! Listen, you had Oscar Wilde ... If you just take England, you had Oscar Wilde, Shakespeare, Byron and so many others ... What are you on about!

NW: Did you feel proud?

JG: Of Byron, of Oscar Wilde? I was never proud of Byron![2]

* * *

JG: By putting me in prison the French rejected me, but at the same time I asked for nothing better than to be driven out of France, to escape from the oppressive French atmosphere and discover a different world. Passports weren't easy to get, but when you had completed your military service, they gave you a passbook, more or less like a passport. I fixed a photograph on it and when I showed it to customs officials, once it had two or three stamps on it, it was as good as a passport!

NW: Did you start stealing because you were hungry?

JG: If you like, there were two things mixed together: on the one hand there was hunger, true hunger, when your stomach is crying out for food, and at the same time it was a game. It's fun stealing, much more fun even than answering questions from the BBC!

NW: But it was no fun when the cops caught you, was it?

JG: When the cops caught me, of course, it was ... like falling into the abyss. It was the end of the world. When a policeman's hand ... I suppose, like this ... [*He stands up and puts his hand on Nigel Williams' shoulder.*] I knew exactly what that meant.

NW: Oh! I'm still afraid of that. When I was a child, I used to steal things, but ... I'm still afraid of the police!

JG: Yes, but the hand on your shoulder from behind ...

NW: Not good!

JG: Yes, but you have to pay for the pleasure of stealing.

NW: Yes.

JG: You have to pay for everything.

* * *

NW: During the Occupation, were you pleased at the Germans being in France?

JG: Overjoyed! Overjoyed! I detested France so much, and I still do, that I was overjoyed that the French Army had been beaten. It had been beaten by the Germans, by Hitler, and I was very happy about it.

NW: Do you still feel the same way? Aren't you at all proud of being French or of writing in French?

JG: Good God, no! Oh no!

* * *

JG: I told you earlier that I started writing my first book on paper for making paper bags. I had written about the first fifty pages of *Notre-Dame-des-Fleurs* and then I was taken to court for the preliminary hearing of my case – I've forgotten which offence it was for – and I had left the sheets of paper on the table. The workshop master had the keys, he could go into any of the cells any time he liked, and while I was in court he went into my cell and saw the sheets of paper covered in writing. He confiscated them and handed them over to the governor of the Santé prison – and since we had that little misunderstanding over the words *amour* and *mort,* I'll tell you that at that time the governor of the Santé was called Monsieur Amor. The sheets of paper were given to him, and so the next evening, when I got back to my cell, they had vanished. So the first part of my novel had vanished. I was called up before the governor the next day and I was sentenced to three days confinement to my cell and to three or six days of bread and water. And my sheets of paper were thrown away. So what did I do? Three days later, when I was no longer confined to my cell, I went to the store, as I had the right to, and asked for an exercise book. Then I got under the blankets and tried to remember the sentences I had written and I started what I had done all over again.

* * *

NW: Let's suppose we meet the writer Jean Genet himself. Is it the real Genet we are meeting?

JG: Is there a false one going around? Is there a false Genet at large? Am I the real one? You ask me if I am the real one. So where is the false one?

NW: Yes, I understand.

JG: Perhaps after all I am an impostor who has never written a book. Perhaps I am a false Genet, as you say.

* * *

NW: Have you always felt yourself as being separate from others?

JG: Listen, you're there, I'm here, and at this very moment I still feel myself separate. I've always been on my own, whether in the Morvan or whether with you.

NW: But have there been moments when you didn't feel so?

JG: No.

NW: Never? Never in your whole life?

JG: No.

NW: Even, I don't know, when you were with someone, or even in love? Do you think man is always alone?

JG: As to man, I don't know, I don't want to generalise. But as far as I'm concerned, yes.

NW: And has that distressed you?

JG: Not at all. It would distress me if there were no space between us.

NW: And how can one person get close to another?

JG: I prefer not to get close.

NW: You prefer to always keep a distance?

JG: Oh yes!

NW: But why?

JG: And you, do you prefer to keep a distance?

NW: Not always, no.

JG: And why not?

NW: Becaue I like the experience of being with someone, of being entangled with someone.

JG: Well, I don't.

NW: Isn't this really what your plays are all about?

JG: The last play I wrote was thirty years ago. You're talking to me of something I've completely erased from my memory: the theatre.

* * *

JG: I had scarcely ever been to the theatre. I had seen a few plays, but very few. Very few and they were plays by Alexandre Dumas or ... But it wasn't so difficult because – what I was explaining to you yesterday, I think – my approach to society is an oblique one. It isn't direct. Neither is it a parallel path, since it crosses it, it crosses the world, seeing it as it does so. It is oblique. I saw the world diagonally, and I still see it diagonally, though perhaps more directly today than twenty-five or thirty years ago. The theatre, or at any rate the theatre I prefer, is precisely that which lays hold of society diagonally.

If you like, what interests me is doing a job as well as possible. (The cameraman is asking me to sit in a certain way.) The work did indeed interest me but whether it was a new approach, I didn't know then and I don't know now. It's not for me to say, but in any case, it intrigued me. It's an approach which, if it isn't new, was certainly clumsy. And by being clumsy, it perhaps acquired a certain novelty. Because it was clumsy.

* * *

JG: I was in the theatre occupied by the students in May 1968. And it wasn't just any theatre: it was the theatre[3] where *Les Paravents* had been performed. If they had been true revolutionaries, they wouldn't have occupied a theatre, above all not the National Theatre. They would have occupied law-courts, prisons, radio stations. In short, they would have acted as revolutionaries, as Lenin did. They didn't do that. So what was going on? The theatre is set out like that, isn't it? It is more or less round, in the Italian style. On the stage there were young people with placards and speeches. The speeches came from the stage into the audience and back onto the stage again – there was a circular movement of revolutionary speeches which went from the stage to the audience, from the audience to the stage, from the stage to the audience, from the audience to the stage ... and it went on and on and never left the theatre. Do you see? Precisely, well more or less, as the revolutionaries in *Le Balcon* never leave the brothel.

NW: Did it make you laugh to see that?

JG: It didn't make me laugh and it didn't make me ... I'm simply saying how it is.

NW: But you don't really support the revolutionaries?

JG: You mean the pseudo-revolutionaries.

NW: Or the true revolutionaries, like Lenin?

JG: I would tend to be on Lenin's side, yes.

* * *

JG: I had a dream last night. I dreamt that the technicians making this film rebelled. While they're taking the preparatory shots for a film, they never have the right to speak. Why is that? And I imagined that they would have the nerve – we were talking of nerve yesterday – to throw me out, to take my place. And yet they don't move. Can you ask them how they explain that?

NW: Yes. Er ... How they ... ?

JG: How they explain that. Why they don't come and shove me away, shove you away too, and then say: 'What you're saying is so stupid that I've no desire to carry on with this job!' Ask them that.

NW: Yes, of course. [*He turns to the technicians and translates Genet's question into English for them.*]

JG: The sound engineer too.

[*Nigel Williams asks the sound engineer, Duncan Fairs, who replies that he doesn't have much to say for the moment, that those who work every day lose their sense of objective judgment about what they are doing and remain trapped in their own private little world. He adds that the technicians make their contribution after the filming; to do so during filming would incur too great a cost for the production company making the film.*]

NW: But is that what interested you in your dream: disrupting order? In a way, you want to break up the order that exists in this room?

JG: Break up order?

NW: Yes.

JG: Of course. Of course. It seems so rigid to me! I'm on my own over here, and facing me there are one, two, three, four, five, six people. Of course I want to break up the order, and that's why yesterday I asked you to come and sit here, of course.

NW: Yes, it's like being questioned by the police?

JG: There is that, of course. I told you – is this being filmed? Fine – I told you yesterday that you were doing a cop's job, and you're still doing the same thing, now, this morning. I told you so yesterday and you've forgotten already, because you're still questioning me exactly as the thief I was thirty years ago was questioned by the police, by a squad of police. I'm sitting here, alone, and I'm being questioned by several people. There is the norm on one side, the norm where you are: two, three, four, five, six, seven, and after that also the film editors and the BBC, and then there is the margin where I am, where I am marginalised. Am I afraid to enter into the norm? Of course I am afraid to enter it and if at this moment my voice is raised in anger, it's because I'm entering into the norm, I'm in the process of entering British homes, and obviously that doesn't please me. But I'm not angry with you, who are the norm, I am angry with myself, because I agreed to come here. And that doesn't please me at all.

NW: But your books are even taught in schools here in Britain.

JG: Oh! What's that you say?

NW: It's true. I studied Genet at university.

JG: Hm! ...

NW: Does that please you?

JG: On the one hand, there is a feeling of vanity, but at the same time it's disagreeable. Of course, there is this double ... this double imperative. Is this being filmed?

NW: Yes, it's being filmed.

JG: Good. So ask me some questions, since the system requires that I'm the one being questioned.

* * *

NW: You don't live in France at present, do you?

JG: No, Morocco.

NW: Do you have a house in Morocco?

JG: No.

NW: So you 'hang out' with friends, if I may use the expression?

JG: No, I live in a hotel.

NW: Why in Morocco?

JG: Can I ask you a question? Why not Morocco? And why this question? Because you, like everyone else, want to transform me into a myth, because you belong to your – what's it called – BBC, eh?

NW: Or else perhaps because there is another reason, because you have an affinity with the country, the people, because you like the landscape ...

JG: Oh! You know, I like all landscapes. Even where they're most desolate, even England ...

NW: Could you live anywhere?

JG: Yes. Yes. Yes. Absolutely. Of course.

NW: It doesn't matter?

JG: No …

NW: And how do you spend your days over there?

JG: Ah! yes … You want to raise the question of time? Well, I shall reply as Saint Augustine did: 'I'm waiting for death.'

[Translated by Ian Birchall from the typescript of the interview in Albert Dichy (ed.), *L'Ennemi déclaré: textes et entretiens* in Jean Genet, *Œuvres Complètes VI* (Paris, 1991), pp. 297–306.]

NOTES

1 The 'older brother' was an inmate selected on the basis of authority and good behaviour to supervise the activities of one of the families into which the colonists at Mettray were divided.

2 Williams is here apparently asking Genet if he is proud of his homosexuality, but Genet, deliberately or otherwise, misunderstands the question. In French, Williams' question allows the two possibilities and could be a reference to his homosexuality or to the preceding list of writers.

3 The Odéon, part of the French National Theatre.

CHAPTER 7

An Erotics of Diversity: The unsuspected sex of Genet's heroes

Mairéad Hanrahan

GENET'S SECOND NOVEL, *Miracle de la Rose*, constitutes a paean of praise to male beauty. The text recounts the narrator's relationship with a series of men whose charm on a preliminary reading seems in direct proportion to their masculinity; the more virile and phallic their appearance, the greater their fascination for Genet. But I would like to argue that, far from shoring up the cult of the phallus, Genet is profoundly subversive of the orthodoxy, most clearly articulated by Lacan, which privileges the phallus as (part-)object of desire. His writing is exceptional not only in the way it insidiously devirilises the images whose maleness it eulogises, but in the high symbolic and erotic value it attaches to the femininity it thus reveals in the most phallic of men. One of the most remarkable aspects of Genet's fantasmatic structure, in terms of sexual politics, is that the 'loss' of phallic status he enjoys imagining for character after character is represented not as a loss, a castration, but as a sexual enrichment. The work of this renowned homosexual (literally, same-sex lover) breaks new symbolic ground by presenting an *erotics of diversity*.

The narrator himself draws attention to the unexpected erotic charm he finds in the loss of the attributes which first aroused his desire:

> I mean that whenever I discovered a ridiculous side to a boy, a blemish, a stain on his beauty, it did not prevent me from being in love with him. I even went so far as to be in love because of it. Too weary of loving, I have followed, spied on kids quivering with grace, until the charm was broken. I would wait for the moment, the glance which would enable me to discover the speck of ugliness, the angle that would be enough to indicate the ugliness, the line or volume destroying the beauty, so that I would be rid of the burden of love, but it often happened, on the contrary, that when I had seen the boy from all sides [*faces*], he would sparkle with a thousand other lights and catch me in the confusion of charms entangled in his multiplied facets [*facettes multipliées*]. And the discovered blemish would no longer be enough to free me. On the contrary. In seeking it, I would discover each time a new point of view of the masterpiece.[1]

The 'stain' on the boy's beauty serves to *increase* both his beauty and the narrator's bewitchment. The ugliness which shows a new angle of the 'masterpiece' adds to its charm, becomes another, equally precious aspect of its beauty, with the result that it is impossible to determine where beauty ends and ugliness begins.

The narrator describes himself observing the boy as a jeweller inspects a jewel for imperfections. The reason the boy sparkles 'with a thousand other lights' is that the 'blemish' discovered is part of the jewel: seeing the boy 'from all sides [*faces*]' enables the narrator to discover the 'charms' of his 'multiplied facets'. It is significant that Bijou (Jewel) is the nickname of Bulkaen, one of the men the narrator loves. The nickname is particularly rich in ambiguity in French: the plural expression 'family jewels' (*les bijoux de famille*) is slang for the testicles, whereas the singular 'jewel', as in English, symbolises the female genitals.[2] These connotations lend a sexual dimension to the 'confusion of charms' entangled in the boy's 'multiplied facets'. It seems that, far from being repugnant to the narrator, the diversity of a boy's 'jewels' enhances his attraction.

Divers

It is especially in relation to that other character with a 'singular' name, Divers, that Genet explores the value of diversity:

> The fact that he was called Divers gave him an earthly, nocturnal dream quality which was enough to enchant me [*m'enchanter*]. For one is not called Georges Divers, or Jules, or Joseph Divers, and this nominal singleness placed him on a throne as if, from the time he was in the children's prison, glory had recognised him. This name was almost a nickname, royal, brief, haughty, a convention.[3]

Divers' name is both single and diverse: the narrator is 'enchanted', as by Bulkaen's nickname, by its numerical undecidability. Note the importance of subjecting Genet's writing to the same close scrutiny he gives the objects of his desire: like them, it always contains a twist which casts its overt meaning in a new light. Thus Divers' 'nominal singleness' distinguishes him from other men – but not from other Divers.[4] And the name the reader has by this stage long since automatically classed as a nickname is declared to be 'almost' a nickname: it is therefore Divers' 'real' name.

Quite early in the novel, we learn that Divers' integrity, in the sense of wholeness, is not intact:

> In Divers, finally, there was that crack [*fêlure*], which was intended by the architect, as was intended [*fut voulue*] the pathetic breach in the Colosseum which

causes eternal lightning to flash [*fulgure*] over its mass. I later discovered the meaning of that crack, a second sign of mourning, and of the even more theatrical one which furrows Bulkaen, which furrows all the hards, from Botchako to Charlot.[5]

Remarkably, Genet asserts Divers' 'crack' (which also furrows the writing: *fêlure, fut voulue, fulgure*, and whose 'architect' of course is no other than Genet) to be 'intended', voluntary, chosen. The comparison of the crack with the breach in the Colosseum in itself holds little that is remarkable; the audacity lies in the calm reinterpretation of one of the most 'monumental' of all monuments. The notion that the breach is an integral part of the building rather than an accident destroying its original integrity shows a 'colossal' freedom of imagination. Genet has recourse to universally recognisable figures to illustrate his thinking, but the 'intended' effect is to render these figures unrecognisable.

The narrator never clarifies the 'meaning' he announces here of the crack which furrows not only Divers, but all the 'hards'. However, this meaning can be gleaned from an extraordinary passage that elaborates on Divers' attraction for the narrator, and that on the surface belies the existence of any 'crack'. Following the narrator's example in our first quotation, the writing surreptitiously shows Divers from 'a new point of view' which, contrary to appearances, has the effect of *heightening* his seductive power:

> He appeared more and more fabulous to me. Everything about him still surprises and enchants me [*m'enchante*]. Even the word 'diversity' seems to me to be born [*né*] of him, as achillea, or the Achilles plant, is born [*née*] of the warrior who treated his heel with it. Divers often said 'Balls' [*Mes couilles*], simply. He said it instead of 'What a fuckup' [*Quelle connerie*]. His face was hard [*dur*]. When I kissed him for the first time, on our wedding night, [...] along with the intoxication of intimacy, with such a beautiful face continued by such a beautiful body, of so rigid a male, I knew the impossibility of communion. That head was hard [*dure*] like a head of marble. It numbed your wrists. And cold. He didn't throb. No flaw, no crack [*Aucune faille, fente*], let out an idea, an emotion [*une idée, un émoi*]. He was not porous. Some men are porous. A vapour emanates from them and penetrates you. Divers' face was less mean [*méchant*] than strange [*étrange*]. It is only by kissing him that I recognise him a little, that he seemed to me to show himself [*il me semblait le voir se présenter*] in a new and troubling light, opening up unknown perspectives.[6]

Divers' 'fabulous' appearance gives him a marvellous, legendary status, immediately reinforced by the comparison with Achilles. According to Genet, his proper name, like that of the warrior, has created a common noun; his name turns out, in effect, to be the very opposite of a nickname, typically suggested by a characteristic feature of the person. Again, Genet's delight in turning received assumptions on their heads is evident in the way he exploits his onomastic resource, deeming Divers to have given his name to diversity, rather than the reverse.

But the comparison between Divers and Achilles extends still further. Like the warrior whose heel was the only vulnerable point of his body, Divers too manifests a vulnerable, feminine side (remember that Achilles spent a number of years disguised as a woman) which is at odds with his very hard appearance. From the beginning of the passage, a sexual 'diversity' is adumbrated in the shift in gender from the word 'born' (*né*) of him (moreover, the fact that something is 'born' of Divers automatically places him in a maternal position) to the plant 'born' (*née*) of Achilles. Graphically, the masculine pronoun *il*, so conspicuous at the opening of the paragraph (it begins two of the first three sentences), acquires a feminine resonance from the play of the signifier: 'Ach*ille*', 'cou*illes*', and even '*Il le* disait'. The visual similarity between the heroic proper name 'Ach*ille*' and the obscenity which follows it closely, that most 'common' of nouns 'cou*illes*' (balls), creates a link between two opposing registers; the suggestion of sexual uncertainty is reflected in the overlapping of the sublime and the vulgar. A typically Genetian paradox: the greater the vulgarity, the greater the refinement. 'Divers disait souvent: "Mes couilles" simplement': the sentence inscribing the obscenity is a perfect alexandrine, with interior rhyme (sou*vent*, simple*ment*) at the caesura. Genet adopts a Racinian style, but does so to sing of vulgarity.[7] Furthermore, the first two sentences, with twelve and eleven syllables respectively, approximate the rhythm of verse. If we added to 'Divers' the *x* which transformed Bulkaen into an undecidable Bijou(x), the text could create a fable of ten lines – *dix vers*!

At first glance, the beginning of the text sketches the portrait of a patently phallic man. Divers' face is hard, his body beautiful and rigid, his head hard and cold; his very name disseminates the sounds of hardness – *dur, raide, froide*, etc. He rejects the slightest trace of femininity, even in his exclamations; he uses the expression 'balls'[8] instead of an expression which in French inscribes the feminine sex, 'Quelle *connerie*'.[9] It would appear that Divers represents a 'perfectly' masculine man, one with 'no flaw, no crack': Genet's idol is a man who seems to have achieved the impossible, warded off all trace of castration. However, the narrator ridicules his hero as much as he rapturises over him, exactly as he claimed to do in his love affairs. With no crack from which 'an idea, an emotion' might emerge, Divers' impassivity renders him both stupid and unfeeling. His cold head is numbing:[10] the 'hard' is *frigid*. His insensitivity is reflected phonically in the proliferation of plosive consonants in the original (for example: 'Cette *t*ête é*t*ait *d*ure *c*omme une *t*ête *d*e marbre') and in the jerkiness of the rhythm, unpleasant on the ear ('And cold. He didn't throb. No flaw, no crack let out an idea, an emotion'). The irony of the description is compounded by the fact that Divers does not emit a 'vapour' – he does not *breathe*. Kissing a 'hard', Genet suggests, is like kissing a corpse.

Nevertheless, shifts in gender in these last sentences again serve to alert us to the undermining of this monolithic masculinity. The inscription at close intervals of the 'hard' (*dur*) face and the 'hard' (*dure*) head signals the beginning of an increasingly marked oscillation between masculine and feminine. '*Elle* engourdissait ... *Il* ne palpitait ... *Aucune* faille ... *une* idée, *un* émoi ... ' It seems that the more manly, i.e. the more inviolable, impregnable, impenetrable, one is, the *less* one penetrates; the vapour 'which penetrates you' emanates from men who are 'porous', permeable, penetrable. In the couple Genet–Divers, it is the narrator who symbolically penetrates the other man by kissing him, in so far as the latter's face is the one that alters,[11] 'opening up unknown perspectives'. But if it is clear that this change occurs *when* the narrator kisses Divers, it is less clear *who* brings it about. 'Il me semblait le voir se présenter ... ': the untranslatable infinitive construction (literally, 'it seemed to me to see him show himself'), with an impersonal subject, makes it impossible to determine whether Divers or Genet is the agent of the transformation. The 'unknown perspectives' are opened *from an unknown perspective*, in the movement from one subject to another. The way Divers is going to 'show himself in a new and troubling light' is in fact by disappearing from the rest of the passage, i.e. by allowing a different 'fabulous' face(t) to appear.

A new point of view

I experienced the same emotion when I cut out Pilorge's photograph from a detective magazine. My scissors [*ciseaux*] slowly followed the line of the face and this slowness forced me to notice details, the skin's texture, the shadow of the nose on the cheek. From a new point of view, I was seeing that beloved face. Then, needing to turn it upside down to facilitate the cutting, it suddenly composed for me a mountainous landscape, with a lunar relief, more deserted and desolate than a Tibetan landscape. I advanced along the line of the forehead [*front*], I turned a little and, suddenly, with the speed of a racing locomotive, shadowy perspectives and chasms of pain closed in [*fonçaient*] on me. I had to make several attempts to finish my work, so thick were the sighs [*tant étaient épais*] which, coming from far away, reached my throat [*gorge*] and blocked [*boucher*] it. The two blades of the scissors remained open, not daring to go further into the paper, so beautiful was the view I had of a certain eyelid. I did not want to finish too quickly. I was abandoned in a gorge [*gorge*] or on a peak [*pic*], struck by the discovery of an assassin's face.[12]

The text is, in every sense, in the process of *changing subject* – firstly, in that the appearance of Divers' 'unknown perspectives' leads directly into a comparison with the 'shadowy perspectives' revealed by Pilorge's face (the guillotined murderer to whom Genet dedicated *Notre-Dame-des-Fleurs*); secondly, in that the narrator is the grammatical subject in the majority of these sentences (as opposed to the first part of the paragraph which is nearly all in the third person). The text is indeed offering us 'a new point of view'. It is important to stress that it is *after* the narrator tells us of his new perspective that he turns the photo and discovers the 'shadowy perspectives' hidden in Pilorge's face: the passage in fact describes a *series* of 'points of view'. The disconcerting effect this shifting perspective has on the reader is exacerbated by the fact that nothing is ever what it seems initially. The narrator's ability to make out the 'skin's texture' (i.e. the pores? Is *Pilorge* one of the 'porous men'?) suggests that the line he is following is the face's surface, not its outline. When he turns it upside-down, the face is suddenly in *relief*: Genet cuts out the photo with his scissors (*ciseaux*) as a sculptor releases a statue with a chisel (*ciseau*). Furthermore, the face becomes the subject: 'it composed for me'. The photograph *comes to life* as it turns, like Galatea coming down from her pedestal.

If we follow the text closely, the important point is that Pilorge's body, as well as his face, seems to be turning. The mountainous landscape, with a 'lunar relief more deserted and desolate than a Tibetan landscape', evokes the behind both iconically and because in French the moon (*la lune*) is slang for the bottom.[13] The narrator follows the line of the *front*, the forehead, which gives in reverse the line of the back(side), until he suddenly finds himself plunged in 'shadowy perspectives' and 'chasms of pain'. There is yet another sudden change of subject: Genet doesn't plunge, the 'perspectives' close in (*fonçaient*) around him, with the speed of a 'racing locomotive'. The scene clearly solicits reading as an anal penetration, where paradoxically the anus is the penetrating agent, in place of the subject it engulfs.[14]

The other side of Genet's idol's face can thus be read as the backside; by gradual displacement, the phallic head at the opening of the passage has turned into an anus. The scene adopts a more and more explicitly sexual rhythm: 'I had to make several attempts [...] I didn't want to finish too quickly [...] I was abandoned.' This thrusting rhythm pervades the writing itself, pounded by [p]s and [t]s, notably in the sequence: '*travail tant étaient épais*'. Every level of the text manifests the narrator's desire for Pilorge.

The masculine slit

However, the scene is yet more complex. The anus is not a sex; were the phallus to be in symbolic exchange with the anus alone, the effacement of sexual difference which is prevalent at all levels of Western culture would remain unchallenged. On the contrary, Genet's writing is exceptional in that the fantasmatic structure it inscribes makes space for a symbolic exchange between *two different, equal sexes*.[15] Thus, in this passage, the more the anal penetration progresses, the less Genet 'cuts' between the sexes. If, for example, 'a certain eyelid' which dazzles the narrator and stops him cutting can be assimilated to the anus, on the other hand its shape, like that of the two open blades of the scissors, evokes the vulva. The penetration leaves Genet abandoned in a space of sexual (con)fusion, as can be seen in the division of Pilorge – both face and name – into a peak (*un pic*) and a gorge (*une gorge*). This (feminine) 'gorge' clearly functions as a *sexed alternative to the peak*, rather than as a neutral, asexual plain throwing into relief the sexual space of the phallic peak. The French word *gorge* is a homonym with at least three meanings; it is used twice in quick succession in the passage, first in the sense of throat, then in the sense of ravine. This antanaclasis invites us to read the second inscription of the word as a lower version of the oral cavity.[16] Furthermore, the passage contains two mouths (*bouches*), the first hidden/revealed in the verb *boucher*, the other highlighted precisely where the text is slit in the middle by an indented line in direct speech:

> I thus caressed that insolent lad a last time, as one caresses a word, thinking one possesses it. That is how, by taking them unexpectedly, by approaching them from unusual angles, one discovers the extraordinary composition of faces and postures, and some of Bulkaen's virtues were revealed to me just as accidentally. By saying to me, on the tenth day of our encounter, on the stairs, while he took my mouth [*bouche*]:
>
>   'A peck [*Une bise*], Johnny, just one.'
>
> Bulkaen had opened for me the door to René Rocky's heart. I was in the habit of calling a kiss a smacker [*un bécot*], Bulkaen had said 'a peck'. Erotic language, the one we use in games of love, being a sort of secretion [*sécrétion*], a concentrated juice which leaves the lips only in moments of the most intense emotion, of moaning, being if you like the essential expression of passion, each pair of lovers has its own peculiar language, heavy with a perfume, an odour *sui generis*, which belongs only to that couple. By saying 'a peck' to me, Bulkaen was still secreting the juice specific to the couple he formed with Rocky. A foreign, because new and unsuspected, body [*un corps étranger parce que nouveau et insoupçonné*] was entering my love for Bulkaen, but at the same time, by that word, I was brought into contact with the intimacy of the couple Bulkaen–Rocky.[17]

It becomes clear that the passage which seemed initially to be an exploration of Divers actually deals with a whole series of 'fabulous' men, all of whom display an unexpected side: it is now Bulkaen's turn to reveal an unsuspected side of himself by his choice of vocabulary. Divers' 'unknown perspectives', Pilorge's 'shadowy perspectives' and 'chasms of pain' give way to 'certain virtues' of Bulkaen which surprise the narrator. Genet makes the transition by again turning a common analogy back to front: he speaks of caressing the 'lad' (but the 'lad' is a *photograph* – the difference between image and reality is blurred) 'as one caresses a word' – here the caress of the *word* comes first. Language and body seem to be equivalents. Just as the narrator was wrong to think he 'possessed' Pilorge, the reader would be wrong to think s/he 'possessed' the sense of Genet's words; it is only by following his example – 'by taking them unexpectedly, by approaching them from unusual angles' – that one discovers the 'extraordinary composition' of his writing. If we take unexpectedly the mouth that Bulkaen takes, its surprising side turns out to be not only what comes out of the mouth, but also the fact that Bulkaen possesses an *unsuspected mouth*.

This reading is corroborated by the end of the quoted passage, where it becomes finally impossible to disentangle body and word. According to Genet, 'the essential expression of passion', generally considered to be the union of bodies, is a *word*, which is in turn a body, a 'sort of secretion' (an anagram in French as in English of 'erections') or 'concentrated juice' which flows from the lips. In other words, the specificity of two lovers' union is most intimately embodied in the language they use together. Each couple has its own erotic language, charged with an 'odour *sui generis*' (reminiscent also of the 'vapour' emanating from 'porous' men which makes communion possible). Are we then to interpret the word 'peck' or Rocky's body as the first meaning of the foreign body which enters Genet's relationship with Bulkaen, and which in turn allows Genet access to the 'intimacy of the couple Bulkaen–Rocky'?

Or is yet another interpretation possible? Let us approach the 'odour *sui generis*' from a different angle. Literally, the Latin expression can mean 'specific to its gender'. Given moreover that the French word *bise*, unlike the alternative *bécot*, is feminine in gender, does the 'foreign, because new and unsuspected body' whose lips secrete a juice with a particular strong smell in moments of the most intense emotion, not incontestably evoke the *female* body? In this passage, the supreme repressed of our culture, the female sex, comes – obliquely – into view, both as another body in the series of bodies the text explores *and* as the 'unsuspected' side of each. The writing in fact insistently disseminates the 'con', the vulgar word for the female genitals: *con*nerie, *con*tinuant, *con*nus, *com*munion, recon*nais, incon*nues, *com*posa, loco*mo*tive, fon*çaient, on *c*aresse, qu'on, *com*position, *con*centré, *con*tinuait, insoup*çon*né.

Etymologically, Achilles' name signifies *without lips*. Just as the warrior's vulnerability evinces the impossibility of foreclosing femininity, the 'crack' which furrows Divers, Pilorge, Bulkaen – indeed, all of Genet's 'heroes', however phallic they may seem – endows them with a symbolic femininity. The difference with Genet is that this femininity is conceived, not as a *lacking* sex, but as a *second* sex. We may recall that 'fabulous' means both 'marvellous' and 'improbable'. 'He appeared *more and more fabulous* to me. *Everything about him* still surprises and enchants me': the rare value of this text exploring Divers' sexual diversity is that it represents femininity not as a tragic flaw, but as one of several glittering attributes which make a hero 'fabulous'.

[The translations in this chapter are by the author; given the importance of the signifier for the reading, she has tried to remain as close as possible to the original French, at the expense of the elegance of the English translation.]

NOTES

1 Jean Genet, *Miracle de la Rose* in *Œuvres Complètes II* (Paris, 1951), pp. 391–2.
2 Another passage in the novel focuses attention on the nickname's ambiguity, all the richer in that the singular and the plural are indistinguishable phonically: 'In his mind he heard himself addressed as 'Jewels' ['Bijoux'] with the aristocratic *x*. But, when it was pronounced, nobody knew whether or not there was this *x*.' (Jean Genet, *Miracle de la Rose* in *Œuvres Complètes II* (Paris, 1951), p. 317.) As a thief of jewel(s), Bulkaen's sex is *undecidable*.
3 Jean Genet, *Miracle de la Rose* in *Œuvres Complètes II* (Paris, 1951), p. 279.
4 The three first names listed all begin with the same consonant, [zh]. Added to his surname, this causes Divers to 'diverge' from the homogeneous identity with which the text is investing him.
5 Jean Genet, *Miracle de la Rose* in *Œuvres Complètes II* (Paris, 1951), p. 292.
6 Jean Genet, *Miracle de la Rose* in *Œuvres Complètes II* (Paris, 1951), p. 387.
7 This is emblematic of Genet's ambivalent attitude towards the classic forms of French literature. He defiles them by using them in relation to the basest of subjects, while at the same time he derives the full advantage of their beauty.
8 But his masculine attributes are feminine in gender: *Mes couilles*.
9 It is interesting that there is no such widespread equivalent vulgarity designating the female sex in English. One could of course debate whether the greater taboo value that attaches to the English expression 'cunt' is indicative of a more or a less misogynist culture ...
10 Literally, Divers' cold head numbs 'your wrists'; the text addresses the reader at the very moment it speaks of the impossibility of communion.
11 The change is also inscribed in the play of the signifiers detailing Divers' evolution: the whole which 'enchants me' (*m'enchante*) – the same verb that was used to describe the effect Divers' name produced on the narrator – at the beginning of the paragraph later becomes 'less mean [*méchant*] than strange [*étrange*]'.
12 Jean Genet, *Miracle de la Rose* in *Œuvres Complètes II* (Paris, 1951), p. 388.

13 One of the first sounds the narrator hears on his arrival in Fontevrault is a voice shouting: 'Hi to your ass [*lune*] from my cock [*bite*]!' *Thib*et may thus be read as the reverse side of the '*bite*'.

14 The invasiveness of the hole can also be discerned in the sudden proliferation of *o* sounds: 'Soudain, avec la rapidité d'une locomotive emballée, fonçaient sur moi des perspectives d'ombres, des gouffres de douleur.'

15 This symbolic heterosexuality is all the more extraordinary in that it appears in a portrayal of male homosexuality which shocked – which can still shock – on account of its explicitness. The point I wish to stress is that Genet's unprecedented attention to the specificity of homosexual relations is not symbolically repressive of sexual difference.

16 This reading is all the more compelling since the third meaning of *gorge*, breast, refers specifically to the female body.

17 Jean Genet, *Miracle de la Rose* in *Œuvres Complètes II* (Paris, 1951), pp. 388–9.

CHAPTER 8

Genet: Gay deceiver or repressed homosexual?

Grace Russo Bullaro

JEAN GENET FLAUNTED his homosexuality at a time when social and psychological survival demanded that it be kept secret. It is therefore relevant to consider whether the ostentatious display of his homosexuality was due to the inner conviction of its acceptability or to other reasons.

My particular concern here is to examine Genet's representation of gender paradigms, the manner in which he subverts these hegemonic models, and his attitudes towards homosexuality. Given the rebellious and contestatory nature of his relationship to society, can we say that his concept of homosexuality was ahead of his time?

Genet is full of contradictions, a 'moralist who stole from friends', both sadistic and masochistic, manic and depressive, cruel and sensitive,[1] who has both treasured and reviled his identity as thief, traitor and homosexual. He has loudly proclaimed his homosexuality, yet not only hated being 'queer' himself but also hated other 'queers' to the point of committing violence against them. How much of this contradiction is genuine and how much literary posturing?

Regardless of the reasons for the secrecy, myth-making and misrepresentation, it is clear that Genet is too elusive and ambiguous a figure to reduce to a simple 'explanation'. If his novels have been 'semantically underdetermined',[2] his life has been, if anything, semantically overdetermined. He gives us plenty of information but most of it is contradictory or ambiguous. In his life, as well as in his work, Genet's emphasis has always been on externals. It is not surprising therefore that his concept of gender relations and gender roles is informed by the primacy of gesture. For Genet 'masculinity' is identified with externals: hard, bulging muscles, gruffness, swagger, and even cruelty. Equally, 'femininity' is not a matter of biological identity but of theatrical self-presentation. Furthermore, we may agree with White that Genet's concept of the individual as a collection of actions, clothes, gestures and setting implicitly denies the existence of an essential self.[3] We see that Divine, the transvestite heroine of *Notre-Dame-des-Fleurs*, enacts a kind of femininity which in its grace and simpering exaggeration outdoes that of any biological female.

It is Genet's lifelong rebellion against the values and societal codes of patriarchy that informs his presentation of gender roles, his ostensible purpose being to subvert them in an attempt to undermine and discredit patriarchy. Whether Genet accomplishes this, or only this, remains to be seen. Genet's discourse in his novels is not explicitly political. He does not fulminate against government and its agencies. Rather, his hatred and rebellion are aimed at the smug bourgeois, who for him embodies all the oppressive conservative values of his society: marriage, family, religion, patriotism; hence his choice to express himself in the classic French prose of the class that he is targeting.

Genet's evaluation of political events was always highly personal, as was his well-known involvement in the controversial causes of the Algerians, the Palestinians, and the Black Panthers. As a ward of the state he felt himself to have been excluded from a normal childhood. Consequently he identified with all marginal or oppressed groups, even declaring at one point, 'Maybe I'm a black.'[4] Therefore it is perhaps more valid to speak of Genet's discourse as being informed by the inside/outside dichotomy, which is more psychological than political in nature. Having grown up as a recognised thief, sissy and foundling, he had thoroughly internalised the identity of the outsider.

Certainly no one would doubt that Genet had an affinity for outsiders all his life or that he exhibited what Kate Millett sees as the psychological characteristics often associated with oppressed and minority status: 'group self-hatred and self-rejection, [and] contempt for himself and his fellows'.[5] Nor should we doubt that he sees the 'insider' as the enemy. Consequently, while his discourse is not explicitly political it is implicitly so in the way that it challenges the system's institutions, codes and values. In the end whether we believe that Genet *chose* to be a thief and homosexual is not relevant. What is relevant is how he uses these activities to protest against the political, moral and legal structures. In *Homosexuality: Oppression and Liberation* Dennis Altman expresses the view that homosexuality is a form of rebellion against the marriage/family/home programme, and that 'there is at least sometimes an element of deliberate choice in the adoption of homosexuality',[6] a point which is hotly debated in the gay community and among gender theorists. In the pre-Stonewall days[7] homosexuals had few options – either they must try to 'pass' for heterosexuals or they must pay the heavy consequences of homosexuality: economic and social deprivation as well as the psychological price of being considered 'failed' men. In as much as Genet did not attempt to 'pass', he chose homosexuality. Indeed, he used his homosexuality as another weapon against a society that he considered both corrupt and unjust.

As a result we might conclude that Genet was a man ahead of his time in his concept of homosexuality and in his rebellion against the established models. Certainly in some respects, chiefly his visibility and his willingness to use his difference to challenge the system, he was. However, while his actions were clearly contestatory, his attitudes were not. Like most homosexuals of his time (and time seems to be a more important consideration than place) whether in France, the USA, or many other countries, he too shared the prevailing attitudes and suffered from self-hatred, shame, and contempt for other homosexual men. Readers of French homosexual writers such as Gide, Cocteau and Proust know that mainstream attitudes towards homosexuality differed little in Genet's country. The dominant elements of shame, furtiveness, self-hatred and the feeling of gender failure reflected the internalised image imposed by the hegemonic models in France as well as in the USA. Hence, the homosexual experience seems to have been characterised more by its commonality than by its differences.

It is generally accepted by the gay community and by gender theorists that the Stonewall riots, started on 27 June 1969, marked a turning point in the homosexual/gay consciousness. The typical pre-Stonewall attitude towards being homosexual is expressed by Donald Webster Cory when he declares, 'I was deeply ashamed of being abnormal.'[8] In fact, 'Cory' was so aware of the consequences of his 'secret' that he deemed a pseudonymous identity necessary.

Many people writing about homosexuality in the 1950s and 1960s talk about these attitudes: Kleinberg in *Alienated Affections*, Altman in *Homosexuality: Oppression and Liberation*, Cruikshank in *The Gay and Lesbian Movements*, Duberman in *Stonewall* and Crisp in *The Naked Civil Servant* are only a few. Crisp tells us that he 'regarded all heterosexuals, however low, as superior to any homosexual, however noble'.[9] It is not surprising that homosexuals should feel this way at a time when all the 'experts' expounded the belief that homo-sexuality was both a physical and moral illness (when it was not an actual crime), a view expressed as late as 1963 by Charles Socarides when he piously stated that 'the homosexual is ill, and anything that tends to hide that fact reduces his chance of seeking and obtaining treatment',[10] thereby implying a fundamental failure transcending the merely sexual.

In the face of such beliefs and hostility homosexuals had little choice but to hide their 'condition' in order not to become victims of contempt, discrimination and occasional violence. This repressive climate changed little until the advent of the civil rights movement in the late 1950s. Genet's flaunting of his homosexuality becomes all the more significant in the light of these facts.

For some people Stonewall proved to be an epiphanic moment. Duberman tells us that for 'Sylvia' Rivera (a transvestite whose life shares some remarkable similarities with Divine's), singing the improvised chorus 'We are the Stonewall girls' had the unmistakable effect of 'lifting something off [her] shoulders'.[11] For the Establishment too Stonewall was epiphanic. Seymour Pine, Chief Inspector of the precinct in which the Stonewall riots took place, has stated that afterwards 'things were completely changed ... suddenly they were not submissive anymore'.[12] The message in the future would no longer be that homosexuals were like straights except for that one difference. The emerging 'gay' philosophy would henceforth emphasise and valorise difference – and the positive good of 'faggotry'.[13] 'Gay Power', the slogan born of the Stonewall riots, signified a new attitude and awareness of political and human rights that henceforth would be fought for. Cruikshank points out that 'homosexuals acquiesced to police brutality; gay people fought back'.[14]

Both 'gay' and its pre-Stonewall counterpart 'homosexual' reflect the hegemonic attitude towards the minority community, the self-image held by that minority and the level of self-rejection or self-acceptance that these terms entail. 'Gays' no longer believed the internalised heterosexual image of homosexuality as disease. Did Genet ever make this transition?

Heavy role-playing, so visible in Genet's work, was considered by many gays to be a residue of the need to win acceptance from heterosexuals by mimicking their dichotomous concept of gender.[15] This would explain in part the hostility shown towards transvestites, who thus became a reminder of the pre-Stonewall climate of enforced submission and necessary deception. Naturally, not every gay person considered heavy role-playing in this light. Even in the 1970s heavy role-playing continued to be widespread in the gay community. Consider, for example, the popularity of the macho and clone looks. Kinsman observes that its adoption signalled what appeared to be a validation (and an assimilation with a vengeance) of conventional masculinity. Kleinberg adds that this unconditional validation of masculinity nevertheless represented a rejection of reality: 'Effeminacy acknowledged the rage of being oppressed in defiance. Macho denies that there *is* rage and oppression.'[16]

Genet's masculine paradigm is founded on what Kleinberg suggests is an almost primitive conservatism, a masculinity that lies exclusively in the glamorisation of physical strength and ignores the more subtle psychological or philosophical dimensions. Millett has referred to Genet's images of gender roles as a 'vicious and omnipotent supervirility contrasted to a fluttering helplessness and abjection'.[17] What Millett says may be true, but only in so far as it is the implementation of a strategy of subversion. Genet does recreate the 'ideal' and quintessential gender roles, but only in order to underline their arbitrary and artificial nature. (If admiration for this kind of masculinity inevitably creeps into Genet's presentation it is not an indication of endorsement on his part but of his internalised ambivalence.)[18]

In his novels Genet replicates gender roles as conceived by the patriarchal system and he carries to 'logical conclusions' the traits that constitute traditional 'masculinity' and 'femininity.' In satirising hegemonic attitudes towards sexual/gender identity, Genet invalidates them by exposing their arbitrary and relative nature. In short, he exposes them as myth, showing us that 'masculinity' and 'femininity' need not even coincide with the respective biological labels of male and female. Indeed, some have argued that 'the most perfect image of what society has defined as woman is the drag queen'.[19] For this reason the portrayal of the drag queen, seen by some as the crystallisation of the fundamentally ironic existence of the gay individual, who so often is obliged to lead a double life to escape victimisation, stands at the very heart of Genet's representation of gender.

Irony is the most important element to consider when discussing both the drag queen and Genet's novels because 'the essential awareness for the drag queen is that his performance is always parody and that he must convey that to the audience at the same time that he asks for their disbelief'.[20] Genet performs this delicate balancing act between illusion and reality by setting up 'manly' characters (i.e. strong, active, assertive) like Armand (*Journal du Voleur*), Querelle and Nono (*Querelle de Brest*), only to problematise that identity by having them genitally consummate relations with other men and by endowing them with 'feminine' characteristics such as making paper lace.

The drag queen is Genet's literary alternative to biological females, a necessary reinvention since masculinity (Genet's true object of scrutiny) can only be defined against the background of its opposite. The affectation of the queens, linguistic and otherwise, is an example of feminine gestures carried to an extreme of parody as Armand and Querelle carry masculinity to exhibitionistic proportions. Divine herself says to Mimosa, 'I'm such a camp!'[21]

The function and nature of camp are the subjects of a wide divergence of opinion. For some, camp means turning the weaknesses (i.e. the 'womanly' in a man) into a strength. For others it is 'a way to obtain power in one's life', or 'the ability to see beyond what is clearly evident; to grasp a reality beneath or totally separate from what is taught'.[22] According to this view it is by changing the world into something controllable and safe that one obtains power. In 'Notes on Camp' Susan Sontag makes the surprising claim that camp is not political[23] while Mike Silverstein in 'God Save the Queen' sees it both as an expression of self-hatred and as a 'guerrilla attack on the whole system of male–female roles our society uses to oppress its women and repress its men'. Indeed, he sees queens as the 'vanguard guerrilla partisans of the gay revolution'.[24] More importantly, Genet has declared that the purpose of a drag queen is 'to mock virility'.[25]

On the other hand, Genet's recreation and representation of the masculine model reveals more clearly the author's fundamental ambivalence. While on the intellectual level he wishes to discredit what he clearly believes to be hollow and vicious devices of patriarchal manipulation, on the emotional level Genet admires what is evidently an internalised image dictated by the hegemonic order. In fact, the reinvention of the masculine model has as its goal more than just the discrediting of the hegemonic concept, its purpose is also to allow the author to conjure up an image of the man he would like to be while exorcising the man he hated being. In this respect Genet's portrait of femininity, the drag queen, unimpeded by simultaneous admiration and rejection, is more singular in its function of protest and subversion. This deep-seated tension between the intellectual and emotional domains remains unresolved for Genet. The 'men' in Genet's work are conceived as glorious representations of manly attributes as conventionally conceived; they are hard and strong both physically and emotionally and they reject human warmth. They are subjects among whose privileges is the possession of other human beings. Armand, in *Journal du Voleur*, whose cruelty, savagery and stupidity are prodigious, is a distillation of the pre-Stonewall image of 'true masculinity' carried to satiric exaggeration. Indeed, Armand tells us that his 'cock is worth its weight in gold'.[26]

The privilege of such unbounded masculinity is the complete submission of creatures like Jean, whom he takes to his room and subjects to his pleasure and scorn.[27] Three things stand out in the portrayal of Armand's masculinity. The first is that, like the macho look as perceived by Kleinberg, it is a definition of masculinity based exclusively on physical characteristics; the second is the irony that this paradigm of masculinity is in the act of having sex with another man; and the third is that Jean (Genet's literary alter ego) both adulates and is grateful to the sadistic Armand for his dubious attentions.[28]

Querelle is another example of exhibitionistic masculinity, yet he too has sexual relations with men. What is more, he is the passive partner. In Genet's novels, sailors and pimps (like Nono) represent the two categories that constitute the *ne plus ultra* of this kind of manliness. They are the supermen, second perhaps only to 'the pure virility of the murderer'.[29] Mignon-les-petits-pieds, the object of Divine's (Jean's) passion and affection, is elegant, supple, indiscriminately violent or gentle, betrayer of Divine's friends for money and for pleasure. He is a superman with virtually no moral obligations or limitations, certainly not that of protecting or advising or remaining loyal to Divine.

Jean's and Genet's attitude towards masculinity and these models is illustrative of Kleinberg's claim that 'most of us [homosexuals] became sissies because we fell in love with men, usually jocks',[30] and suggests another important point to consider. In *L'Amour cannibale* Maurice Chevaly refers to Genet's cannibalistic concept of homosexuality, a concept that White sees as another form of theft.[31] Both authors are discussing Genet's implicit belief that it is possible to *become* like the chosen model through imitation. According to White, 'homosexual roles are often redundant or a form of admiration and envy'.[32] This function of homosexuality is corroborated by Genet himself when he tells us that the earliest kind of love that he could remember 'took the form of my desire *to be* a handsome youth ... whom I once saw bicycling past ...'[33]

For White 'the first act of homosexual love, then, is impersonation'.[34] This form of mimicry works on two levels: in the text the characters, especially the Genet persona who reappears in most of the novels, attempt to take on the masculinity of the brute they emulate. This is the case when Stilitano, one of Jean's love interests in *Journal du Voleur*, 'enters' Jean, thereby symbolically transferring to him traits of virility: his muscles, his manly gestures, and his 'heaviness.' It is also the meaning behind Mignon's cry that 'a male that fucks another male is a double male'.[35]

On another level Jean Genet, the author, recreates for himself through language, the ideal and quintessential masculine identity as his desires dictate. The fundamental ambivalence towards this so-called ideal is revealed by Genet's dual operation, for he aims to discredit the validity of the ideal that he so obviously admires and perhaps even longs to be. This is the same ambivalence that the author bears towards his reader and, by extension, towards the mainstream attitudes that he represents in his texts. Statements like 'I aspire to your recognition, your consecration'[36] must be balanced against others that inform us that 'since rectitude was your domain, I would have none of it'.[37] Moreover, the hostility evident in his cry 'I thus resolutely rejected a world which had rejected me'[38] is clearly born of wounded feelings.

Genet's later marginality and exclusion take on multiple forms and his subsequent rejection of the rejecters is also linked to a sense of powerlessness and a desire for revenge. In addition, while he never stopped showing contempt for that reader, heaping insult and obscenity on him, he also never stopped currying his favour: 'I feel such a need to complain and to try to win a reader's love!' he tells us in *Notre-Dame-des-Fleurs*.[39] Even allowing for Genet's usual dose of literary posturing and mythomania, the evidence for a sincere craving for such approval and love coexisting with its opposite is overwhelming.

Genet's characters further undermine the validity of the established order by rejecting the rest of its values. Almost without exception, his characters refuse to make any positive contribution to society. They live not by the fruit of honest work but by that derived from crime or prostitution and rarely are they placed in the context of the family; when they are, as is the case for Divine's/Louis' relationship to her/his mother, Genet depicts the bond as unrewarding rather than as a source of human warmth and fulfilment.

However, although Genet deliberately subverts, devalues and rejects gender roles and all that society prizes, he does not present homosexuality and homosexuals in a more positive light. It is associated with vice, crime and evil and is another cause for ostracism by that society. In a long letter that Genet wrote to Sartre around 1952 he explicitly declared homosexuality to be an embodiment of the wish for death and the significance of homosexuality as a refusal to continue the world, a way of proclaiming that 'I will not embody the principle of continuity'.[40] Homosexuality as negation, sterility and death is a far cry from the post-Stonewall slogan, 'Say it loud, we're gay and we're proud'.

Hatred and shame of homosexuality were typical of Genet's time. The fact that he dared to flaunt it in the faces of the established order was part of his strategy of living life, without apologies, according to a standard of moral inversion consisting of what he believed to be the three cardinal virtues of theft, homosexuality and treachery. Indeed, Genet chose to present homosexuality as 'entirely evil'.[41] Ironically, society's agreement on this issue effectively neutralises Genet's rebellion, at least on this score. To Genet homosexuality is another form of self-degradation. This should not surprise the reader. Self-contempt is common in Genet's fiction. For example, in *Notre-Dame-des-Fleurs* Divine masochistically relishes Mignon's beatings. In *Journal du Voleur* Armand's brutality and the resulting fear act as an aphrodisiac on Jean.[42]

Jean's self-degradation also manifests itself in his deliberate betrayal of friends to whom he has become attached. The pleasure he experiences in shattering the bonds of friendship is double, consisting of both the satisfaction of rejecting another bourgeois value and of violating his true nature, considered by him to be weak because affectionate. Rejection of friendship is thereby compounded by an absence of love in the life of Jean and the other characters; and it is paradoxical that despite their consuming search for love and approval they throw away any opportunity to form bonds of affection. Perhaps the fear of exposing himself to another rejection makes Jean wary. Armand's rebuff amply justifies this fear. Perhaps it is an indication of a deeper self-loathing. He thus punishes himself by renouncing that which he craves. Finally, it is also an expression of misogyny because he identifies anything 'womanly' with weakness.

In *Saint Genet* Sartre speaks of 'a systematic labour of devirilisation' on the part of the queens in Genet's novels. According to Sartre the object of the queens' compliance to the 'men' (i.e. those homosexuals who play the masculine role) is to figuratively emasculate them for 'the aim of his caresses is the softening of the male ... they are caught in his pestilential swamps and their virility abandons them ... fellatio is castration'.[43]

In Sartre's interpretation, although at first Mignon ignores Divine's worship of him, he gradually grows attached to her, and thereby becomes feminised, accepting Divine's own exaggeratedly feminine gestures and inadvertently adopting them for himself. Now, 'little by little, they were conquering the stronghold' and working equally well on Notre Dame.[44] White suggests that in Genet's cosmology a 'real man' is corrupted by prolonged exposure to homosexuality, even if he himself always plays the active role, the result being that one day he will lose his desire for women.[45] This view of homosexuality and the feminine as a 'pestilential swamp', a contaminating and corrupting influence on true masculinity, further elucidates the fact that the queen in Genet's work represents less 'a nostalgia about the idea of the woman one might have been', than 'the bitter need to mock virility'.[46] The reverse side of this condemnatory attitude towards homosexuality and femininity is the covert endorsement of the superiority of traditional masculinity that we have already examined, always tempered, of course, by Genet's naturally pessimistic and cynical view of human nature in general.

There are other negative aspects in Genet's depiction of homosexuality. For example, the homosexual sex act is always shown to be merely mechanical and associated with vice and shame, lacking a spiritual side. Moreover, it engenders nothing, neither love nor companionship, and of course by nature it is infertile from a biological perspective. To illustrate this negativity, consider that Querelle chooses to have homosexual sex with bisexual Nono as a form of self-imposed expiation for his murder of Vic.

Indeed, we cannot even point to a sense of community among homosexuals themselves, for both in fiction and in real life Genet saw homosexuality as promoting alienation. In *Journal du Voleur* Jean willingly rolls queers to obtain money or blackmails them for their 'dastardly deed'.

This attitude is consistent with that which Genet held in real life. In an interview with Hubert Fichte, Genet admitted in a matter of fact manner that he had done queer-bashing in France, Spain and Holland, concluding with, 'So what? I took their money by beating them up or by making them come; the goal was still the loot.'[47] Robbing homosexuals was, according to White, considered by Genet as a huge joke, all the more because he was never attracted to homosexuals at all. Thus he saw no reason not to feel alienated from the homosexual community, an association which at that time most homosexuals rejected only too willingly. That Genet feels no attraction for homosexuals is ironic because, feeling no attraction for women either, the only remaining object of sexual desire could be a macho man similar to Armand. But as Crisp has commented, '[Homosexuals] set out to win the love of a "real man". If they succeed, they fail. A man who "goes with" other men is not what they would call a real man ... '[48]

Genet's loyalty is to the brotherhood of criminals. Indeed, he finds in it the sense of 'family' that he claims he never enjoyed in the more traditional manner. However, notwithstanding Genet's mythomania, we learn from White that Genet was rejected by the criminal world as a 'cave', i.e. a dupe or a fake.[49] Perhaps this misplaced solidarity should be taken as another indication of his compelling need to seek acceptance from any source since, at least in his view, his life can be read as a series of rejections, starting with his mother's.

The significant fact is that in Genet's own hierarchy of values homosexuals were devalued while criminals were glorified. He goes so far as to deny homosexuals a political voice because 'in politics nothing new can be contributed by a homosexual'.[50] On all fronts, the psychological, the social and the political, both in his fiction and in his real life, Genet's treatment of homosexuality can be summed up in White's scathing statement that 'no religious zealot could attack the hell of homosexuality with more vigour and spleen'.[51] It is therefore out of the question to consider Genet a 'gay' man *ad litteram*. Nowhere in his life or fiction do we find either a positive portrayal of homosexuality, a set of values and attitudes similar to what came to be known as a 'gay consciousness', a sympathetic view of fellow homosexuals, or an acceptance, let alone a joyful acceptance, of his own homosexuality and feeling of community with others. Homosexuality is identified with negation, sterility and death, homosexuals as weak, vicious individuals corrupted by the womanly and in turn able to contaminate 'healthy real men', and his own homosexual experience is seen as an alienation from society and even from other homosexuals.

Although he vigorously contests and ultimately invalidates dichotomous gender roles, showing them to be based on arbitrariness, relativity and artifice, this too is done not in a spirit of affirmation but in a spirit of negation, out of hatred for the hegemonic order that was the source of his rejection. All told, Genet's portrayal of homosexuality is better represented by Cory and Socarides – the mainstream view of homosexuality as disease and failure (both as men and as human beings) – than by the Gay Liberation Front's slogan equating being gay with being proud.

NOTES

1 Edmund White, *Genet* (London, 1993), p. 377.
2 Edmund White, *Genet* (London, 1993), p. 391.
3 Edmund White, *Genet* (London, 1993), p. 394.
4 Edmund White, *Genet* (London, 1993), p. 24.
5 Kate Millett, *Sexual Politics* (New York, 1969), p. 56.
6 Dennis Altman, *Homosexuality: Oppression and Liberation* (New York, 1971), p. 6.
7 For a full account of the Stonewall riots and their repercussions and implications see Martin Duberman's *Stonewall* (New York, 1993).
8 Quoted by Tony Marotta in *The Politics of Homosexuality* (Boston, 1981), p. 4.
9 Quentin Crisp, *The Naked Civil Servant* (New York, 1968), p. 68.
10 Charles Socarides, 'The Growth of Overt Homosexuality in the City Provokes Wide Concern' in *The New York Times*, 17 December 1963.
11 Martin Duberman, *Stonewall* (New York, 1993), p. 201.
12 Martin Duberman, *Stonewall* (New York, 1993), p. 208.

13 Dennis Altman, *Homosexuality: Oppression and Liberation* (New York, 1971), p. 87.

14 Margaret Cruikshank, *The Gay and Lesbian Movement* (New York, 1992), p. 69.

15 Martin Duberman, *Stonewall* (New York, 1993), p. 237.

16 Seymour Kleinberg, *Alienated Affections* (New York, 1980), p. 130 (emphasis in the original).

17 Kate Millett, *Sexual Politics* (New York, 1969), p. 340.

18 For the sake of clarity, and because I believe that such a distinction is necessary, I use 'Genet' to refer to the author and 'Jean' to refer to the fictional autobiographical character found in Genet's writing.

19 Dennis Altman, *Homosexuality: Oppression and Liberation* (New York, 1971), p. 21.

20 Seymour Kleinberg, *Alienated Affections* (New York, 1980), p. 137.

21 Jean Genet, *Notre-Dame-des-Fleurs*. All quotations from this work in this chapter are from Bernard Frechtman's translation *Our Lady of the Flowers* (New York, 1963), here p. 153.

22 Michael Bronski, *Culture Clash: The Making of Gay Sensibility* (Boston, 1984), p. 43.

23 Susan Sontag, *Against interpretation and other essays* (New York, 1967), pp. 275–7.

24 Michael Silverstein, 'God Save the Queen' in *Gay Sunshine*, November 1970.

25 Edmund White, *Genet* (London, 1993), p. 442.

26 Jean Genet, *Journal du Voleur*. All quotations from this work in this chapter are from Bernard Frechtman's translation, *The Thief's Journal* (New York, 1964), here p. 135.

27 Jean Genet, *The Thief's Journal* (New York, 1964), p. 134.

28 Jean Genet, *The Thief's Journal* (New York, 1964), p. 135.

29 Kate Millett, *Sexual Politics* (New York, 1969), p. 347.

30 Seymour Kleinberg, *Alienated Affections* (New York, 1980), p. 130.

31 Edmund White, *Genet* (London, 1993), p. 38.

32 Edmund White, *Genet* (London, 1993), p. 38.

33 Edmund White, *Genet* (London, 1993), p. 31 (my emphasis).

34 Edmund White, *Genet* (London, 1993), p. 38.

35 Jean Genet, *Our Lady of the Flowers* (New York, 1963), p. 106.

36 Jean Genet, *The Thief's Journal* (New York, 1964), p. 268.

37 Jean Genet, *The Thief's Journal* (New York, 1964), p. 194.

38 Jean Genet, *The Thief's Journal* (New York, 1964), p. 87.

39 Jean Genet, *Our Lady of the Flowers* (New York, 1963), p. 202.

40 Edmund White, *Genet* (London, 1993), p. 441.

41 Edmund White, *Genet* (London, 1993), p. 199.

42 Jean Genet, *The Thief's Journal* (New York, 1964), p. 134.

43 Jean-Paul Sartre, *Saint Genet, comédien et martyr*. The quotations from this work in this chapter are from Bernard Frechtman's translation, *Saint Genet, Actor and Martyr* (New York, 1963), p. 129.

44 Jean Genet, *Our Lady of the Flowers* (New York, 1963), p. 84.

45 Edmund White, *Genet* (London, 1993), p. 149.

46 From the letter from Genet to Sartre cited on p. 79 above. See Note 40 above.

47 Albert Dichy (ed.), *L'Ennemi déclaré: textes et entretiens* in Jean Genet, *Œuvres Complètes VI* (Paris, 1991), p. 170.

[48] Quentin Crisp, *The Naked Civil Servant* (New York, 1968), p. 63.

[49] Edmund White, *Genet* (London, 1993), p. 389.

[50] Edmund White, *Genet* (London, 1993), p. 443.

[51] Edmund White, *Genet* (London, 1993), p. 447.

CHAPTER 9

Gender in Genet's Poetry

Jeremy Reed

IN THE PHOTOGRAPH of Jean Genet I keep on my writing table, he stands contemplatively with his back to the Seine, his eyes focused on Philippe Halsman, who is out of the picture. It's 1951, and Genet is forty. He's informally dressed in a white cotton shirt, open at the neck, a suede zipper jacket and jeans. All his defiance, vulnerability, and deeply wounded poetic sensibility are concentrated in Halsman's shot. You can't hear the traffic in a photograph, but you can imagine the audial backdrop to a late afternoon in Paris. Genet looks not only at the camera, but also at the configurative poem he carries in his head. The poet's preoccupation with an unconscious archetypal text, and its externalisation through bits of autonomous imagery, invests the person with an air of distraction. Poets are distracted by virtue of bilocation, and their inhabiting parallel worlds. Inner and outer realities, unconscious and conscious states are differentiated, but unified, by the poetic line. The image is the big 'now', the immediate, the mythopoetic arrival. As Jung tells us, 'image and meaning are identical; and as the first takes shape, so the latter becomes clear'.

Genet's poetry, as opposed to the prose poems he called novels, belongs to the high-octane imaginative tradition of Baudelaire, Lautréamont and Rimbaud. It was Rimbaud who propagated the notion of the poet as *voyant*, inspired visionary, and, pertinent to Genet, as the great criminal or social outcast. The poet lives in a metaphoric desert. He is an exile, the one who refuses to be demystified by ideologies, and who inhabits an imaginal universe. The sand in a poet's shoes turns to gold.

Genet's dictum that 'poetry is the art of using shit and making you eat it' may be seen as iconoclastically subversive, or simply alchemical in its coprophiliac reference. His inversion of all moral precepts, and most principally his exclusion of women from the uniformly homoerotic microcosm of his poetics, instates a world of psychophysical gender substitutes. In an interview with Madeleine Gobeil in 1964, Genet commented, 'Homosexuality was imposed on me like the colour of my eyes, or the number of my feet. Even when I was still a child I was conscious of being attracted by other boys, I have never felt desire for women.'[1]

In Genet's poetry gender transference, or in his terms 'a refusal to continue the world', involves not only altering sexuality, but implies subscribing to a passive attitude, one in which the adoption of feminine characteristics suggests sexual sterility rather than the manifestation of a failed woman. Genet equates the unregenerative qualities of homosexuality with his lengthy periods of creative impotence. He is blocked by his inability to become his fluent opposite. In Genet's first literary creation, the poem *Le Condamné à Mort*, which he published at his own expense while imprisoned in Fresnes during 1942, he evokes the androgynous blueprint for his later intensely lyrical and homoerotic novels. His masturbatory ideal, envisaged as a tough blond kid, is equally transposable into the feminine role of a princess in a tower. Genet writes:

> Don't sing *Bullies of the Moon* tonight.
> Blond-haired kid, be a princess in a tower
> introspectively dreaming of our love
> or a tight-jeaned cabin-boy up on deck.[2]

While the poem is dedicated to Maurice Pilorge, a murderer who (Genet claims) was executed at the age of twenty, it also represents the romantic idealisation of a gay fraternity and the celebration of an invincible thug who will be the self-appointed King of the Underworld. Within the formal structure of rhymed alexandrine quatrains, Genet pitches a subversive sexual current against his constraining form. In what is in fact a paean to fellatio, Genet instigates a conflict between romantic diction and criminal slang, and in the process succeeds in criminalising poetry. And it's not so much that the poem consciously excludes women, it's more that Genet writes as if they don't exist. Genet's prototypical thugs double for women because there are no other options. His poetics recreate the universe, and they do so by imaginatively transforming gender. Genet's problems are not so different from Sade's on a physiological plane. He would like to reconstruct anatomy, and find in his felt androgyny a corresponding physical completion. A new species, but one generated without the mediating force of women. Genet's poetic universe is at all times fantastic, surreal, and structured out of the mythopoetic contents of the unconscious. Genet saw the role of the poet as mediumistic. The poet makes himself especially receptive to occult and irrational forces which exist independent of the intellect. The visionary poet is set apart by this difference; his life is spent waiting and listening for the voice to come through. The aural desert is constellated by images. The poet catches them like falling stars.

'The author of a beautiful poem is always dead,' Genet tells us in *Miracle de la Rose*, and Genet's overriding sense of a dead childhood, which can only be redeemed by poetry, was one of the psychological determinants of his creative impulse. Rimbaud's belief in the poet making himself a seer, through an inner programme involving 'the systematic derangement of the senses', finds a corresponding practice in Genet's liberal use of amphetamines while writing, and in the belief that the poet animates the explosive force situated in objects or things. Genet makes his lovers into poems, in the sense that the word inseminates myth, it gives tangible form to an ideal which had previously existed only in the imagination. For Genet, poetry is like masturbation; it embodies the fantastic through concentrated manipulation of the image. Genet's characters exist only through his creating them as constructs within the poem. They are exact replications of his sexual fantasies. The poet is omnipotent in this sense, he has absolute power over a subjective state. And so it is that Genet invents his murderers, queens, pimps, and boys who are transposable to girls. In *Le Condamné à Mort* he celebrates his conception of the immutable legendary hero who was to become the prototype for his novels:

> Let's dream together, love, of a hoodlum,
> big as the universe, body splashed with tattoos.
> He'll strip us, lock us into bondage cells,
> and show us how between his golden thighs
> and on his smoking stomach, a hot pimp
> works it up on carnations and jasmine.[3]

Genet had begun work on *Notre-Dame-des-Fleurs* at this time, and the poem and the novel share a corresponding lyric thrust. The explicit homoeroticism in both works, the opulent poetic diction contrasting a classic literary language with prison slang, and the uninhibited dynamic behind the celebration of taboo, invested Genet's work with a sense of individuated and scandalous genius. Genet's mythologems had been externalised as seething jewels. They studded his work with the fascinating glitter of poetic evil. They sat on the page like sapphires or black rubies.

In *Journal du Voleur* Genet professes how the wound or the death he experienced in childhood had him seek to narrate his life as a legend, or to subjectify living until the experience became in itself the poem. 'I refuse to live for any other end but that contained by the wound. My life must be a legend, or legible, and the reading of it must give birth to a particular new emotion which I call poetry.'

Genet's insistence on transforming the ordinary into the legendary, and in constantly inventing a life for himself, make all of his biographical statements appear suspect. Poetry substitutes imaginative truth for reality, it hypostatises the moment in a way that has the poet lie in the act of revealing truth. The intended contents of the poem are altered by the fiction of writing it. The poet becomes the magician, the word-thief, the image conjuror. And language in its mediating between inner and outer realities establishes at best a meta-truth.

Where do we look for Genet? In the poem or outside of it? His grizzled head, small figure, suffering eyes, his inveterate leather jackets, his sartorial oscillation between dandy and thug, his image as international writer and scandalous criminal, all the tension and discord in his conflicting personae make Genet into one of the most concealed of writers. Not even Edmund White's exhaustively researched and superbly eloquent biography succeeds in bringing Genet to the light. He evades exposure. He remains like a fish which stays in the depths, rather than coming to the surface. There's a sharp, realistic taste of the man in Mohammed Choukri's pithily minimal *Jean Genet in Tangier*, a book which catches Genet at a certain time in a certain place and evokes the natural angularity and perversely hostile presentation of his views on life, politics and literature. The real Genet is essentially in his poetry, in the romantic and celebratory impulse behind a self-created world, one over which he presides by the directed psychic energies of the imagination. In his poem *Le Pêcheur du Suquet* Genet creates the object of his desire, and the writing of the poem is the extension of libido. 'A gold dust floats around him, and keeps him at a remove.'[4] This boy could be anyone, but he is apotheosised in the process of being created by Genet. 'A complicity, a consent are established between my mouth and the cock – still concealed in his blue shorts – of this eighteen-year-old fisherman.' The desire for fellatio becomes the poem's entry point. *Le Pêcheur du Suquet* has themes in common with Hart Crane's marine sequence, *Voyages*, in which love and death are celebrated through tidal flux and the exotic imagery of drowned sailors and subaquatic cities. Genet's imaginary love is both compliant and resistant to his advances; the autonomous contradictory energies which inform the poem also connect with the tensions that govern a real relationship. But more often the legend overtakes:

> I wade into love as one does the sea,
> palms first, blinded, my grief
> holding back to keep your presence alive,
> you're heavy, eternal, and I love you.[5]

Genet is similar to Rimbaud in that he makes the subjective conflict of writing poetry the subject of the poem. Imaginative conception cries out on the line. It is blood, fire, tears and anguish, an emotional arena in which the poet risks everything for a charged inner reality. The qualitative power of that truth is assembled through imagery which is in turn the vocabulary of psyche.

In keeping with Genet's instinctual attraction to the androgyne, the masculine image in *Le Pêcheur du Suquet* is feminised as part of Genet's need to unify opposites within the same. He becomes she while remaining he. 'But he's melting in my mouth. Only one verse. For which girl and what garden? What dream makes him drowsy, tumbles him into himself, delicately torments him, and twists his stomach in anticipation.'

In an undated letter to Sartre, probably written in 1952, which Edmund White quotes in full in *Genet*, Genet attempts to struggle against the feelings of pessimistic sterility that he associates with homosexuality. Writing, for him, represented transcendence over the sexual nihil, an activation of 'funereal themes in the imagination'. The act becomes the writing of the poem, and the latter itself is seen as a generative symbol. He writes as a postscript to his letter to Sartre, 'A poem is only the activity of a funereal theme. It is (definitely) its socialisation, a struggle against death. The themes of life propose action and forbid the poem.' And so it is that Genet lives inside the poem, and dies within life. Most of his lifelong anomie, and passive resignation to suffering, were occasioned by his increasing inability to write. Without the inspirational act of poetry Genet squandered life. In his post-prison years, the magic of a closed, homoerotic ethos denied him, he seems never again to have found the same creative centre to his life. An increasing addiction to Nembutal which acted as a downer to his neurophysiology, his unfocused peripatetic life, his quasi-affiliation to revolutionary political causes – most of Genet's later life was a distraction from his dead creative energies. In fact, as early as 1950, that is, after the writing of *Journal du Voleur*, Genet seems to have been disinherited from the poem. If prison symbolised a metaphoric castle or fortress from which he wrote, separated from society, then his eviction from that site left him exposed to liberty, and all the diversity, diffuseness and chaos implied by that state. Given freedom, Genet became imprisoned by creative sterility. It was as though he had left his genius on the inside, and was unable to recreate that phenomenon in the social world.

It's in his poem *Un Chant d'Amour* that Genet gives most eloquent expression to the excessively sensual voice by which he recreates gender. Nowhere is the poem more interchangeable with the imaginatively created body of the lover. The poem makes itself available to be fucked, and in a very real sense Genet is observed writing the poem with his penis. Sexual and psychic energies are orchestrated into a singular dynamic. The poem explodes at orgasmic pitch. It detonates with romantic longing for the impossible love:

> From blood on stones or an open wound
> who will be born, what page-boy or angel of ivy
> will choke me? What soldier wearing your dead nails?[6]

Genet sees himself 'naked on a blue staircase',[7] and foundering in a dream. The poet fights to externalise the poem. He is terrified of his vision collapsing, and of being unable to sustain the tension between subjective and objective universes:

> Tired of dying on the brink of my lips
> the horizon fell asleep in your folded arms.[8]

Everything will close down if the poet loses breath. His imaginal, and by extension physical, universe will black out. Genet assumes deistic responsibility for the poem. It exists because of him, the whole psychophysical infrastructure of its organism rests on his energised thrust to sustain inspiration. If the poem runs out on the poet, or the poet deserts his source, then the continuity of creation is interrupted. The Big Bang short-fuses. In the context the poet is a star-thrower, one who constellates and extends a continuous galaxy. Writing poetry means lighting up the world. Throwing a switch to the stars. Everything jumps into place.

Nor does the intense, white-hot fever of homoeroticism in Genet's poetry preclude heterosexual interest. All love is one love, if it's fired by passionate sensuality. 'How I love any kind of love,' Marc Almond sings in his composition *There is a Bed*. *Un Chant d'Amour* is shot through with unrelieved gender confusion:

> In his torso, asleep, and cream-coloured
> like an almond, a little girl lies coiled,
> blood tinkles along the blue avenue
> and evening stamps a bare foot on the lawn.[9]

Here the instance of androgyny is not only psychically visualised, but also physically realised. The feminine is envisaged as curled like a foetus in the male torso. Genet, who professed contempt for fags and drag queens, and who idealised straight-looking lovers, nevertheless writes a poetry of androgynous consciousness, and often dresses his syntax in drag. A Genet sentence is heavy with rhinestones. Out on the street it attracts attention to itself, and is in trouble. Genet writes of 'a thief's five fingers with carmine nails'.

There's a breathtaking lyrical beauty to Genet's poetry, a hauntingly ambiguous quality to his search for islands, undiscovered paradises, apolitical utopias and legendary states, which invests it with a visionary luminosity. In the tradition of Lautréamont, Rimbaud and Saint-John Perse, Genet sets out to discover the subject of the poem in the course of writing it. Lyric impulse becomes the experiential meaning of the poem. And there are times when Genet sounds like the Perse of *Amers*:

> But the green flag of the sea wanderers
> has to keep watch somewhere, stretched between poles.
> Shake the blue night, powder your shoulders with it,
> drill air columns into your sandy feet.[10]

One of the dominant features of Genet's work is his defacement of beauty, his subversion of the underlying dynamic to his work. Genet fears to look on beauty; he can only imagine it. His fear of demystifying the world of things has him turn inward to a world of psychic autonomy. He tells us something of this excruciating paradox in *Journal du Voleur*. 'I dared not even look at the beauty of that part of the world – unless it were to look for the secret of that beauty, the imposture behind it, to which one falls a victim of trust. By rejecting it, I discovered poetry.' By rejecting Andalusia, he recreates it through poetry. It is a country made real through the externalisation of the contents of the poet's psyche. An Andalusia which is a sounding-board of the poet's organism.

There will always be two kinds of poetry. One which turns inwards and recreates the universe through imaginative transformation, and one which is concerned purely with observing and experiencing objective phenomena. The Dionysian and Apollonian, unconscious and conscious energy channels. Genet belongs to the tradition of poets who amaze us by their discovery of a transcendental quality in the ordinary. The poet either heightens or debases reality, and through the substitution of metaphor for observed phenomena, stands back from a world he has created through image-mythopoetics. You walk down the same road every day, and suddenly it's a highway to the stars. Everything observed becomes something else in the transformative flash. The poet closes his eyes and dreams of freedom. Genet does this in *Le Condamné à Mort*:

> O the sweetness of impossible islands,
> delusional skies, the sea and the palms,
> transparent mornings, mad evenings, calm nights,
> heads that are shaved, and satin skins.[11]

Something of Genet's need to make poetry into a subversive raid on the established order of things, a psychological impulse not so dissimilar from theft, is expressed in his attitude to Hitler's Germany in *Journal du Voleur*. Granted the freedom to commit crime, Genet found himself impotent to steal. 'If I steal here, I perform no singular act that might appease me. I obey the customary order; I do not destroy it. I'm not committing evil. I'm not disturbing anything. The outrageous is prevented me. I'm stealing in the void.'

And so it is with his poetry. The anarchic opposition to civilisation is the drive behind lyric impulse. And in the process gender is also re-evaluated and re-arranged. The imagination is the weapon with which the poet violates hierarchies. It is also the liberator from passivity. It breaks down pre-existent orders and imposes unconditional freedom. A freedom which extends to everything including gender.

I began with a photograph. The picture will never change. Genet was different before the moment in which Halsman isolated him against the backdrop of the

Seine. He was different for the remaining thirty-five years of his life. But in that instant he has become a frozen image. It's an afternoon in Paris. His books are behind him, but he doesn't know it. Nobody knows him. He can slip anonymously back to the book-stalls along the *quais* and browse, drift with the afternoon, telephone a friend, arrange a rendezvous at a bar. He's in the same process of becoming as he was at the moment of his death.

[The translations in this chapter are by the author.]

NOTES

1 Interview with Madeleine Gobeil in Albert Dichy (ed.) *L'Ennemi déclaré: textes et entretiens* in Jean Genet, *Œuvres Complètes VI* (Paris, 1991), p. 12. This interview was published in English in *Playboy*, April 1964.

2   Ne chante pas ce soir les 'Costauds de la Lune'.
       Gamin d'or sois plutôt princesse d'une tour,
       Rêvant mélancolique à notre pauvre amour;
       Ou sois le mousse blond qui veille à la grand'hune.
   Jean Genet, *Le Condamné à Mort* in *Œuvres Complètes II* (Paris, 1951), p. 179.

3   Rêvons ensemble, Amour, à quelque dur amant,
       Grand comme l'Univers mais le corps taché d'ombres,
       Il nous bouclera nus dans ces auberges sombres,
       Entre ses cuisses d'or, sur son ventre fumant,
       Un mac éblouissant taillé dans un archange
       Bandant sur les bouquets d'oeillets et de jasmins.
   Jean Genet, *Le Condamné à Mort* in *Œuvres Complètes II* (Paris, 1951), p. 180.

4   Une poussière d'or flotte autour de lui. L'éloigne de moi.
   Jean Genet, *Le Pêcheur du Suquet* in *Œuvres Complètes III* (Paris, 1953), p. 165.

5   J'arrive dans l'amour comme on entre dans l'eau,
       Les paumes en avant, aveuglé, mes sanglots
       Retenus gonflent d'air ta présence en moi-même
       Où ta présence est lourde, éternelle. Je t'aime.
   Jean Genet, *Le Pêcheur du Suquet* in *Œuvres Complètes III* (Paris, 1953), p. 168.

6   D'une plaie ou du sang sur les pierres
       Qui peut naître, quel page et quel ange de lierre
       M'étouffer? Quel soldat portant vos ongles morts?
   Jean Genet, *Un Chant d'Amour* in *Œuvres Complètes II* (Paris, 1951), p. 401.

7   Pour me remonter nu sur de bleus escaliers.
   Jean Genet, *Un Chant d'Amour* in *Œuvres Complètes II* (Paris, 1951), p. 400.

8   Las de périr sans fin à deux doigts de mes lèvres
       L'Horizon s'endormait dans vos bras repliés.
   Jean Genet, *Un Chant d'Amour* in *Œuvres Complètes II* (Paris, 1951), p. 400.

9   Dans son torse, endormie – d'une étrange façon
    Crémeuse amande; étoile, ô fillette enroulée
    – Ce tintement du sang dans l'azur de l'allée
    C'est du soir le pied nu sonnant sur mon gazon.

  Jean Genet, *Un Chant d'Amour* in *Œuvres Complètes II* (Paris, 1951), p. 401.

10   Mais le vert pavillon des rôdeurs de la mer
    Doit veiller quelque part, se prendre dans les pôles.
    Secouer la nuit, l'azur, en poudrer vos épaules
    Dans vos pieds ensablés percer des sources d'air.

  Jean Genet, *Un Chant d'Amour* in *Œuvres Complètes II* (Paris, 1951), p. 400.

11   Ô la douceur du bagne impossible et lointain!
    Ô le ciel de la belle, ô la mer et les palmes,
    Les matins transparents, les soirs fous, les nuits calmes,
    Ô les cheveux tondus et les Peaux-de-Satin.

  Jean Genet, *Le Condamné à Mort* in *Œuvres Complètes II* (Paris, 1951), p. 180.

CHAPTER 10

Death, Murder and Narrative Form in Pompes funèbres

Sharon Cornford

THE THEMES OF death and murder recur like an obsession throughout Genet's texts, but it is in *Pompes funèbres* that the narrator's preoccupation with mortality is the most graphic and sustained. It is also in *Pompes funèbres* that the narrator's own stated circumstances and the themes he probes in his narrative are most tightly linked, as he explores his immediate preoccupations within the imaginary arena of the narrated world. This chapter aims to examine the nature of this relationship between narrator and narrated world, between narrator and characters, and ultimately between theme and narrative form in *Pompes funèbres*.

Far from the narrative form of *Pompes funèbres* simply being an arbitrary framework within which themes are presented, the narrator uses the construction of his narrated world not just to explore the themes of death and murder objectively but, more personally, to deal with his own bereavement. The form of his narrative becomes at once the vehicle through which his immediate preoccupations are expressed and the tool he uses for their exploration. It is my contention that the narrator does not simply exorcise his grief by articulating it but exploits his relationship to his narrated world and its characters in an attempt to transform his relationship to his bereavement from unbearable passivity into activity.

Before examining the link between the formal and the thematic relationship of the narrator to the narrated world, it is important to establish the key characteristics of the narrator himself. Following Genette's terminology, the narrator of *Pompes funèbres* is a 'fictional author', an author-narrator who is not just story-telling but writing a book. As a fictional author, the narrator's relationship to his narrative is, significantly, not simply that of a witness but of a self-conscious creator who can take aspects of his 'reality' and transform them in his imaginary narrated world into pure fantasy over which he has total control. Genette also categorises narrators as homodiegetic (present as a character in their narrative) or heterodiegetic (absent from it). In *Pompes funèbres* the narrator is homodiegetic in relation to the primary narrative – Jean

D's funeral, his visit to Jean D's mother's house, his cinema visit, memories from his relationship with Jean D – but heterodiegetic when narrating the secondary narrative, the Erik–Riton story. Generally, then, the narrator is homodiegetic when narrating what he presents as his real situation but heterodiegetic when constructing pure fantasy, although there is some slippage. The fact that the narrator's formal relationship to the secondary, fantasy narrative is different from the primary narrative is significant to the way he utilises his relationship to it in his response to bereavement.

The narrator also exploits his formal relationship to the Erik–Riton narrative by blurring and collapsing conventional distinctions between narrator and character in 'narrative metalepses'. Although heterodiegetic, the narrator projects himself into his fantasy by merging with characters through the substitution of first for third person pronoun.[1] Camille Naish calls this 'transgressive identification'.[2] As Naish suggests, rather than 'becoming' the character in a shift in focalisation, the narrator merges with him while simultaneously remaining himself and retaining his omniscience in a temporary dual focalisation. For example, when the narrator merges with Hitler, he still also reports Paulo's thoughts: he looks through the character's eyes through his own. By merging with his characters, the narrator does not just control his characters' experiences but participates in them vicariously. Thus, there is clearly a connection between the themes the narrator explores, his manipulation of narrative form to explore them, and what he is proposing to achieve.

It may appear problematic to suggest a narrator's motivation for constructing his narrated world. However, in *Pompes funèbres*, where the narrator's personal circumstances and his fantasy – his primary and secondary narrative – are inextricably enmeshed, the narrator states his intention explicitly. If the catalyst for his narrative is his bereavement – he talks of 'the death of Jean D which provides the pretext for this book'[3] – the narrative itself aims to effect 'the prismatic decomposition of my love and my grief' (p. 17). The narrator experiences his bereavement as impotence in the face of an unalterable death – 'Jean had been taken from me' (p. 22) – which emphasises his own inescapable mortal condition. His narrative constitutes an active imaginary response to this passivity, an attempt to transform the humiliation of impotence into the dignity of control by transforming the humiliating defeat of death, which Jean D's sordid state funeral magnifies, into the glorious victory of his own aesthetic 'funeral (w)rites': 'Jean needed a compensation. My heart prepared to offer him the pomp that men refused him' (p. 23).

Although the narrator's poetic response to what is changes nothing in external reality – 'words are words ... they did not alter the facts in any way' (p. 42) – the imaginary is his only option. Powerless before 'the facts', he turns inward to take active control at least of his attitude to them. Using the 'inner gaze' (p. 53) of his imagination, he attempts, through a process analogous to Nietzschean *amor fati*, to 'will backwards' and declare with Zarathustra's Übermensch, 'But I willed it thus!'[4] The narrator endeavours to eliminate a grief which betrays his humiliating passivity by transforming it into something not only willed but actually loved. He cannot undo his grief because he cannot undo Jean D's death, so he aims instead to extinguish his grief by, paradoxically, willing its intensification in his narrative until he is no longer its passive victim but its active master: 'I know this book is only literature, but I am hoping it will permit me to exalt my grief to the point of making it dissolve until it is no more – as a firework disperses after its explosion' (p. 218). The narrator intends to bring his relationship to his grief and to death itself within his control by manipulating his relationship to an aesthetic medium which *is* within his control.

The most significant mechanism the narrator utilises in the poetic transformation of his response to his lover's death is the manipulation of his heterodiegetic relationship to his secondary, fantasy narrative to merge with characters through dual focalisation and explore various confrontations with death vicariously. He thereby fuses theme and narrative form almost indissolubly as he experiments with experiences in an imaginary, narrated world that would lie beyond his experience in his 'reality'. The narrator does not, therefore, simply delegate characters to kill or die in his place, as the 'narrator' in *Fragments* … suggests he will use his 'enfant perdu': 'If he kills, he kills himself: prison, scaffold, penal colony, so many deaths that he will live in my place.'[5] The narrator of *Pompes funèbres* moves beyond a 'Heliogabalan' relationship with his characters, no longer simply using them to live in his stead as the emperor Heliogabalus used his soldiers,[6] but participating vicariously in imaginary experiences through them.

In the first incident of merging, exceptionally the narrator merges with Erik in the primary narrative before beginning his fantasy. Here, the narrator offers a straightforward reason: he is reconstructing Erik's past by thinking himself into Erik's life and being: 'The first time I met him, leaving the apartment, I endeavoured to retrace the course of his life and, to make it more effective, I climbed into his uniform, his boots, his skin' (pp. 31–2). The narrator shares Erik's sexual encounter with the executioner, and initially neither the experience nor the process of participation appears significant to the narrator's attempt to transform his relationship to Jean D's death. However, the second time the narrator talks of reconstructing Erik's past, he makes a direct connection between his bereavement and this fantasy. On the second occasion, which is narrated immediately after and grows out of his cinema visit, the narrator introduces into Erik's past Riton, a purely imaginary character who is not part of the 'real' primary narrative. The link between the Erik–Riton fantasy and the narrator's bereavement, and between the narrative form of this fantasy and the themes explored within it, is therefore to be found in the narrator's experience in the cinema.

In the cinema, as the narrator watches on screen a rooftop battle between a militiaman and a French soldier, he transforms it in his mind so that he is witnessing Jean D being shot. He then uses his imagination to transform his relationship to his bereavement from impotent victim to master of it by changing not the facts themselves but his role in them. Because Jean D's 'real' death is completely beyond the narrator's control, rather than using his imagination to prevent Jean D's on-screen representative from being killed, he transforms his passivity into a semblance of activity by 'willing backwards', willing Jean D's death after the event by instigating and demanding it at least in his imagination.[7] He will then seal the event as absolutely chosen by loving Riton, who kills Jean D for him, in a literal expression of *amor fati*:

> I was suffering so badly from Jean's death that I was prepared to use any means to rid myself of his memory. The best trick I could play on that savage monster we call fate, which delegates a kid to do its work, and the best trick I could play on this kid, would be to invest him with the love that I bore for his victim. I begged the image of the young lad: 'I would like you to have killed him' (p. 51).

There follows an extraordinary internal struggle in which the narrator desperately takes control of his situation by controlling his attitude to it, transforming himself from victim of Jean D's death to his posthumous killer using the murder weapon of his imagination. This is one of the most magnificent passages in Genet's prose fiction, yet it is often misunderstood. The narrator does not simply love the militiaman whom he hates because love and hate are the same in Genet, as some critics, rather oversimplistically, suggest.[8] When the narrator says, 'My hatred of the militiaman was so strong, so beautiful, that it amounted to the strongest love' (p. 51), he is stating that his love and his hate are equivalent in intensity, not that they are the same or interchangeable. If they were, the narrator could love the militiaman immediately, but he cannot. He declares near the beginning 'I want to love Riton', but admits 'I did not love Riton, all my love was still for Jean' (pp. 51–2).

What is crucial is the effort required to transform his hatred of Jean D's imaginary murderer into love and thereby to take control of his grief, again reminiscent of Nietzsche: 'The value of a thing sometimes lies not in what one attains with it, but in what one pays for it – what it *costs* us.'[9] This process costs the narrator dearly, but if crying out 'Kill him!' causes him intense pain, he can only augment his control by willing even more: 'My heart felt torn apart. I wanted my suffering to be even more intense, to rise to the supreme song, to death itself' (p. 52). Building up his love for Riton gradually, he has his first breakthrough, 'a little love passed onto Riton' (p. 53). He pushes his Nietzschean self-overcoming further:

> A third silent invocation rose out of me and drew me out of myself:
> 'Do him in, I'm giving him to you.'
> From out of my motionless, bent body, slumped in the seat, another wave of love
> flowed firstly onto Riton's face, then onto his neck, his chest and his whole body
> imprisoned in my closed eyes (p. 53).

After a supreme effort, the narrator finally declares 'The same rivers of love flowed onto Riton yet not a drop was removed from Jean' (p. 54).[10] As Maurice Chevaly comments, the agony of the narrator's 'victory' of self-overcoming resembles an extreme assertion of Cornelian stoicism; he is Chimène admiring her father's murderer and torturing herself with delight.[11] And as with Chimène, the pain renders the narrator's victory over himself all the more glorious. He has played the first leg in his 'game which consists of conning fate' (p. 54) and has won.

I wish to suggest that the narrator, having achieved a temporary inner victory in the cinema, constructs the Erik–Riton narrative to sustain and develop the experience of transforming his impotence before death into control. The narrator's superficial reason for the fantasy is to continue his reconstruction of the 'real' Erik's imagined past, and he incorporates Riton into the story as the militiaman Erik fought alongside in the 'revolt of Paris'. But if this is the superficial connection between the narrator's 'real' situation and the fantasy, the deeper link is revealed by another statement: 'I am trying to portray these characters to you in such a way that they are lit up by my love, not for them but for Jean, and above all in such a way that they reflect this love' (p. 55). Crucially, the narrator has just transformed his love of Jean D into willing his death by killing him through a substitute. If, on a thematic level, the Erik–Riton fantasy represents the narrator's attempt to assume control of his grief by experimenting with further chosen confrontations with death and murder in his narrated world, on a formal level the way the narrator manipulates his relationship to this narrated world constitutes the formal, aesthetic means through which he brings about this imaginary experimentation.

Thus the narrator's relationship to what he sees on screen is duplicated in his relationship, both in formal and thematic terms, to the Erik–Riton story which he generates out of it, and the cinema scene itself constitutes the link between the primary, 'real' narrative and the secondary, fantasy narrative which becomes the arena in which he experiments with a method of dealing with 'reality' through fantasy. The method the narrator explores in the cinema to assert an active imaginary response to the passivity of his bereavement and thereby to effect the 'prismatic decomposition of his love and grief', the mechanism of

Nietzschean *amor fati*, is gradually pushed to the limit in the Erik–Riton fantasy. Indeed, because this inner process for dealing with his grief is essentially imaginary, the narrator's further exploration of it is ideally suited to an aesthetic medium – the book he writes – where it can be more easily sustained.

On a formal level, the shift from 'real' to fantasy narrative involves the narrator's transition from participating observer to creator-fantasiser. This transition is illustrated by Erik's passage between 'reality' and fantasy. There are two Eriks in *Pompes funèbres*, the 'real' one whom the narrator meets at Jean D's mother's house, and the fictional Erik, an imaginary construct partly based on the 'real' one, whom the narrator invents in his fantasy about Erik's life. The narrator describes the way fantasy Erik is pieced together: 'I take gestures chosen from young people passing by. Sometimes it's a French soldier, an American, a thug, a barman … They suddenly offer me a gesture which could only belong to Erik' (p. 67). Fantasy Erik's status as pure construct is reinforced by a transgression of chronological coherence: fantasy Erik is shot dead before the narrator meets 'real' Erik and begins the fantasy about him. Shifting his narrative from 'reality' to fantasy, the narrator even asserts his control over logic and time.

On a thematic level, the significance of the shift from 'reality' to fantasy, and the key to the relationship between theme and narrative form, also involves taking control: when the narrator alters his formal relationship to his narrative he changes his thematic relationship to his grief, and thereby brings about his own transformation from victim of circumstance to master of it.

In the fantasy, the actual moments when the narrator projects himself into his creatures are not arbitrary but follow a pattern or progression which both reflects and embodies the narrator's endeavour not to be a victim of Jean D's death. In the cinema, because the narrator could not alter the fact of Jean D's death, he chose rather to transform his passivity into activity by willing his death, using an imaginary substitute killer to shoot an imaginary substitute for Jean D. In the Erik–Riton fantasy, the narrator reinforces and extends the decomposition of his grief through a sustained exploration of confrontations with death in which the narrator participates vicariously. There is a clear progression in the experiences the narrator shares, from indirect confrontations with death through to outright murder, reflecting the narrator's own progression from victim of his lover's death to his imaginary killer.

When the narrator first merges with Erik, he appears simply to be reconstructing Erik's past, but even here, before the cinema and the fantasy, the sexual encounter with the executioner which the narrator experiences through Erik reflects his aim gradually to assert control over death. The narrator uses this sexual experience to begin to overcome his horror of death and killing. The executioner repeatedly asks whether the narrator/Erik is frightened of who he is, forcing the narrator/Erik to transcend his terror. Even before merging with Erik, almost in preparation, the narrator emphasises the self-overcoming required for Erik/himself to love the executioner: 'To hate is nothing, but to love what one hates is sickening. Kissing him or being kissed by him was not terrible but getting an erection and coming because of these kisses received and given certainly was' (p. 111). In order not to be defeated into passivity by death's apparition, he must push his willing to the limit, and 'follow it through to the end' (p. 72). To assert his liberty from death's reign of fear he must not just tolerate but actually love the executioner, as he must eventually will and love death itself to avoid being its victim: 'He had without doubt overcome the first fits of disgust and, little by little, had got used to the idea of being the executioner's lover' (p. 83). For Erik, loving death's accomplice constitutes his first indirect step towards domesticating death, while for the narrator, his vicarious experience through Erik represents a further step in his endeavour to alter his relationship to his bereavement by first of all altering his attitude to it.

The second occasion that the narrator merges with Erik occurs within the fantasy. Before entering his creature, the narrator emphasises that, although externally Erik is a composite of the 'real' Erik and various other attributes taken from passers-by, internally Erik is a vehicle for the narrator himself: 'The feelings are mine' (p. 67). Later the narrator states explicitly that he is at once participating in Erik's experiences and pursuing his own through him, 'reliving Erik's anguish and bringing him to life through my very own anguish' (p. 126). This time, the narrator/Erik progresses from familiarity with killing gained through intimacy with an executioner to assisting with an execution. The narrator/Erik declares that assisting another to take life is his psychological preparation for committing a murder himself:

> One day I insisted on being present at the execution of a criminal as an assistant, a second-in-command. I was the one who held his head on the block. I was not aspiring to the executioner's position as a state employee, but I was killing myself so that I would be able to kill later without danger (p. 67).

On the next occasion, the narrator merges with Riton after killing the cat. The narrator/Riton tells us that before this he had tried to attack a stranger but his nerve had failed him:

> Before the incident with the cat, I had tried in vain to beat a guy up … At the top of the rue du Temple I spotted a guy, not too tall. I have a good cosh … Every yard I said to myself, 'No one's around, I'll do him in here' … I jostled him as I passed him, then I insulted him and hit him: a punch in the face. He was the stronger. I had to get the hell out (p. 99).

The narrator does progress to shooting a victim, but significantly he firstly merges with the executioner meeting Erik, as though using this brief self-insertion into an experienced 'killer' to boost his own courage to kill. The narrator does note the way Erik's relationship with the executioner has inspired him, and it is certainly with redoubled courage that, when the narrator next projects himself into Erik, he dares to share the experience of shooting a young boy.

The way the narrator/Erik describes killing the boy places it firmly within the progression of vicarious experiences up to this point: 'The moment that I looked at the face of the boy, which had an ironic boyish delicacy, I understood that the moment had come to know what a murder was like' (p. 120). In his desire to uncover 'the secret of death' (p. 121) through this experience, the narrator shares every detail through Erik, from noticing the boy to pointing the gun, pulling the trigger and watching the boy fall. The instant of firing is described as a supreme victory of courage and self-possession, of self-liberation from the fear and horror of death, a triumphant moment of control over death itself: 'My finger on the trigger. The highest moment of freedom had been attained. To shoot at God, to wound God and make of Him a deadly enemy. I fired. I fired three shots' (p. 122). In the cinema the narrator willed the shooting of Jean D by a substitute, but now he overcomes his impotence before the death of another by not just willing such a murder but performing it in his imagination. He does not want to understand Erik's experience of murder, but uses him for his own vicarious experimentation. CJ Rawson also makes this point, commenting on the ambiguity when the narrator (whom she calls Genet) merges with Erik:

> Genet's lordly determination not to clarify emphasises that it is of little consequence whether the act was done or who is deemed to have done it, and that the real issue is his own involvement in it in the now of the narrative ... He is ... enacting a total unconcern with understanding Erik as a separate being, at the very moment of giving him and his introspection the centre of the stage. What he is in effect declaring is his participatory exploitation of the personage.[12]

Rawson's comment re-emphasises that the characters within the narrated world are not primarily independent agents but the narrator's pawns exploited as vehicles for his own experimentation.

Once the boy is dead and the moment of control over death is passed, the narrator/Erik's self-possession diminishes as his horror of the physical reality of the death grows: 'I felt horrified at being in contact, physically and magically, with a warm corpse' (p. 122). Having fought to transform his passivity into activity and won, the narrator/Erik is loath to let his victory over himself be undermined by a return to the humiliation of inner limitations: 'I was ashamed of my cowardice' (p. 123). He draws on the executioner's influence to strengthen his power to will: 'He taught me courage. I will' (p. 123). Imagining the executioner holding his waist,[13] the narrator/Erik confirms and reinforces the self-overcoming he has achieved in willing the boy's murder by forcing himself to look at the corpse. When Erik becomes afraid now, having sustained his self-assertion to the end, the narrator emphasises that he is 'frightened, not by remorse or by possible punishment, but by his glory' (p. 124).

If shooting the boy vicariously constitutes a major victory for the narrator over himself and over death, the subsequent occasions of merging reflect and further explore this new control over his impotence. The next time, he merges with Juliette when she is exploring the possibility of informing on Jean D. The connection between this experience and the narrator's situation is that the narrator describes his willing of Jean D's death as betrayal, and the narrator now experiments with mustering enough self-possession to betray Jean D through Juliette, as though testing further the freedom he has won thus far. He draws strength from this vicarious experience – 'I felt strong with my freedom, intoxicated by my freedom, a little intoxicated' (p. 131) – and even though Juliette does not go through with this betrayal, the episode constitutes a testing out of 'I can' before the act is completed in 'I will'.

The narrator briefly merges with Erik, trying to leave the executioner, as though his personal victory over death means he no longer needs the executioner's influence, and then, significantly, the next merging is introduced explicitly as a betrayal of Jean D. The narrator overcomes his pain faced with his lover's corpse and asserts his self-possession by replacing his respect for Jean D with the shameful insult of indulging in a sexual fantasy about Hitler. It is not in spite of but because of his recognition that 'one feels somewhat ashamed at thinking about acts of sensual pleasure while in mourning', that the narrator proves his control over himself and his grief by doing just that: 'I had to force myself to write the preceding erotic scenes … I mean that, once I had overcome my disquiet at having defiled a corpse, this game of which a corpse is the pretext gives me a great freedom' (p. 148).

The 'erotic scene' between Hitler and Paulo represents a progression from Erik confronting his fear of killing through a sexual encounter, since this episode does not involve a mere executioner, who has taken perhaps hundreds of lives, but Hitler who has ordered the death of millions, the very personification of death. It is also a progression since the narrator does not merge with the one who must overcome his fear of death but chooses to savour through Hitler the experience of inspiring the fear of death in others.

The fantasy Hitler has not just murdered one lover, and not just in his imagination, but many, in the secret alcove where 'Hitler loved and killed his victims' (p. 148). This Hitler has not simply shot a boy but explored death in all its conceivable forms. The narrator shares in this as the narrator/Hitler declares 'I have already done the rounds of every possible kind of death' (p. 157), for the first time exploring the deaths of others as vicarious rehearsals for his own as equally willed and chosen: 'I have chosen every kind of death. None will surprise me. I have already died often and always magnificently' (p. 158).

Having reached these heights there is apparently nowhere further for the narrator to progress. The remaining instances of merging simply play out further opportunities for self-assertion, such as the narrator/Riton daring to instigate sex with the older, more powerful Erik, and the narrator/Erik deciding he wants to kill the executioner, to kill the 'killer'. And then, like the narrator's momentum in creating his narrative, the instances of merging simply peter out.

The penultimate scene of *Pompes funèbres*, in which Riton shoots Erik, is rather hurried as the narrator's creative energy dwindles. The narrator does not project himself into the killer this time, but the scene is significant because it brings the narrator full circle to a final re-enactment of his original endeavour, first attempted in the cinema, to achieve the prismatic decomposition of his love and grief and transform the passive humiliation of his bereavement by willing the shooting of his lover. Riton's whole *raison d'être* within the fantasy is as the narrator's chosen substitute for carrying out his willed killing of Jean D after the event: 'I have the soul of Riton' (p. 133). Moreover, this re-enactment of that earlier scene, this time with Erik as victim, parallels the narrator's own situation more closely than the cinema film, since now Riton is not killing the enemy but has to find the added strength to shoot his lover. As such, it represents a fantasised, symbolic compensation for the earlier episode in which the narrator imagined himself putting his gun in Jean D's mouth at a fairground but was unable to pull the trigger: 'I tremble with shame at the memory of that instant ... I was the one who lost his nerve' (p. 92). Characteristically, the narrator achieves vicariously what he cannot even imagine achieving himself. The parallel between Erik and Jean D is reinforced in an earlier remark that 'Erik was fulfilling his destiny with the same ardour that Jean D fulfilled his' (pp. 115–16).

There is another important difference between the two re-enactments. Whereas, at the end of the cinema scene, the narrator treats his initial victory there as a starting point for further exploration in the fantasy he begins, the final scene ends, after the narrator's extraordinary inner struggle, with a final assertion by his substitute of victory over death: Riton does not simply kill his lover, but dances on his body. Through a sustained process of merging with his characters and self-substitution, the narrator of *Pompes funèbres* has finally transformed his humiliating passivity before his bereavement into a supreme moment of active control and self-possession. He has exploited his relationship to his narrated world in order to alter his relationship to his grief and indeed to death itself, and has apparently emerged victorious.

[All translations of quotations in this chapter are by the author.]

NOTES

1 This process of substitution is apparently prefigured, although for different reasons, in *Miracle de la Rose*, although attention is only drawn to this fact in *Journal du Voleur* when the narrator makes the following comment: 'In a book entitled *Miracle de la Rose*, when the friends of a young convict are spitting on his cheeks and in his eyes, I assume the disgrace of his position myself, and speaking of him I say: "I".' (Jean Genet, *Journal du Voleur* (Paris, 1949), p. 181.)

2 Camille Naish, *A Genetic Approach to Structures in the Work of Jean Genet* (Massachusetts, 1978), p. 119.

3 Jean Genet, *Pompes funèbres* (Paris, 1953), p. 8. All references are to Gallimard's 'L'Imaginaire' integral edition of *Pompes funèbres*, and will hereafter be signalled in the text by a page number in brackets.

4 Friedrich Nietzsche, *Thus Spoke Zarathustra: A Book for Everyone and No One*, translated by RJ Hollingdale (London, 1990), p. 163. The idea of the Superman constituted one of the two key concepts in Nietzsche's philosophy that Genet told Barbezat he found particularly pertinent to his own thought. See Jean Genet, *Lettres à Olga et Marc Barbezat* (Décines, 1988), p. 261.

5 Jean Genet, *Fragments ... et autres textes* (Paris, 1990), p. 91.

6 Indeed, Genet was fascinated by this idea (Edmund White, *Genet* (London, 1993), p. 203; Jean Genet, *Fragments ... et autres textes* (Paris, 1990), p. 90), and wrote a play for Jean Marais entitled *Héliogabale* in 1943 (Jean Marais, *Histoires de ma vie* (Paris, 1975), p. 151), the year before *Pompes funèbres* was completed. We find a similar idea expressed by the narrator in *Journal du Voleur* who calls Lucien 'my ambassador on earth' (Jean Genet, *Journal du Voleur* (Paris, 1949), p. 275).

7 White suggests a Freudian explanation for this process: 'Partly, of course, this action arises from what Freud called the repetition compulsion – the desire to repeat painful events from which one suffered passively but which this time one engineers, precisely in order to overcome the original sense of helplessness' (Edmund White, *Genet* (London, 1993), p. 279).

8 For example, Richard Coe states that 'Genet finds himself not hating but loving Riton' because 'at this point of white-heat, the two emotions become interchangeable' (Richard Coe, *The Vision of Jean Genet* (London, 1968), p. 149).

9 Friedrich Nietzsche, *Twilight of the Idols or How to Philosophise with a Hammer and The Anti-Christ*, translated by RJ Hollingdale (London, 1990), p. 102.

10 Michael Stephen Henderson describes the narrator's achievement in the following terms: 'In an effort to rid himself of his grief, the narrator begins an operation of betrayal, negating all that Jean D represented by transferring his desire onto the image of his killer' (Michael Stephen Henderson, 'Discourses of the Self: Confession in the Works of Jean Genet' (doctoral thesis, University of California, 1991), p. 139). However, this statement reveals a fundamental misunderstanding of the narrator's inner process. The narrator himself makes it quite clear that his aim is not to transfer his love from Jean D to Riton but to love Riton as much as he loves Jean D. The narrator's entire attempt to transform his relationship to his bereavement is not undertaken in order to stop loving Jean D, but precisely because of his continuing love for him.

11 Maurice Chevaly, *Genet II: L'Enfer à Fleur de Peau* (Marseilles, 1989), p. 52.

12 CJ Rawson, 'Cannibalism and Fiction, Part II: Love and Eating in Fielding, Mailer, Genet, and Wittig' in *Genre*, Vol. 2, No. 2, 1978, p. 305.

13 The narrator later comments that, just as Erik draws his inspiration and support from the example of the superior self-assertion of the executioner, so too the power of the executioner is supported by the figure of Hitler, who stands hierarchically above him, not just in terms of social standing but chiefly in terms of the degree of control over death that each man has achieved: 'The great shadow of the executioner was walking at his side supported by the greater and slightly paler mass of Hitler' (p. 83). In this context, 'size' is clearly a question of degree of inner self-overcoming as it is manifested in outer acts rather than actual physical mass.

CHAPTER 11

Jean Genet's mots dialectophages

Angeliki Rosi

GENET'S RECENT BIOGRAPHER Edmund White, in the preface to his book, writes about the difficulties he encountered in reconstructing the author's biography, pointing out: 'Jean Genet had remarkable powers of self-transformation. The art of biography is often supposed to trace the small steps an individual takes in a clear direction, but no one could logically account for the extraordinary leaps Genet made from the beginning to the end of his life.'[1]

Jean Genet had a literary perception of reality. For him, the fictional universe of his novels and plays was closer to his perception of the real than the course of his private life, and it is in this light that we may interpret his belief in the power inherent in image-making. Genet was aware of the artificial dimensions an image possesses, but also of the important influence it exerts upon the other's perception of one's social attitude. He therefore transformed into an art the process of shifting personae throughout his career, and remained a silent spectator watching his legend being built and acquiring almost mythical dimensions.

Recent research has forced certain important changes to the 'legend' of Genet, certifying his image-making abilities, and proving that for him such a procedure was a conscious choice serving specific intentions. His personae may be seen as forming versions of his different subjectivity, since the deviation from the norm was the force sustaining both his personal and literary adventures. Genet's subversive attitude against the norm was not limited to the level of praxis, but was mainly expressed by means of his writing.

From very early in life Genet was aware of the power of language to perpetuate the dominant ideological myths, in that he experienced the social system from a marginal perspective that allowed him to observe its operation without falling into the trap of mystifying it. This detached perspective towards the norm led him to realise that to express his revolt successfully he must first master the idiom of the dominant class so as to undermine it from within.

Genet was particularly sensitive about writing 'proper' French and he worked very hard to achieve the formal skills that can be traced in his early literary style.

The recently uncovered data reveal him to have been a passionate reader and a devoted writer who started making literary experiments from an early age. The path towards the discovery of a literary style was a time-consuming process, and it could be suggested that early difficulties he encountered led to the development of a perfectionism which he maintained throughout his career. Indeed, it was only after a long period of experimentation that Genet decided to publish his first text, *Le Condamné à Mort*, judging it good enough to be read by others.

After this inaugural publication in 1942, Genet proved particularly productive; by the end of the 1940s he had published five novels and two plays, and had become a recognised writer. Success, however, seemed to lead him into a period of reflection. Questioning his literary achievements, he was particularly critical of the emotional background that inspired and defined his narrative adventures.[2] The outcome of this crisis was that Genet, in an attempt to detach himself from his erotic inspirations, decided to abandon the intimacy of his narrative world in order that his text might acquire a public dimension.

Genet's decision to assign this public dimension to his artistic idiom was concomitant with the recognition of the social role he had to perform as a writer. The narrative adventure was a sort of therapeutic experience for him, in that by giving a fictional expression to his revolt, he came to terms with his difference and felt eligible to speak in the name of others. Theatre was the appropriate domain to assist his effort towards socialisation. Yet the formulation of a social discourse was not his primary objective, his intentions being aesthetic rather than ideological. During the 1950s, when he completed his major plays, Genet elaborated a theoretical context which served as the aesthetic support to his original theatrical idiom.

At the core of his dramatic preoccupation lies the exploration of language. Unlike his novels, where he plays with semantic juxtapositions and mystifies the invocative power of language, in his plays his linguistic preoccupation is formal and his intentions are deconstructive.[3] Placing the text at the centre of the theatrical unfolding, Genet carries out a meticulous study of the verbal element in order to demonstrate its artificial dimension. What he wishes to show is that the only real dimension language possesses is its audible or written form, and that its validity as signifier is as illusory as any other action performed on stage.

Genet develops his ideas about the signifying potentials of language in the appropriate setting; it is the entire world of the stage that declares its incompatibility with reality. In order to succeed in his intentions, he challenges the traditional distinction between the dramatic context which sustains the play's fictional universe and the theatrical enactment of this universe on stage. In the attempt to eliminate the distinction between the stage and reality, Genet gradually demolishes the notion of the dramatic context, and reaches the point where the action on stage has no other referent than the reality of its performance.

Genet focuses closely on the function of each scenic element in the process of performance and invents two principles that model the structure of his theatrical universe. The first refers to the process of making manifest the artificial dimension of every scenic element, the second to a dynamics of contradiction defining the articulation of these signs according to the laws of contrast. The operation underlining the artificial dimension of the stage primarily concerns the visual outcome, including the setting, the costumes, the diction and the acting procedure. The dynamics of contradiction defines the mode in which the scenic elements interact within a framework of contradictory patterns. The logic of juxtaposition refers primarily to the intermingling of the supposed dramatic reality with its theatrical enactment. More often than not Genet relates the various scenic signs by means of contradiction, aiming at the elimination of any trace of realism from the stage. This logic also affects the verbal element – the characters often speak a highly sophisticated idiom which is incompatible with their supposed dramatic reality.

In an attempt to subvert the distinction between the dramatic and the theatrical in *Les Bonnes*, Genet intermingles the apparently separate levels of the sisters' performance. Yet the outcome does not succeed in entirely eliminating the dramatic, but rather in confusing the two levels, since the play was written at an early stage in the development of his innovatory theatrical patterns. In *Le Balcon*, Genet exposes his original techniques by writing a play where theatre itself is at stake. He therefore attentively intermingles the dramatic and the theatrical in each moment of the unfolding of the play so as to prove in the final scene that what appeared as the dramatic reality of the play was only one of the illusory scenarios acted out in the course of the performance. Moving from the general context which defines his perception of the theatrical representation, in *Les Nègres* Genet focuses on the actors' collective performance. The play develops more than one theatrical level and it is the acting that sets the boundaries of each scene and juxtaposes the play's different 'realities'. In *Les Paravents*, he concentrates on the performance of the actor as the major theatrical sign that signifies the unfolding of the scenes; in this play, both the process of underlining the artificial dimension of the stage and the dynamics of contradiction are generated almost exclusively by the performance of the actors, who are not only called upon to act out a particular character but also to create the setting in which the situations of the play develop.

Within the framework of his aesthetics of the purely theatrical, Genet succeeds in formulating a subversive discourse. In order to serve his purposes, he creates characters who for the most part speak versions of the dominant discourse within the context of specific power relations. He does not juxtapose the idiom of the social margins to that of the dominant class in order to deify the former, as he does in his novels. What he intends instead is to expose on stage the operation by means of which the dominant discourse moulds the individuals' utterances, regardless of the class to which they belong. It is the dominant ideological myths that are at stake in his dramas, and his undermining intentions are to make manifest their artificial dimension. Any form of authority, whether political, cultural or social, exerts its power by exploiting the mystifying potentials of language, and since its idiom is fake, its power also acquires only a fictional validity. For Genet, the exercise of power is an acted-out performance respecting the rules of a well-made play.

Genet's subversive intentions towards language should be interpreted in the context of his wider ideas concerning language as the means by which a writer represents his perception of the world. In an attempt to challenge the mediating role of language, Genet wishes to adopt the more objective view of the artist and therefore focuses on the visual arts, a domain where the process of creation is non-mediated. The painter or sculptor has a visual perception of his or her model and is called on to reproduce this perception by means of a raw material whose tangibility excludes artificiality. The writer, however, is called on to represent his or her perception of the world by means of words, a procedure involving a socially determined mediation.

Genet associates the social dimension of language with the notion of historical time; for him, the artist's objective view should register the point lying beyond history. 'The goal of theatre is to take us outside the limits of what is generally referred to as "historical".'[4] Yet in order for the writer to transgress the historical, he needs to go beyond perception by means of language, as this is modelled in the context of everyday experience. Genet therefore focuses on the notion of death, a word describing the only 'perceptible' state that negates the dimension of historical time.

The transgression of the historical acquires obsessive dimensions in Genet's mind, and in order to give expression to his preoccupation, he develops an entire aesthetic context on the basis of death. It is in this light that he writes his conclusive vision of how theatre should be, and the texts registering the relevant ideas are *L'Étrange mot d'* ... and *Les Paravents*. The two texts bear close affinity and may be seen as forming a unity comprising Genet's philosophical meditation on theatre aesthetics: in *L'Étrange mot d'* ... he describes his vision of theatre and narrates his experience as a dramatist, and in *Les Paravents* he attempts to provide a theatrical illustration of these ideas.

On an open-air stage, situated near the cemetery of a modern city, Genet invokes the figure of the funeral mime, whose role was 'to lead the funeral procession and mime the most important acts of the dead man's life',[5] and he writes his theatrical testament for the generations of dramatists to come. The deeds he sings are his literary adventures, and the conclusions he reaches summarise his life-long struggle with language.

> If we are clever enough, we can pretend to understand, we can make believe that words are stable, that their meaning is fixed or that it has changed because of us who, voluntarily, people seem to believe, if we modify their appearance slightly, become gods. As for me, faced with this enraged herd encaged in the dictionary, I know that I have said nothing and that I never will: and words don't give a damn ...
>
> Therefore ... the funeral mime will have to discover, and dare to say, those dialectophagous words which in the presence of the public will devour the life and the death of the dead man.[6]

Concluding his theatrical adventure, Genet has indeed discovered the dialectophagous words (*mots dialectophages*)[7] and his intention in writing *Les Paravents* is to place them on stage and celebrate them. In this play, Genet constructs a spectacle in which he accommodates his literary adventure in order to demystify it. Speaking from the perspective of his maturity, Genet realises that what he should finally offer to his audience is the truth of his artistic endeavour, which belongs to that category of 'truths that must never be applied, those that must be made to live through the song they've become'.[8]

In *Les Paravents*, Genet repeats his artistic experience and to transform it into a song he uses dialectophagous words. Their power has explosive potentials, and indeed it is not only colonial discourse that is deconstructed in this play, but also the playwright's entire theatrical mythology. In order to succeed in his intentions, Genet organises a spectacular feast where the ensemble of his literary idiom is deconstructed into signs performing acrobatics. Genet's celebratory mood is manifest in the play's carnivalesque world; *Les Paravents* recalls a circus programme offering a variety of turns which aim to thrill the audience. The circus aesthetics may be traced in the visual pandemonium reigning on stage and in the outbursts of laughter that are heard throughout the performance. It is the first time that laughter intrudes into Genet's world, a laughter expressing the detached sense of humour he adopted when he reached the state of maturity.

In order for the performance of *Les Paravents* to reach the point lying beyond the historical, Genet constructs a theatrical system which actualises the operation and simultaneous deconstruction of its sustaining principles. He invents a representational mechanism which gradually shows its malfunction; the reigning rhythm is irregular and the development of the actors' performance is unexpected. Verbal and gestural obscenities abound and a disarticulated power seems to dictate the unfolding of the play. For this theatrical parade, Genet provides the appropriate setting; the abstract drawings on the screens and the multiplicity of contrasted colours and fabrics create the visual impression of an uproar accompanied by a cacophony of strident noises.

Genet envisages an open-air theatre for the performance of *Les Paravents*, but since he cannot ensure that this space would be near a cemetery he brings the dead onto the stage. In the geometrical organisation of the stage into three levels on which the action develops in parallel, death is placed on the summit, denoting the ultimate referent of the entire action. The world of the dead operates as a reference point, which, instead of sustaining, invalidates what is acted out on the lower levels of the play's dramatic reality.

Genet decides to talk about death and to transgress the limits of the perceptible by using history as the background context of the play. Such a decision serves his intention to transgress the historical, first by mystifying it, then by deconstructing this myth and transforming it into a song. The subject he chooses is the Algerian War, an event responding to his ideological preoccupation concerning the imperialistic dimension of Western colonial discourse. Genet places on the one side the colonisers, who represent the rational dimension of the dominant discourse, and on the other the Arabs, who are in the course of discovering the mystifying potentials of the political idiom. Between these two groups, he places a number of figures derived from his literary mythology. These characters do not take sides in the conflict but are the ones who speak the dialectophagous words.

Saïd, Leila, the Mother, Warda and Ommou act out their own story, refusing to integrate into either of the two opposing camps. Yet, although they do not involve themselves in the conflict, they participate in its theatrical development. Their participation is of the utmost importance, in that by speaking aloud their own version of words they succeed in undermining the meaning the other characters try to utter. These figures may be seen as incarnating Genet's perception of dialectophagous words which demolish the signifying potential of language. Genet's intention is not the invention of these words but rather the exposition of their operation – their explosive power is not due to their form but to the particular pattern of their articulation. So Genet does not isolate the characters who speak these words but places them in the middle of the conflict. Their participation may appear minor, but their influence is crucial, since by means of their presence the discourse of the others is rendered meaningless. When confronted with the colonisers they uncover the theatrical dimension, the playing of roles, on which their authority relies, and when they engage with the Arabs they indicate the rationalising trap into which the new regime is falling.

The most accurate metaphor for the dialectophagous procedure which these characters act out in *Les Paravents* may be traced in the Mother's lines, when she attempts to draw her self-portrait:

> Hello! I'm Laughter – not just any laughter, but the kind that appears when all goes wrong ... Through the lords of old, go back to the Fairy, back to the Virgin,

I've known since childhood that I belong ... to the nettle family. Near ruins,
tangled with shards, their bushes were my cruelty, my hypocritical meanness that
I kept, with one hand behind my back, in order to hurt the world.[9]

The metaphor of the nettle perhaps summarises the mode by which Genet's
dialectophagous characters subvert on stage the mystifying power of language.
Despite their harmless appearance and the marginal position they maintain in
the unfolding of the conflict, they succeed in undermining both the colonial
discourse and the political myth on which the Arabs built the reality of their
independence. Genet, concluding his theatrical career with *Les Paravents*,
reveals to his audience that his artistic idiom has a similar dialectophagous
dimension, aimed at denouncing the dominant myths on which contemporary
society relies.

NOTES

[1] Edmund White, *Genet* (London, 1993), p. *xxxix*.

[2] The text registering Genet's relevant conclusions is *Fragments* ... (in Jean Genet, *Fragments
... et autres textes* (Paris, 1990), pp. 69–97). Critics suggest that a major factor which
reinforced Genet's self-critical mood was the publication of Sartre's *Saint Genet, comédien
et martyr* (Paris, 1952).

[3] The terms 'deconstruction' and 'deconstructive' throughout this chapter do not derive from
Derrida's system of thought, but maintain their literal meaning, referring to an act or
attitude challenging the notion of a coherent structure.

[4] Jean Genet, *The Strange Word 'Urb'* in *Reflections on the Theatre and other writings*,
translated by Richard Seaver (London, 1972), p. 64.

[5] Jean Genet, *The Strange Word 'Urb'* in *Reflections on the Theatre and other writings*,
translated by Richard Seaver (London, 1972), p. 72.

[6] Jean Genet, *The Strange Word 'Urb'* in *Reflections on the Theatre and other writings*,
translated by Richard Seaver (London, 1972), pp. 73–4.

[7] The term 'dialectophagous', invented by Genet, is a compound word which derives from
Greek words: *dialektos* (διαλεκτοζ), from the verb *dialegomai* (διαλεγομαι), relating to
'speech' (ομιλια), 'discussion' (συνομιλια), 'conversation' (συζητηση), that is, the act of
communicating a meaning by means of language; and from the past participle of the verb
trogo (τρωγω), meaning 'to eat/devour'. Hence the term 'dialectophagous word' may be
interpreted as a word which has the power to 'devour' language, that is, to prevent
language from communicating a meaning.

[8] Jean Genet, *The Screens*, translated by Bernard Frechtman (London, 1963), p. 195.

[9] Jean Genet, *The Screens*, translated by Bernard Frechtman (London, 1963), p. 112.

CHAPTER 12

The Uses of Monotony: Repetition in the language of Oscar Wilde, Jean Genet, Edmund White and Juan Goytisolo

(The William Matthews Lecture, delivered at Birkbeck College, London, 17 May 1994.)

Neil Bartlett

Editor's note: The William Matthews Lectures have been held annually at Birkbeck College, University of London since 1982, alternating between medieval and language topics. Professor William Matthews (d. 1975) was a graduate of Birkbeck College and lectured at Westfield College, University of London before becoming Professor of English at the University of California, Los Angeles. He edited an edition of Samuel Pepys' diary with RC Latham.

BEFORE I BEGIN, I would like to say that I shall be speaking from notes, not reading a written paper. I do this for several reasons. Firstly, I want to read things to you quite a lot – the four authors that I am going to be talking about are four men for whom and for whose work I have almost boundless admiration and so my main intent is to get you to read their books – and as I do so I want there to be a clear distinction between my own speaking voice, which will be rather disorganised, and the extremely organised and distinctive prose from which I shall be reading. Secondly, I have chosen to speak, rather than to read, because that will allow me room to ramble a little, which, as I hope will become clear, is actually pertinent to what I want to talk about, which is partly why one might ramble and what rambling can achieve as a literary device. I have also chosen to speak in this way because much of what I have to say seems to me to be about speaking – about speaking out loud. One of the characteristics that these four authors have in common is that their use of punctuation, for instance, reflects the punctuation of the speaking voice. If you just try to punctuate the last sentence that I have spoken, it would not be a literary punctuation, it would be what we would call (I suppose) a dramatic punctuation. And so it is important that you know that I am speaking out loud, and in some sense improvising on themes, because that is a quality of written text – a quality of improvisation – which I think is too little thought about. We all think because books are written down that they are primarily conceived in terms of text. This seems to me deeply untrue, particularly in the case of the four authors about whom I am going to be talking.

So let me start by saying why I have chosen these four authors: Oscar Wilde, Jean Genet, Edmund White and Juan Goytisolo – two alive and two dead, all men. I will start by reading a piece by Oscar Wilde, which I rather hope is where the title of my lecture comes from, because I am not sure if I have remembered it right. We will find out as I am quoting. (The reason for me giving this lecture, actually, is that I am currently writing a stage version of *The Picture of Dorian Gray* by Oscar Wilde and so in some sense this lecture is the work in progress. It gives me an opportunity to clarify in public my thoughts towards that adaptation, which is going to be staged at the Lyric Theatre, Hammersmith, in September 1994.)

I would like to read to you from the close of Chapter 10 of *The Picture of Dorian Gray*. This is the turning-point of the plot of the novel. I do not know whether all of you will know it. The thing which changes Dorian's life most is a book, which is a little extraordinary. Considering that he is also a drug addict, an adulterer, a pederast, a murderer, it is extraordinary that the thing that really counts is when someone gives him a book. This is rather a long quotation. I make no apologies for that.

> His eye fell on the yellow book that Lord Henry had sent him. What was it, he wondered. He went towards the little pearl-coloured octagonal stand, that had always looked to him like the work of some strange Egyptian bees that wrought in silver

(the word 'strange' occurs over six hundred times in *The Picture of Dorian Gray*)

> and taking up the volume, flung himself into an armchair, and began to turn over the leaves. After a few minutes he became absorbed. It was the strangest book that he had ever read. It seemed to him that in exquisite raiment, and to the delicate sound of flutes, the sins of the world were passing in dumb show before him. Things that he had dimly dreamed of were suddenly made real to him. Things of which he had never dreamed were gradually revealed.
> It was a novel without a plot, and with only one character,

(I would like you to remember that)

> being, indeed, simply a psychological study of a certain young Parisian, who spent his life trying to realise in the nineteenth century all the passions and modes of thought that belonged to every century except his own, and to sum up, as it were, in himself the various moods through which the world-spirit had ever passed ... There were in it metaphors as monstrous as orchids, and as subtle in colour. The life of the senses was described in the terms of mystical philosophy. One hardly

knew at times whether one was reading the spiritual ecstasies of some medieval saint or the morbid confessions of a modern sinner. It was a poisonous book. The heavy odour of incense seemed to cling about its pages and to trouble the brain. The mere cadence of the sentences, the subtle monotony of their music, so full as it was of complex refrains and movements elaborately repeated, produced in the mind of the lad, as he passed from chapter to chapter, a form of reverie, a malady of dreaming, that made him unconscious of the falling day and creeping shadows.

I think I would define the four writers I have chosen as the potential authors of that imaginary book, even though only one of them was actually alive when that description of the book was written.

Not surprisingly, a large number of people contacted Mr Wilde after the publication of *The Picture of Dorian Gray* and asked what this book was. Now he, of course, denied that it existed. This, I have to say, was a complete lie, since *Dorian Gray* is largely a reworking of passages from Huysmans and especially from Pater's unfinished *Gaston La Tour* and also various other books, including the Department Guide Books to the South Kensington Museums, of which Wilde must have had a complete set, since he quotes from them at such length in the twelfth chapter of the book. In particular, in April 1892, Mr E W Pratt, whose address was High Road, Lower Clapton, wrote to Wilde, wanting to know where he could obtain a copy of this book, and Oscar took it upon himself to write back, 'Dear Sir, The book in *Dorian Gray* is one of the many books I have never written but it is partly suggested by Huysmans' *À Rebours* which we know as *Against Nature* which you will get at any French booksellers.' So at least he was honest on that occasion.

There is a sense in the work of these four authors that they do not write real books. You could say of Wilde, of Genet, and of Goytisolo certainly, that they write books unlike anybody else's, that have few points of connection with the way that books, or especially novels, are meant to be written or are supposed to be about. It seems to me that they are all authors who are endlessly negotiating the idea of a book that they have never written. Their books characteristically are littered with projects which are never developed, promises which are never kept, and particularly with sentences that seem to go on for ever and never get quite where you thought or hoped they might get to. I think they could all have been authors of Dorian's mysterious book.

Another way of connecting these four authors – who, I should say, are very unlike: one a London Irish gentleman, one a convicted French criminal, one an American midwesterner in exile, now living and working in Paris, and one a Spaniard in exile, now spending half the year where he works in North Africa – I think the thing which connects them most of all is the sound of their sentences. It is said that the hallmark of a good writer, by which people always mean a writer whom one enjoys reading, is that you can recognise their work without being told that it is by them. You know, play me a phrase of Wagner and I will tell you that it is Wagner. Well, read me a sentence of Oscar Wilde and I will tell you for sure that it is Oscar Wilde. So what is the sound of the typical sentence which, I want to argue, would connect the four of these authors? Now, of course, you will have to go away and read the books and hear quite a lot of their sentences to decide whether you agree with me or not, but let me try some samples on you.

I think the Wilde quote is probably the most familiar piece to people. I think probably more people have read *The Picture of Dorian Gray* than any of the other books that I have been talking about. Remember what it said about Dorian's book:

> The mere cadence of the sentences, the subtle monotony of their music, so full as it was of complex refrains and movements elaborately repeated, produced in the mind of the lad, as he passed from chapter to chapter, a form of reverie, a malady of dreaming, that made him unconscious of the falling day and creeping shadows.

I think that is the archetypal sentence from my lecture, not only for what it describes but the way that it is itself constructed. '*Cadence* of the sentences', not the *meaning* of the sentences. 'The subtle monotony of their music' – that they are musical, so full, the idea of prose which is *full*, which is brimming with something, rather than of prose which is pointed, direct, economical, mechanical. 'Complex refrains and movements elaborately repeated' instead of sentences which get to the point and then move on. They are complicated, elaborate, repetitious, these sentences producing 'in the mind of the lad, as he passed from chapter to chapter' the sense, not of 'Right, what have you got to say to me? Just say it and let me move on' but of, as one passes 'from chapter to chapter' (the rhythm of that phrase itself, almost as if one was moving from room to room), 'a form of reverie, a malady of dreaming, that made him unconscious'. I think that is an extraordinary ambition for writing. Of all the things that we think writing could or should do: to make us dream, to make us ill, to make us unconscious! We normally think of writing as a healthy and purposeful project and certainly one that is an activity of the conscious mind, but here it is one that will make us 'unconscious of the falling day and creeping shadows'.

In the case of Proust, who is the great missing example from my catalogue, it really is true that sometimes the commas will run for almost a page, and indeed they can make you dream, they can make you ill, they can really make you unconscious. After reading a page of Proust it is very difficult to say, often, how long it has taken you to read, very difficult indeed. And to take that to its logical conclusion – 'How long does it take you to read Proust?' – I think the only intelligent answer would be to say 'I haven't finished yet'. Again, I am trying to point out alternative possibilities for the way that we might think about sentences and books operating. (Oh good, I've started to ramble, we're loosening up.) What I was trying to say was that in an archetypal sentence of a monotonous kind, a deliberately monotonous sentence, you can hear a hammering, insistent, repetitious, tolling rhythm. On to my next example.

I wonder if anyone here is familiar with the work of Goytisolo? Only two of you. A treat is in store. These are the two books which I am going to be quoting: *Makbara* – *makbara* is the place in a Moorish cemetery in which people meet to make love – and *The Virtues of the Solitary Bird*, which is a text originally written by St John of the Cross. St John of the Cross was forced to eat it by the Spanish Inquisition and it is reconstructed in this book by Juan Goytisolo. Goytisolo, a Spanish writer who went into exile under Franco, now lives half the year in Paris and migrates – he follows the storks. When the storks leave Europe to go to North Africa, he goes with them. I am going to read the opening two pages of *The Virtues of the Solitary Bird* and I wonder if you can hear in this, written almost exactly a hundred years later, any of the formal characteristics that I am proposing as inherent in Wilde's work. *The Virtues of the Solitary Bird* begins on page 11. The reason why I know this book is because it is published by Pete Ayrton from Serpent's Tail, who is here this evening. I remember Pete telling me he sent it to a reviewer who phoned up and said, 'There seems to be some terrible mistake. What's happened to pages one to ten?' The answer is, 'They're not there'. Because with this kind of writing, they do not need to be. It is not stupid to say that you can begin to read Proust anywhere or indeed *The Picture of Dorian Gray* anywhere. Eventually you will go back to the beginning and read it from the beginning. In order to be made sick or be made to dream or be made to forget or reconsider the passing of time, you certainly do not need to begin at the beginning of the sentence. You can become addicted, wherever you begin.

The Solitary Bird begins in the middle of a sentence, 'the apparition had materialised, had appeared to us' – straightaway, repetition; there is no reason to say that 'the apparition had materialised, had appeared to us'. Well, of course, it 'had appeared to us' if it 'had materialised' – if it had appeared to us, then the apparition must have materialised.

> the apparition had materialised, had appeared to us, at the top of the staircase on a day like the others, no different from the others
> (no, don't start asking me about dates, what does a misleadingly precise month, day, year mean at this point, after what's happened?)
> as we sauntered nonchalantly back and forth from the salon to the dressing rooms, crossed the foyer next to the showers where several still sprightly young things and

older, more experienced ones much the worse for wear were devoting themselves
with the same pleasure to the lustral rites, and leaning on the Lady's counter or the
shelf with the illustrated weeklies,

(one thing about this prose is that it requires immense resources of breath, as
you can hear – the only other thing that it is like is Racine. You really have to
have lungs to get through this)

we contemplated the couples on the side benches, the tables carefully set out by
the waiter, the lamps with translucent glass shades, each with a twisted bronze
foot, aligned like the fasces of lectors, the proprietress of the place used to say on
evoking its history, the pomp and splendor of the imperial inauguration
(imperial, yes, imperial, don't be skeptical, Napoleon and Eugénie did live, did
reign, it was a great event attended in its day by the cream of society)
step by step, carefully, because of the weight and bulkiness of its footgear
(the giant clodhoppers of clogs of a peasant woman)
we saw its endlessly long legs appear, its incredible scarecrow trousers belted about
its ghostly silhouette of a puppet moved by tiny invisible strings or wires
had it entered like everyone else through the arch of the carriage gate, crossed the
little courtyard with nineteenth-century bath-tubs ingeniously planted with
perennials, proceeded toward the staircase and its gas lamps of outworn majesty,
opened the door giving access to our ravaged and destroyed kingdom, paid sixty-
five francs to the blonde cashier who gave out tickets, little individual bars of soap,
shampoo, and other beauty products and aids to bodily cleanliness?
it's no use asking questions after all this time, as though you'd like to relive the
minutes preceding the blinding mushroom of Hiroshima or the burial of Pompeii
or Herculaneum

It goes on. It carries on for the rest of the book. It never stops. Does anybody
know what this is describing? What Goytisolo reveals later is that it is
describing the arrival (as he calls it) of 'the obscene monosyllable' – I love the
idea that he finds monosyllables so obscene – he is describing the arrival of the
obscene monosyllable 'Aids' in a gay sauna. That passage, describing a
mysterious feminine figure arriving, materialising somewhere in a sauna and
passing through it, is described numerous times in the course of *The Virtues of
the Solitary Bird*. It comes again and again and again, until at the end of the
book what, as I have shown, on first reading is more or less incomprehensible
– one has the sense of a momentous, ritualised event but also of one that is
more or less meaningless. By the end of the book it becomes very much
meaningful.

So we have had Wilde, we have had Juan, whom shall I turn to next?
Edmund? Let us have a short one. Genet. I did not know how to even begin to

quote from *Notre-Dame-des-Fleurs* (*Our Lady of the Flowers*) since I would really like to read you the whole thing but I thought I would choose one sentence, going back, remember, to *The Picture of Dorian Gray*, 'the subtle monotony of their music'. One quotation from the centre of the book, 'The Sayings of Divine', the leading character of *Our Lady of the Flowers*. This is a little collection of her 'verbal greatest hits' in the middle of the book. My favourite has always been, ever since I read the book as a very young man,

> Divine: 'My heart's in my hand, and my hand is pierced, and my hand's in the bag, and the bag is shut, and my heart is caught.'

which I think is a perfect sentence. Five commas in that one. The cadence of that sentence is unforgettable. The sense, I do not know. What does it mean?

> My heart's in my hand, and my hand is pierced, and my hand's in the bag, and the bag is shut, and my heart is caught.

Yes, it sort of makes sense, but the primary impression you get is of a queen starting a sentence, going on, thinking to herself 'Oh, this sounds fabulous. I'll just carry on.' Then ending with a flourish. And I think that is very much what Genet intends. That it is the *gesture* of the sentence, the *cadence* of the sentence rather than the *sense* (in the ordinary rather po-faced English sense of that word 'sense') that matters.

Edmund White. Three sentences which close three of the chapters of *Nocturnes for the King of Naples*.

> And yet there they were as fascinating as a swarm of butterflies descending on a particular old tree, the thousands of bright wings pivoting on black bark. In their midst sat the only child, a boy in a sailor suit with eyes as large and serious as yours.
>
> And then, once we're in the light, I see he's one of your old admirers, the crazy one who gave you the dog. We smile and begin to talk about you.
>
> A gipsy boy shined my shoes under a street lamp and then, without asking permission, briskly hammered taps into the rubber heels – an 'improvement' he charged me for. I paid him without a word and tap-tap-tapped my way into the shadowy botanical gardens. I sat on a bench under a banana tree and cried. Someone put a friendly arm around me. It was you at last.

Each of the chapters of *Nocturnes for the King of Naples* ends with the word 'you'.

So, I am trying to find things which these four men might have in common: the sound of their sentences.

Now, something which, it seems to me, connects them profoundly in my own mind, referring to my own title of 'monotony'. I do think that literature is not supposed to be monotonous. Nothing is *supposed* to be monotonous. Everything is supposed to be exciting, various, distinctive, attractive. Monotony is considered to be unattractive but it seems to me that the texts of these writers reverse that proposition. One of the particular qualities that I find attractive in their monotony is their insistence on going on about things at great length. All of them and all of their characters do go on and on. Rather than getting to the point they love to wander around the point, to elaborate the point, to embroider the point, and it seems to me that there is a direct connection between that sense of going on and on monotonously – if you like, droning on (the idea of a musical cadence droning on) – which is connected to the fact that these four writers are all homosexual artists. They do what all homosexuals, but especially homosexual artists, are accused of: going on and on about it, endlessly making up a set of variations on a single subject, being obsessed with just one thing. It seems to me that it is quite right to say that these writers are obsessed with just one thing, that their work revolves around that one thing, and I think that revolving is built into the very structure of their sentences, not just into the structure of the canon of their collected works.

Another point of contact between these four writers would be the way in which I discovered them, and this is also pertinent. This is a ramble but it is pertinent to my theme. Genet's *Our Lady of the Flowers*, written in 1943, was the first book that I ever bought because it was a dirty book. It seems to me there is something about this writing which is improper. One of the reasons why they go on and on and on is because they want to get to you. They want to tamper with you. They want to induce a malady, which may or may not be the 'malady of dreaming'. That is certainly the case with me and Genet. When you are fourteen and you read *Our Lady of the Flowers* things begin to look up.

Edmund White's *Nocturnes for the King of Naples* (1978) was the first book by a contemporary writer that I bought because I knew that he was a gay artist. I remember shaking with fear when I went and ordered the copy of this book from a bookshop in Bristol. The reason why I did that was because again I knew that this was an improper form of writing, that it was writing from the twilight world, 'a form of reverie, a malady of dreaming'. I did not really want to tell the bookseller that that was what I wanted from this book, a book that would make me 'unconscious of the falling day and creeping shadows'. It is all right if the author is dead, but it is really shaming if they are still alive to admit that you want to be exposed to this kind of writing.

Oscar Wilde I came to very late. I have since discovered why. My father tells me that there was actually a first edition of *The Picture of Dorian Gray* (1891) in my family's possession, but my grandfather removed it from the family bookcase and would not let my father read it. My grandmother has since thrown it away. And so I did not discover Oscar Wilde until I went to Oxford and I went to Magdalen College – and was totally infected as a result.

Juan Goytisolo I discovered completely by accident because his work is published in English by my publisher.

I would say just in passing – this really is not pertinent to my title – it is very important to me that these writers for me do represent the real tradition of gay writing. I have always thought of coming-out narratives, sensitive first novels, stories about Jeff and Steve having problems in middle America, as deviant. I am now told that it is supposed to be the other way round, that we are supposed to see Genet, White, Wilde and Goytisolo as being the deviants, the shady operators, the peculiarities, the perverts, who are operating somehow either behind or before or to the sides of the mainstream of the tradition of gay writing. I have to say that I think that is completely the wrong way round.

More things that connect these writers: it seems to me that as we acquire language, we are supposed to move from the babbling and the repetitious towards the articulate, the mature, the distinctive. Children start to speak by sing-song, babble, repetition, nonsense. They say the same thing over and over and over and over again for the pleasure of the sound of saying it. They then grow up and start to become more or less articulate. They learn to say what they mean. It seems to me that these four writers proposed, through the use of monotony, i.e. the idea of not getting to the end of your sentence or the end of your point, a completely different idea of what mature writing might be. That it might not be about saying what you mean, but about manipulating the pleasure of 'saying' itself. Pleasure of saying, rather than saying what you mean.

There is also a collection of very particular connections between these writers. Edmund White, at a time when he does not have any time to waste, has chosen to spend years writing the official biography of Genet. There is no evidence that Genet ever read or quoted from Wilde but it does seem to me that Genet's poem *Le Condamné à Mort* (*The Man Condemned to Death*) is very close to Wilde's text, and I cannot believe that he did not read *The Ballad of Reading Gaol*. I also think the title of *Miracle de la Rose* (*Miracle of the Rose*) is taken from *The Ballad of Reading Gaol* which describes roses blooming from the heart of a condemned man. That passage is paraphrased, it seems to me, in *Miracle of the Rose*, but I would love someone to try and find out and prove that. And Goytisolo knew Genet, and said there are two kinds of writers in the world: Genet and the others. Another set of connections.

There is a list of omissions from this little clutch of writers, writers who write in this peculiar and recognisable way. I think in particular I should have included James Purdy, William Goyen and Tennessee Williams, all of whose prose seems to me to have precisely the same qualities, of repetition, insistence, decoration, elaboration and devotion to the pleasures of saying, rather than the pleasures of sense, as the prose of my chosen foursome. This rather raises the question: 'Well, is what Neil is really saying just kind of, you know, well, gay writers *talk like that*?' No, it is not what I am saying. I do not think being gay determines an operation of the voice, any more than it determines an operation of any other part of your body, but I would have to say that, somewhere in all of this, there is an argument for the most remarkable consistency of gay culture. That is not at all the same thing as saying that there is a distinctive gay voice or gay sensibility or anything like that. But to be able to trace an ancestry of the sentence from Proust through to authors as various as Edmund White or Tennessee Williams or Juan Goytisolo, to be able to see a form of sentence making its way through history in that way, well, it means that there must be something going on.

Let us jump completely sideways now from these books. I would like to talk about some of the things that were happening to me when I first read them, which I think bears some relation to why I find monotonous prose attractive and important. I was first reading these books in the late 1970s and early 1980s (although I did not come to Goytisolo's work until much later). Other things were happening then, which seemed to me in some way to be models for the way that this kind of prose operates. Now you may think that I am mad to suggest some of these things. That is fine.

At the same time that I was reading these books I was listening to a lot of disco music, necessarily, since I was a homosexual in the late 1970s. It seems to me that disco music – I am not being flippant here – operates in a way that is remarkably similar to the prose of Dorian Gray's magical book. It is insistent. It insists on repetitions, variations on a formula, on repeated motifs; and it makes deliberate use of banality. In much the same way the word 'strange', the word 'languid', the word 'marvellous', the word 'brilliant' reappear so many times in *The Picture of Dorian Gray* that you get sick of them, but because they are repeated they begin to acquire an energy beyond the value of the words themselves. And that seems to me precisely the function of the phrasing, both verbal and musical, of disco music.

Also at that time there was the historical phenomenon known as cloning, which I am sure some of you in the audience will be familiar with. This was the idea that one of the basic principles of gay culture was the notion of multiplication, the notion of plagiarism, the idea that a motif, a gesture, which was valued for being unique and beautiful, could then be repeated a million times; but, because it was repeated a million times, it would become more beautiful and more valuable. That is an idea which runs opposite to many ideas about why we value things.

There was also central to our culture at that time the idea of promiscuity, the idea of non-cumulative incidents, i.e. the point about one-night stands is that they do not get you anywhere. You do one and then you do another one and you do another one and you do another one and you do another one. The sum is more than the total of the parts but they do not add up in a *sensible* way, in the same way that the units of Wilde's sentence do not add up in a sensible way. They accumulate, rather than make a point.

I think, lurking under all of these authors' writings also, there is a form of writing that we overlook at our peril, which is pornography. Like these writers, the primary structural principle of pornography is monotony. All pornography is the same by definition. It is repetitious. It is tedious. It is insistent. It does do precisely what Dorian's book does to you. It induces 'a form of reverie, a malady of dreaming, that made him unconscious of the falling day and creeping shadows'. Well, it sounds to me as though he was reading pornography.

I would just like to unpack the word 'monotony' a little to say what I think the characteristic features of this monotonous prose that I am proposing are. One, which you have heard already in my speaking voice, is the idea of insistence, of a throbbing bass – this is where the disco music analogy is useful – but also where the analogy of pornography is useful. The rhythm of pornography is the pounding of blood and the bass line of the disco song is also the pounding of blood in your head and, it seems to me, that under this prose there is something similar. Here, for instance, is Dorian Gray being seduced by Lord Henry:

> 'The only way to get rid of a temptation is to yield to it. Resist it, and your soul grows sick with longing for the things it has forbidden to itself, with desire for what its monstrous laws have made monstrous and unlawful. It has been said that the great events of the world take place in the brain. It is in the brain, and the brain only, that the great sins of the world take place also. You, Mr Gray, you yourself, with your rose-red youth and your rose-white boyhood, you have had passions that have made you afraid, thoughts that have filled you with terror, day-dreams and sleeping dreams whose mere memory might stain your cheek with shame –'
> 'Stop!' faltered Dorian Gray ...

– as well he might. That incredible pound, pound, pound – it is not the tolling of a bell, though, it is the pounding of blood. There is an extraordinary sense of compulsion, of obsessive return, that there is something being talked about and I am going to talk about it and talk about it and talk about it until finally we get there. Something will give way. This pounding or driving can operate within the sentence itself, it can also operate within the entire plot of a novel. I have said, for instance, Edmund's *Nocturnes for the King of Naples* is structured around the idea that every chapter in the book ends with the word 'you' because the book is a piece of devotional literature dedicated to a dead lover and so every sentence of the book arcs towards that word. Lord Henry Wotton in *Dorian Gray* is asked if he had ever thought of writing a book and he says, 'Yes, I would like to write a book like a Persian carpet', by which he means a book whose plot would be a series of convoluted patterns revolving around a single central point, a non-sensical novel, in other words. Well, that novel has now been written and it is *Makbara* by Juan Goytisolo, which, really, is structured very specifically like a Persian carpet. Technically it is a series of arabesques, in the sense that the sentences are derived from the decorative traditions of Moorish culture, where to execute a graceful gesture is justification in itself, where sense is not an issue but then, when all those gestures are put into one coherent arrangement, they form a dedicated pattern, a pattern with a point, if not with sense.

There also seems to be lurking under this prose the idea of intoxication: *Dorian Gray* – to induce 'a form of reverie, a malady of dreaming'. Basically the prose is trying to get him stoned. This prose drugs you. It drugs you so that it can do things to you or make you do things that you would not do if you were sober. White, an ex-alcoholic at the time he wrote *Nocturnes for the King of Naples*; Goytisolo, whose Moorishness includes the regular use of intoxicants; Wilde who actually in the character of Lord Henry Wotton elevated speech itself to the form of a drug (he says that Lord Henry Wotton could not only intoxicate himself, he could intoxicate an entire dinner party just by speaking); Genet, whose whole project in writing *Our Lady of the Flowers* – well, he makes it quite clear all the time by telling you literally that he is writing with one hand and masturbating with the other. He is writing in a condition of euphoria and it seems to me that the prose itself aspires to mimic the symptoms of euphoria, however induced, whether by sex, alcohol or drugs or by talking.

Monotony – this morning when I was writing this, for some reason Radio 3 played the prelude, the opening phrase to *Tristan and Isolde*, eight times in a row. I am not quite sure why they did this. They were trying to explain some point about the structure of the phrase. That reminded me of Pater's famous line 'all art aspires to the condition of music'. It does seem to me that this is musical prose *par excellence* and it seems to do to you some of the things that music does rather than speech does. In 1893 John Todhunter wrote a spoof on Oscar Wilde called *The Black Cat* which was produced by J T Grein (who also produced the first Ibsen performances in London) in which there is a character called Cyril Vane, who is a sort of spoof Wilde character. Someone asks him to explicate the meaning of a poem which he has written and of course Cyril Vane is totally outraged by the suggestion and says, 'Meaning? It is a piece of music in which I have skilfully eluded all meaning.' That is meant to be funny but it is also a serious comment. It is necessary, in order to communicate some meanings, to elude the notion of meaning, i.e. to make the reader stop worrying about what this means so that he or she can then be properly exposed to the meanings which are resonating under the prose. If you worry what this means too much, you will never get the meaning. Therefore this speech must be cadenced, must be musical. It must operate in the realm of the senses. For we do forget all the time that text operates in the realm of the senses, not in the realm of the intellect, that it is about the reverberation of something, the reverberation of meaning and also particularly about the reverberation of the voice, which is why I believe very much that these authors intend in some sense their text to be spoken.

One of the consequences of that idea of speaking, that these are sentences that require the resonance of the voice, is that you do have a sense that this is text without characters in it, text with only one voice. By the time you get to Goytisolo, you abandon all notion of character. There is merely a kind of whirling interplay of voices. But even in a novel which works so hard to have characters as *The Picture of Dorian Gray*, Wilde continually blows it and a speech which was given to one character in Chapter 6 will reappear in its entirety given to someone else in Chapter 12. The language itself, with this insistent repeated energy that it has, does not belong to a character. The notion that this is someone's voice, a person's voice, is completely wrong. This is the sound of the text itself, rather than the sound of a character's voice. Oddly enough, that creates an extraordinary sense of personality. I think these are all texts which have a very vivid and immediately recognisable personality, which should not be the case logically if they are destroying or working against character in this way.

The title of my lecture was 'The Uses of Monotony' because in the end I have to say that I am not interested in these writers because they are beautiful or because they have this extraordinary literary technique. I am interested in the uses to which they put their techniques.

I am going to try and wind up now, which is an odd thing to do in dealing with this subject matter.

The only way of getting to the end of *The Picture of Dorian Gray* is that he just has to die. Otherwise it would go on for ever and ever and indeed the other text that I am quoting from, *The Solitary Bird*, never does end. In *Our Lady of the Flowers* Genet stops by saying, 'Well, that is the end of this book. I am going to write another one now' (which he never did). *Nocturnes for the King of Naples* ends with a fugue, where all the characteristic images of the book are brought back together in one whirling final replay of the whole thing; but that does not constitute a conclusion. It is merely laying out the pattern of the whole work in one paragraph.

So, to try and conclude …

'The Uses of Monotony': to what use is this particular technique of monotonous prose put in the work of these authors? I was thinking about what other rhythms I hear underneath this prose. It seems to me that there are two particular rhythms. One I have touched on already, which is the rhythm … well,

I have mentioned pornography, but it seems to me more than that. It seems to me that it is no accident that these are four writers who mostly write about sex, and in a very particular way. It is their commonest subject matter, Wilde included, once you learn how to locate the actual sex life of his characters in the historical context. And, it seems to me, that the caressing, stroking, insistent, cumulative rhythm of the prose is very much to do with the male experience of sex, especially the male experience of masturbation. It is themselves that they are seducing, as they write, rather than anybody else. They are not writing duets. They are all writing solo. I recall a lyric from Sondheim's 'Liaisons' from *A Little Night Music*: 'a pleasurable means to a measurable end'. It is a wonderful description of a certain kind of sex, and also of a certain kind of writing.

It also seems to me that underneath that prose there is a very strong religious element. *Nocturnes for the King of Naples* is a re-writing of devotional literature, dedicated, as it happens, to a lover rather than a minor saint. *The Picture of Dorian Gray* stinks with late nineteenth-century Anglo-Catholic revivalism. All of Goytisolo's work is an interplay between the traditions of Spanish medieval Christianity, the Inquisition, and Moorish, Muslim, Arab spirituality. *Our Lady of the Flowers* is called *Our Lady of the Flowers* and is soaked in the rituals of Catholicism but, more than all of that, it seems to me that this way of writing does lay claim to the power of religious writing, of religious text, in quite a particular way. The thing about religious text is that it is necessarily repetitious. It is reiterated. There is no point in a church service, there is no point in a liturgy of any religion if you only hear it once, the whole point is that it is monotonous. It is familiar to the point of tedium. If you did not know the words, there would not be any point to a church service and so I think that, lurking under this prose, there is also the prose of liturgical religion, the idea of an insistently repeated act, which, through the gesture of repetition, will once again achieve a miracle.

And now I come to my point, which is that, despite Dorian's desires for reverie, dreaming and unconsciousness, this is prose which is very precisely unhallucinatory, i.e. this is not prose which makes us dissolve, which makes us slippery, which makes us wet, which makes us delirious, but prose which makes us *ecstatic*. It seeks to achieve that particular end through the effort, the labour of monotony. This prose, although it appears to have been so sensual, so caressing, so much of and about the body, is actually a system, a system for the achievement of transformation. These are the most exact, exacting and polished of writers; their prose is not liquid or messy or slippery. They never are as careless as pornography. They aspire to the true rigour of religious writing. I think they are using this technique of monotony – well, I kept on thinking when I was writing and thinking about this lecture about trout tickling. Have you ever seen it done? You tickle the fish under the gills for ages till it gives up and when it gives up, you grab it – and I think this prose is all working to a point where it grabs you. It has intentions. Genet wrote *Our Lady of the Flowers* in order to get out of prison. Edmund wrote *Nocturnes for the King of Naples* in order to bring a dead lover back to life for the space of the text. Wilde wrote *The Picture of Dorian Gray* in order to murder Dorian, to categorically kill Dorian, and Goytisolo wrote *The Virtues of the Solitary Bird* in order to rescue from the oblivion of the Spanish Inquisition that destroyed text by St John. They have all very determined, specific intentions. The trout gets tickled but in the end it gets grabbed. They are going to do something to you. I do not know whether that constitutes a conclusion really.

I am going to finish where I started by continuing the quotation (it is nearly seven o'clock) from *The Picture of Dorian Gray*:

> Cloudless, and pierced by one solitary star, a copper-green sky gleamed through the windows. He read on by its wan light till he could read no more. Then, after his valet had reminded him several times of the lateness of the hour, he got up, and, going into the next room, placed the book on the little Florentine table that always stood at his bedside and began to dress for dinner.
> It was almost nine o'clock before he reached the club, where he found Lord Henry sitting alone, in the morning room, looking very much bored.
> 'I am so sorry, Harry,' he cried,

(they are always crying in *The Picture of Dorian Gray*)

> 'but really it is entirely your fault. That book you sent me so fascinated me that I forgot how the time was going.'
> 'Yes, I thought you would like it,' replied his host, rising from his chair.
> 'I didn't say I liked it, Harry. I said it fascinated me. There is a great difference.'
> 'Ah, you have discovered that?' murmured Lord Henry. And they passed into the dining-room.

CHAPTER 13

Interview with Neil Bartlett

Barbara Read

Editor's note: This interview with Neil Bartlett took place at the Lyric Theatre, Hammersmith on 28 June 1995, during the run of Neil Bartlett's production of *Splendid's*.

Neil Bartlett: So how did you come to Racine and Genet?

Barbara Read: In a very odd kind of way. I first became interested when I did a course including Genet at Middlesex University, and I was expecting not to like him. I had the impression that he was very outrageous. When I actually studied him I had quite the opposite response, I was very enchanted by him. Then I saw the 'Arena' interview and also read *The Thief's Journal*, and that was really it. I'd not been that inspired by anyone for a long time. With Racine I became interested because I read just a very small part initially of *Phèdre*, and then went on to read the other plays. I just really liked what he was doing with language and the themes of the plays. I felt there was a similarity between what Racine was doing and what Genet was doing, in the sense that they present the characters initially in one way and then slowly the personae are peeled away to reveal this very raw emotion underneath. I'm also interested in the oppositions between Genet and Racine. Genet's language can be very basic and raw, and Racine's is very stylised. But sometimes Genet's language can also be very stylised. Would you agree?

NB: No. I don't agree that Genet's language is ever basic or raw.

BR: You mean in the plays?

NB: No, not really. I know much more about *Splendid's* than I do about the others, so I'll mostly talk about that. My impression, having just spent so long rehearsing the piece and translating it, is that his language is very derivative.

Whereas he has a reputation of being the *idiot savant*, the person who'd never written a word in his life and then sat down and wrote five plays. The reason I say that is very specific. I think *Splendid's* is very heavily and directly influenced by the American detective thriller writers of the 1940s, especially Jim Thompson, all of whom were published at that time by Gallimard as part of the *série noire*, in translation. It seems to me that's who Genet means when he says that 'when we were in prison we used to read cheap detective novels'. As well as the French *policiers* there were also the American writers. So I think he's quoting a pre-existent language. I don't think his descriptions or transcriptions of the criminal world were ever uninflected by the criminal world which exists only in films and detective novels.

BR: Do you think that he was influenced by the *film noir*?

NB: It's hard to say that historically; he doesn't give any accounts of that. He doesn't say that he saw such and such a film. Although it's very clear – Edmund [White] makes this point very well – it's very clear that in the writing of the plays, and often in the writing of the novels, he's formally much more indebted to the techniques of cinema – basic notions of non-establishment of character, of jump-cut, of collage of simultaneous scenes. Of course those are the techniques of the experimental novel, but I don't think that was where he was getting them from. He was getting them from cinema. Certainly the stage directions and the editing of the dialogue in *Splendid's* are completely cinematic; they're not theatrical in any respect at all.

BR: Edmund writes about this in the introduction to Jane Giles' book [*The Cinema of Jean Genet: Un Chant d'Amour*].

NB: That's right. One thing that's been really overlooked in the whole examination of Genet as a stylist is that people tend to think of homosexuality or homosexual culture as being his only subject matter.

BR: I don't think that's right.

NB: Right. Whereas it seems to me that the important thing is that a lot of the things that we think of as being the stylistic trade-marks of Genet: linguistic inversion, gender-swapping, travesty, especially the habitual construction of the sentence to mean what it doesn't say – i.e. to use an endearment as an insult or to use an insult as an endearment, or to describe a prostitute in the terms that would normally be reserved for a Racinian princess – that's actually something which is endemic to gay language. Of that period and, indeed, of this period.

Somebody said to me, 'Oh, isn't it interesting that it's almost as if the plot of *Splendid's* is a Racinian palace intrigue, and the characters seem in some way to think that they are all members of the aristocracy?' I replied, 'Yes. You may find that a striking idea, but as a gay man, I don't find that a striking idea at all, because we habitually refer to ourselves as members of the aristocracy. We are, after all, called queens.' A lot of the name-calling that you get in Genet – the assumption of a court-name which most people see as being just about drag but is often about the assumption of a court-name rather than just a drag-name, the world of coterie, of very elaborate and potentially deadly social etiquette, the use of language as a weapon, the idea of taking a word which doesn't belong to you and then using it as a weapon against those people who deprived you of ownership in the first place – all those ideas are absolutely second nature within the world of gay language.

BR: But that idea of using language as a weapon against those who oppress you is not just intrinsic to gay culture, it's intrinsic to a lot of minority cultures.

NB: Yes, but I think very strongly that that's where Genet got it from, and that he wasn't doing it deliberately, he wasn't making that up. That was the way that he and his colleagues in Montmartre talked. That was the way people talked in Graff's café after the war, and I think that's where it comes from. It's been interesting working on this piece. I cast *Splendid's*; the seven members of the gang are all gay, they're all queens. I did that absolutely deliberately. They don't find Genet's language at all odd. They find it very comfortable; they know how to speak it, because it's more or less the way that we're used to talking, in a gay social situation still. The linguistic structures haven't changed. I think that's something that's underestimated. There's the big scene of travesty in *Splendid's* where one of the characters says, 'Are you scared that he's going to turn into a woman? Now that she walks out onto the balcony.' Is that an error, is that a very deliberate little linguistic trick? No. Actually at bottom it's because this is a queen talking. Of course he would refer to the 'he' as a 'she'. It's not an extraordinary thing for him to do at all. It's actually a very normal thing for him to do linguistically. And I think that's overlooked, and I think it's overlooked because people don't see gay culture as a culture in the same way, certainly within academic studies. They don't address gay culture. It's always headed under theories about sexuality. I'm talking about the actual heritage; I'm talking about the fact that I, as a gay man, use words which were current in 1726 and I use them in exactly the same sense as then. That's what I mean by 'culture'. I mean lived, concrete, historically verifiable cultural continuum.

BR: But you're saying these words are used in the same way that they were used two hundred and seventy years ago? Has there been no progression?

NB: Oh yes. Within that there are enormous changes. We ostensibly don't control the culture – the Culture with a capital C – we're born into it, but because we're not identifiable as a culture by skin colour or by race, therefore we're considered a sub-culture, whatever that might mean, in contemporary academic studies; no-one seems to quite know.

BR: But there are other cultures that you could say are not identified by skin colour. Working-class culture you can't identify by skin colour.

NB: But I'm not talking about a culture which all gay people share; I'm talking about a specific metropolitan, urban, post-Renaissance gay culture. So I'm not talking about something that all men who have sex with other men share. I'm talking about a specific British tradition which goes back basically to the Renaissance.

BR: But it can't be just British if you're including Genet in it.

NB: It's a different version of it. Although it so happens that the particular world that he was engaged in – which is basically Montmartre and Pigalle pre-war and post-war – is remarkably similar to the British world, to Soho. In that respect it's of the same period.

BR: Is it true of other cities?

NB: I would say it's true of Newcastle, Riga (the capital of Latvia), Toronto. That's a random list; those happen to be places where I've engaged in the gay culture. The gay culture which I knew in San Francisco isn't anything like the one that I'm talking about. I'm talking about a very particular culture that's to do with queens and small-scale, gay-owned, gay-run cafés, bars, night-clubs and cabarets, and it's a mixture of a hard-core sex-industry metropolitan clientèle and immigrant suburban queens. It's incredibly specific and it's tiny. So it's not Gay Culture, capital G, capital C, it's very tiny. Graff's café in 1947 I think is very like the As You Like It in 1962. Graff's in Montmartre is where *Our Lady of the Flowers* is set – that world. I think Edmund places it very precisely in his biography. I think one thing that he points out really strongly and really well is that Genet's depiction of power relationships is rooted in the system of the orphanage and then the system of Mettray and then the system based around prostitution.

BR: He actually sees the system of Mettray as being determining.

NB: Of course. Because everybody's experiences at that age are the ones which set the patterns of your life. What's interesting is that the real-life scenarios of Mettray are now the fantasy scenarios of eighties and nineties American-influenced gay S-and-M sub-culture. Now they have actually got nothing to do with each other. For instance in *Splendid's* there's a moment where Johnny says 'I am the top'; now that doesn't mean 'I'm the top' as in contemporary sado-masochism. He specifically uses the word *caïd*, which is the head-boy of the dormitory in Mettray, who had the right to adjudicate who was whose sexual property. It's a technical term from that period. Sometimes I think people are careless. They say 'Oh yes, Genet – drag, S-and-M,' and you go, 'Wait a minute! Do you actually know about this history? Do you know the difference between what drag meant in 1947 and 1962, and what it means now? It's completely different.' That was one of the things that we discovered when we were rehearsing *Splendid's*. When you read it you tend to think of the assumption of the drag being melodramatic, triumphal and poetic; and actually when you rehearse the piece you find out it's very ugly, it's very quick, it's very cheap, it's very nasty, it's very funny.

BR: So you found a difference between reading it and rehearsing it?

NB: Absolutely. You begin to understand how very realistic it is. Being English we have this theory: Genet is difficult, Genet is poetic, Genet is theatrical. (Whatever that means. What non-theatrical theatre is, I don't know.) When you work on it with a roomful of actors you find that *Splendid's* is very rigorously plotted, very precisely plotted; it has an immense plot, to do with the interrelationships between the seven people, who is doing what to whom, where and when; all the entrances and exits are very elaborately plotted. The sense of time, the sense of place, and the games people play with language and with role-play are not fantastic at all. That's the great mistaken English assumption about Genet, that game-playing is fantastical, whereas Genet insisted again and again when children play, they are not playing. Nothing is simpler or more in earnest than the way in which children play or queens play or characters in a Racine play play; they play without irony – they can't even spell 'irony', irony doesn't exist in the world of Genet. When someone says 'I am a queen' they don't mean 'I sort of feel like Marie-Antoinette', they mean 'I *am* Marie-Antoinette. As I speak this sentence I am Marie-Antoinette.'

BR: So there's no difference between the role and the identity?

NB: I think that's one of the places where the parallels with Racine are very exact, Racine only takes place in the present tense, i.e. all the other events, I don't know how to express it ...

BR: I know what you mean, in a sense they almost don't exist.

NB: Yes. When a Racine character says 'I am dying', they are dying. Whereas in another kind of play, when someone says 'I'm dying', what they mean is 'My heart is breaking, I feel as though I might die.' When Bérénice says, 'Let me at least breathe the air that you breathe', she means 'I am on the verge of suffocation, and if I leave this room I will actually die like a fish out of water.' It's completely literal and it doesn't work on any other level. The actors must reach that literalness. And that happens in *Splendid's* as well – when someone says 'I'm imagining being at a funeral', and someone else says 'No, you're there. As we speak you're laid out on the bier.' And they are. As the other person says it, it happens. So it's only written in the present tense, and I think that's a very specific parallel with Racine. Of which there are many. For example, there are several instances in *Splendid's* where the characters speak in unrhymed alexandrines, which is astonishing; and I can't believe that Genet did it deliberately. I think it's unconscious. I think his ear was attuned to that phrase and it happened.

BR: Edmund said to me that Genet was not actually influenced by Racine but that Racine was one of his favourite writers.

NB: I'd love to know what the answer is historically. Had Genet read any Racine in 1947? I don't know, but there are alexandrines in the play, and the opening stage direction of *Splendid's* is a corridor in a palace, with doors to the left and right, at the rear windows opening out to a view over the city, and a chandelier. Well, if that's not a direct quote from Racine, then it's very hard to account for. Because he's describing exactly the setting of an antechamber in a palace with a door to the left and door to the right and an unspecified aperture which may or may not be visible in real terms through which you hear the sound of the city which is in turmoil or quiet, depending on what's happening within the antechamber of the palace. And the only sound which enters that room is the messenger who reports the outside world. Well, in this piece you have the radio. So if he hadn't read Racine, then it's the most extraordinary case of formal synchronicity. So I don't know; I'd love you to find out.

BR: I've been trying to find out.

NB: I don't know how we would find out what he had read by what stage. But I can't imagine ... There are too many references in *Splendid's* to crowns, robes, court, very specific. The gangsters know, they say that they know that they are in some sense parodying court ritual. The newspaper, the radio says there are many columns crowned with outrageous headlines describing the exploits of these gangsters. And someone says, 'You see, crowns, columns! This is how they talk about you!' – meaning you should be behaving as if you were in an aristocratic tragedy; stop being a bunch of whinging treacherous B-movie gangsters.

BR: Do you also see parallels with, say, *The Balcony*? Where you've got characters who are gasmen and plumbers and then dress up and play different roles.

NB: I think that's a different thing. I think that's what happened in the gap. *Splendid's* is the last work before the gap, before the silence.

BR: Before the seven years silence?

NB: Yes.

BR: When was it written?

NB: It was started in 1947 and finished in 1948.

BR: So it would have been written around the same time as *Deathwatch*.

NB: It's after *Deathwatch*, it's the same time as *The Thief's Journal*. It's after *The Maids*. *The Maids* and *Deathwatch* had already been written; he was working on, or had just finished, the scenario for the ballet, *'Adame Miroir*, which has a lot of really useful parallels with *Splendid's*. So it's at the end of the sequence of the five novels. Edmund has written a preface to my translation which pins it into the chronology exactly.

BR: Has it been published?

NB: Yes, it's just been published. It was published last week. *Splendid's* has the same central motif as *The Balcony* – it has people appearing on a balcony, and the idea of fooling the populace by the assumption of costume. And a group of people locked up in space playing experimental, kinky games with each other. But *The Balcony*, it seems to me, is entirely deliberate – I think *The Balcony* is contrived, in the best sense. And I think the writing of *The Balcony* is incredibly different. The writing of the whole trilogy is contrived and is intellectual and is dramatic in a way that *The Maids* and *Splendid's* just aren't.

BR: What do you mean when you say 'the trilogy'?

NB: *The Blacks, The Screens* and *The Balcony.* I think there's every evidence internally, in the writing of *Splendid's,* that he transcribed something which existed fully in his head, that he merely wrote down scenes that he was imagining. As an artist, as someone who rehearses plays, and knows how to spot the nuts and bolts of a dramatic construction, I'd stick my neck out and say I think that the writing of *Splendid's,* as, indeed, of *The Maids* as well, is instinctive, is gestural, that he saw those things happening and he heard those people saying those words and he wrote them down. In the same way as when the first manuscript of *Our Lady of the Flowers* was destroyed or lost (whatever the real version of the story is) he sat down and wrote it again. Because it was there.

BR: Do you think that really happened?

NB: I don't mind if it really happened or not. I think it's a terrific story, and I think it dramatises perfectly the way that he made those early works, which is that sense of 'It belongs to me. And actually I don't mind if I write it down or not.' It seems to me that *The Balcony* is a play that wanted to be performed in front of an audience, I think he was writing for theatre; whereas I think *The Maids,* and certainly *Splendid's,* have no notion of theatre. He didn't know what an actor was, what a theatre was, what a theatre audience was, or if he did there's no evidence of it in the plays.

BR: He actually says, doesn't he, in the 'Arena' interview, that he'd never been to the theatre and that what he wrote was a clumsy kind of theatre.

NB: See, I don't think *The Balcony* is clumsy at all; I think it's an expert piece of dramatic writing. But *Splendid's* isn't; *Splendid's* is entirely instinctive and also cinematic, and I think all those terrible things that he said later about 'I want my plays only to be performed once, and preferably in the cemetery' – I think he meant that, I think he was right.

BR: That is in the letters to Roger Blin.

NB: Yes. In some sense he wrote them for himself. He needed to. He just needed to get down on paper what was inside his head, but he didn't need anyone to understand it. Most people write, or ostensibly write, in order that the reader or the performer will understand what they've written; that's not the case with Genet at all.

BR: You think it's a need?

NB: Well, I wouldn't describe it as a need. I wouldn't presume to know that much about what was actually happening to him. The act was complete in itself. You see most playwrights, when they write a playscript, they're thinking about: 'I've got to say what I mean, but I've got to make sure that the actors understand what I mean so that they will be able to communicate.' But Genet didn't have any of that very fundamental playwrighting apparatus in his head at all.

BR: Yet he was very concerned that his plays *were* put on and how he wanted them put on, because when *The Balcony* was first produced he made such a fuss that he was banned from the theatre [on the occasion of the world première at the Arts Theatre Club, London, 22 April 1957].

NB: Well, all the time he basically did everything he could to fuck up every single one of those productions. In *The Screens*, insisting that the Comédie Française could do it but only if they employ Maria Casarès, knowing full well they would not employ Maria Casarès. He knew what he was doing. In a very real way, one of his great weapons was to say, 'I've created this fabulous thing which I know you really want. I'm not going to let you have it.'

BR: Why do you think he did that?

NB: Why? Well, because he hated them. And of course he hated them. The world was only ever Genet and the rest of the world, and then there's that strange other group of people, which are people like Genet, i.e. fellow prisoners, fellow queens, whatever, fellow Palestinians … as he saw it at the end of his life.

BR: But he didn't like homosexuals. That's one of the things that Edmund is at great pains to point out, that most of his relationships actually were with heterosexual men.

NB: Yes. Well, in that, of course, he is more or less entirely typical of most gay men of the 1940s. If you'd asked any gay man of the 1940s 'Who would you like to spend time with?', they'd say, 'I want to spend time with a real man.'

What's a real man? Well it's not a homosexual. So that's not an idiosyncrasy of Genet's. That's actually very familiar from that period. The idea that homosexuals would be happy with other homosexuals is a small idea that's taken hundreds of years to come to fruition. There have always been groups of queens who hung out together, and who loved each other, but they were the queens. They were the queens from *Our Lady of the Flowers*. Those are the homosexuals who love their sisters. But Genet wasn't. Genet was the most difficult of all creatures, which is a butch queen, a 'queenly butch' – which is an absolutely impossible position to maintain, as anyone would tell you who knows. So it's very specific. The butch queen has very little interest in other queens by definition.

BR: So who would they have interest in?

NB: Real men. As in the world of the novels. But to return to what we were discussing earlier, why he wanted his plays not to be produced – because he wrote his plays, he wrote everything he did to insult, damage and humiliate the world, not to celebrate, contribute or explicate the world.

BR: Yes, he does do this. For instance, in the 'Arena' interview he subverts the whole interviewing process, plays with it; and my feeling about that is that it's partly in terms of the world and the world represented by the BBC and so on, but also in order to show something about the actual contrivedness of the interview situation. But it's not only in order to be petulant and difficult and contrary.

NB: No, I don't think it's petulant or difficult or contrary at all. I wouldn't use any of those words of it. And, certainly, like everybody, you can only sustain absolute hatred for so long. Eventually your hatred has to become strategic. And clever. And he was very, very clever. His ability – that was his artistry – was the ability to take *any* gesture and explore it, turn it round, show it in a new light. And he did it brilliantly in that interview, but he was doing in that interview the same thing that he was *doing* to a gesture, or a word or a sentence in all of his works – taking it, stopping it, freezing it, repossessing it, replaying it, investigating it.

BR: That takes an extraordinary awareness, to be able to do that. Don't you think so?

NB: No. I don't think it does. Speaking again as a homosexual, it's possible to do those things absolutely unaware, because they're the air that you breathe. So if someone says to me, 'You raging poof', I don't stop, think, deconstruct, turn round and say, 'That's quite right, dear – far too many homosexuals working in the theatre.' I say it like that. Straightaway. Genuinely without thinking. I'm now thirty-seven, when I make a piece of work, all that instinctive gestural heritage, which is mine by right as a member of this culture, I am now able to redeploy in unexpected ways. And I think that's what Genet did as well. I think the difference in level of contrivance, of artistry in the technical sense of the word, between the first plays and the last plays is very, very different. And I think there's an amazing trajectory in the prose writing as well. From the absolutely unconsidered brilliance of *Our Lady of the Flowers* – you just go, 'OK, give up, I believe in God', how could a human being just sit down and write *Our Lady of the Flowers*? It's inexplicably wonderful as a piece of art. Then something like *The Thief's Journal* or *Funeral Rites*, which is reaching towards a much more considered, contrived, exploratory, genuinely exploratory kind of writing. Through to *Prisoner of Love*. Then the middle period of the essays and the theatre criticism which are so, so intellectual, that they are practically incomprehensible. You know, things like *What remains of a Rembrandt* ... They make you work so hard.

BR: Oh, I think that's wonderful.

NB: Yes, I agree with you, but it's so tough and considered.

BR: I think it also works at a level of dreaminess, but I don't mean dreaminess as in thoughtless; it has a logic, it has its own logic, which isn't like normal logic.

NB: Yes. It has a gestural language. And then you get to *Prisoner of Love*, where he wrote in a way that I don't think any of us have yet understood. It's beyond ... I can't think of any other writing that is like the writing of *Prisoner of Love*.

BR: But what's quite extraordinary is that it seems as though he was very quiet about the fact he was writing this novel. In the 'Arena' interview he never mentions it and you get the impression that he hadn't written anything for years, and then when he dies this great novel is discovered. And one wonders if he meant it for a readership, or whether he was writing it just for himself.

NB: That we can't know. We'd like to think that he was saving it up just for us. That's one of the great tricks of his art, which he shares with Proust; is that you do feel that no-one else has ever read this novel except you. Proust is very anti-social, not only in the world that it describes, but you can never imagine, you never think 'all over the world people are reading Proust'. In the way that if you are reading other writers, like Ruth Rendell or even Edmund, you think lots of people are reading this, this is a social event, this text. But if you read Proust or if you read Genet, you go, 'No-one else in the world understands this like I understand it – this was written just for me. He didn't know it, but I'm the only person who can ever really be touched by what he's written.' That's a great trick to pull off. I think that's the secret of a lot of his power, that unconscious sense that this is not a public text.

BR: In relation to the Palestinians Genet wasn't against society. In one way, one can understand it because the Palestinians are criminalised. But on the other hand, it's perhaps a bit curious that he allowed himself to be so embraced by a whole society. There's a quote from Edmund in the biography from a Palestinian who said that the Palestinians are looking to become new men. Like Jean Genet. He cites Genet as the new man that they want to emulate, which is very curious in a way.

NB: Yes. I don't know if I understand that. The way that he writes about them in *Prisoner of Love*, the only level on which I can understand it is the image I have. There are two levels of it: there are the relationships with the women and the relationships with the men. The women seem in some fabulous way to be the opposite of how he must have experienced the violence of his foster-parents. Not because they were necessarily violent people (I don't know anything about them) but the emotion of having foster-parents, the lack of care.

BR: And Edmund says in the biography that Genet was the *favourite* of the foster-mother, even more so than her own son.

NB: But the hatred of mothers is a conspicuous feature all the way through – the woman who must be punished is a recurrent figure in the work. Those extraordinary idylls of the welcoming mother, the brave mother, the beautiful mother, the dignified mother, whom you glimpse in *The Screens*, but then you meet as a real person in *Prisoner of Love*. Then the descriptions of gorgeous men carrying guns, playing cards by starlight in abandoned criminal space – incredibly sexy yet sexless in the sense that there's none of the awful price to be paid that's involved in the negotiation with homosexual culture and heterosexual culture. Well, it's exactly what happens in the first act of *Splendid's*. A group of handsome young men playing cards who aren't going to fuck each other – but they all have anyway. Play cards by starlight. I just think he was intensely happy in that environment. That moment in the book that he describes radiates contentment and joy in those people's company.

BR: Have you read his essay on the Sabra and Shatila massacres? Where he says, 'The Palestinians are in the right because I love them; but would I love them if they were not a dispossessed people?'

NB: Right. That I really understand. I think it's a really good question. But the hardest thing in all of that is you knew even before he said it 'the day that they get the homeland is the day I cease to be interested', basically. And you know that from the way he writes, and that's very hard to take, because good liberals that we are, we're brought up to believe that 'the purpose of struggle is to achieve a result', and that's not what he's saying and it's not what he's feeling. That's why he remains such a provocation, I think. It isn't what he asks you to think about.

BR: But he always takes this position. In the 'Arena' interview he says that 'I am here and there you are, you are part of the norm and I am on the margins.' And he wants to remain on the margins; and I suppose it's the same thing with the Palestinians. What's perhaps so paradoxical, in one sense, is that his writings about the Palestinians seem so utterly sincere. It seems as though it's not just simply because they are a dispossessed people or because they're engaged in a struggle and he admires this. But also that he feels very much for their need for justice. Even though he says if they achieve it, he wouldn't be on their side.

NB: Well, what he's saying, of course, is, 'If the world gave me justice I would cease to be Genet and I don't want to cease to be Genet.' A lot of people have said to me, 'Why was *Splendid's* never performed, and why the years of silence?' And you go, 'Well, just think about what happened to him between 1944 and 1947.' He went from being a kind of starvation-diet wartime prisoner in Paris, fighting on the rooftops, orphan, pederast, criminal; and four years later he's Jean Genet. 'Would you come and have dinner with Jean-Paul Sartre, he'll introduce you to the president; we'll organise your state pardon; you've just published five novels.' Well, no wonder he fell silent. It's the most extraordinary, traumatic change of his life, of his identity. The Jean Genet of 1944 and the Jean Genet of 1948 are incredibly different people. People go, 'Why was he so interested in role-playing?' You go, 'Well, why do you think? Look at the roles that he took in his life.'

BR: But do you think his interest in role-playing is also to do with the gay culture that he inhabited?

NB: Well, I think it's to do with it in the sense that it provided him with the first language in which he explored it.

BR: But you think he went beyond it?

NB: Yes, I think he went far beyond it. I think that *The Screens* and *The Blacks* go far beyond any kind of notion of it. He understood that role-play is about power. He didn't only understand that, he *knew* that. That was the culture he lived in. I was talking to somebody who'd seen *Splendid's* and who'd said, 'Oh, I didn't understand it.' This other queen who'd seen it said, 'What do you mean, you don't understand it? Do you mean you've never wanted to shoot people and get away with it?' So the person said, 'No', and the queen said, 'Oh, alright then. I suppose that's why you didn't respond to the piece, but I know how that feels and so does everyone I know.'

BR: Why would he feel like that? That he would like to shoot someone and get away with it?

NB: Because you do. It's those repeated moments of unqualified rage where you just feel 'I've been pissed on for so long I just want to pick up a gun and shoot people, and get away with it'.

BR: But from what we've both been saying, it would seem that Genet would enjoy to remain in that gap where he doesn't go over to the other side, where he is accepted; he doesn't want to be accepted, he doesn't want people not to piss on him. Would you agree?

NB: I suppose I would say that. I'd find that hard to argue for, but I would say that instinctively because I would say he, good Catholic that he was, he didn't believe in forgiveness. What I mean by that is that the crimes which had been committed against him by the time he realised they'd been committed were of such an enormity that the idea of someone trying to atone for them or mend them or heal them is in itself a further crime. That's what I feel.

BR: That forgiveness would be too easy?

NB: Yes, it would be another insult. Kind of to say, 'I vilify you, I humiliate you, I break you, I destroy you, I erase your identity and now you forgive me for doing all those things, don't you?' That's just the final straw.

BR: But forgiveness also implies that the other party is genuinely sorry.

NB: But also implies that the other party has the power to forgive you. To let them forgive you would be to acknowledge one more time that they have the right of forgiveness over you. And that's a right which one will not concede. So when someone says, 'I don't mind you being gay', you don't say to them, 'Oh, that's really nice, I feel much better'; you say, 'Who the fuck do you think you are to mind or not?'

BR: Because it implies a position of superiority?

NB: It implies that you have a position of superiority over me and that I will not allow. Because if I allow you that then we're just back where we started. It's not a politics, it's not a theory, it's a life – that's how he lived. That's what I think.

BR: Why did you particularly choose *Splendid's*?

NB: I didn't; *Splendid's* chose me really. Because I found out that the play existed, so I thought I must read that and so I read it, and thought I must do that so I did it – with the assistance of the Genet estate, who gave me permission to do it and do the first English translation.

BR: Why do you think it's not been translated or produced before?

NB: It was only published in 1992 or 1993 by Marc Barbezat. L'Arbalète published it. It has been produced. It was produced in Germany. Peter Handke translated it with Klaus Marie Gruber and Peter Stein. It's had two or three productions in France in the last six months. There's a Dutch production opening next week, and there's an Australian production in the next weeks. So it's actually coming to life very fully and very quickly.

BR: Is it your translation that's being produced in Australia?

NB: No. That's what I heard, that someone's doing it. And so I don't know what the translation is or who's doing it or, indeed, if it's still happening.

BR: How did you actually find the process of translating it? Did you remain quite loyal to the original French?

NB: Yes, I mean to the point of obsession. It's fantastically faithful. I try and obey wherever possible the internal assonances of Genet, which is the great thing that French does so much better than English. Twentieth-century English isn't very good at internal assonance. I've also preserved Genet's punctuation. It's very interesting, when I submitted the translation to the publishers they sent me back the proofs and someone had repunctuated the entire thing. So I said, 'You put it back according to my original manuscript!' Because the punctuation is completely ungrammatical. It's theatrical punctuation.

BR: You talk about the use of punctuation in 'The Uses of Monotony' [the 1994 William Matthews Lecture; see Chapter 12 of this book].

NB: Well, I think it's really important. Punctuation is music. I also work in music theatre so I'm very aware that once you've got the breathing worked out, that's it – that's all there is to do. And that's true of Racine and it's true of Genet, in the same way as it's true of Hammerstein or Mozart. If you can obey the technical rules of the breathing, then the sense of the text will reveal itself as a matter of course. I mean as a rule of thumb. It doesn't always work out like that. So it's obsessively faithful on the issue of punctuation and stress. Sometimes, of course, very inventive solutions have to be found to the puns, because it's full of puns.

BR: Would you say that what you say is true of the novels is also true of the plays? That the language shouldn't be looked at for interior meaning, but for the actual effect of the language itself. Do you think that's true? One would expect it to be more true of the plays than of the novels.

NB: Yes, I think it's very true of this piece. The text has a life independent of the people who speak it. It has a rhythm and a meaning, so the meaning doesn't belong to what people say. The problem with trying to express that argument clearly is that people go, 'Oh, you mean the text is meaningless, and it has a purely musical effect?' Which isn't what I mean at all. I suppose I use the word 'effect' – effect and meaning are very interestingly interrelated in the theatre. So, the 'effect' of Bob's first line. Bob comes on dancing. And his line is: 'Waltzes, show tunes, it's grand opera.' Now actually if you reproduce Genet's stresses and punctuation, that line is spoken in waltz time. 'Waltzes, show tunes, it's grand opera.' It's got the one, two, three. It actually has the rhythm of the event that is being described, which is a man dancing; it's actually present in the stressing. I can't really explain it, it's very difficult to explain because it's a deeply technical thing.

BR: According to the biographical evidence Genet's first experience of writing literature was through his association with René de Buxeuil, who was a blind poet and songwriter. And he talks in the novels about songs as well, so he would actually seem to have this sense of music you refer to.

NB: Well, it's the use of the speaking voice, isn't it? If you ever think that Genet is kind of difficult to read, you just read him out loud and you realise what you're hearing is this voice conjuring up this whole world of people.

BR: You talk in 'The Uses of Monotony' about the text having its own voice, its own personality, one main personality that all the other characters kind of slot into.

NB: Yes, I think that's very true.

BR: Do you think that's true of the plays too?

NB: Yes, I think that is true. It's the way of speaking, and the development of the way of speaking, and the changes of the ways, that are the primary events of *Splendid's* – which is something that you don't realise when you're watching it. But that is what happens. It's the changes of speech which are of significance. And the main character in *Splendid's*, the person who possesses the play, the person who is addressing the audience, is the dead woman, who he describes as ascending to heaven to the sound of the Mozart requiem in *Prisoner of Love* – the woman in the white dress and diamonds, who also appears in the ballet, where she's dressed in violet, not in white. It is death, or as we call her in this translation, Miss Death, who is the speaking voice of the play; she's not a character. And that's not specified, that's my opinion. It's not specified anywhere in the text. And death is speaking through these people.

BR: Would you not say that's also present in *The Screens* when he describes the incident when Saïd dies and goes straight to a realm of nothingness?

NB: Well, that's why the play is called *The Screens*. It's the screens that are speaking. That's what *The Screens* is about. The screen is about: 'What is the nature of the line between one world and the next? Can one pierce it? Can one pierce it in two directions? Who patrols the screens?' That's why it's called *The Screens*. *The Blacks* is about blacks, *The Screens* is about the screens. The screens aren't props in *The Screens* – it's *about* the screens. It's the screens speaking, commanding speech.

[At this point the interview concluded, as Neil Bartlett had to return to his commitments in the 1995 Lyric Theatre production of *Splendid's*.]

CHAPTER 14

Genet's Splendid's

David Bradby

Editor's note: This review is of Neil Bartlett's translation and production of Jean Genet's play *Splendid's* during its run from 15 June to 15 July 1995 at the Lyric Theatre, Hammersmith.

IN 1953 GENET tore up the manuscript of his play *Splendid's* in front of a friend of Bernard Frechtman (his American agent and translator). Frechtman wrote that

> *Splendid's* is done for, unless someone brings it out after Genet's death. It's bound to happen sooner or later. It will become one of those literary sensations that occur from time to time.[1]

Although Genet refused to allow the play to be performed or published during his lifetime, and it was thought lost, a copy had been kept in the files of Marc Barbezat (of L'Arbalète, Genet's first publisher). As Frechtman had predicted, it appeared in print (in 1993), was much discussed and much produced, both in France and elsewhere.[2] The first English-language performance took place at the Lyric Theatre, Hammersmith on 15 June 1995, as part of the London International Festival of Theatre. Written in 1947–8, the play belongs to the same burst of Genet's creative energy that produced *Notre-Dame-des-Fleurs*, *Miracle de la Rose*, *Pompes funèbres*, *Querelle de Brest*, *Un Chant d'Amour*, *Haute surveillance*, *Les Bonnes*, *Journal du Voleur* and a ballet entitled *'Adame Miroir*. It seems to have been the last play that he undertook before his second major creative period in the late 1950s, when *Le Balcon*, *Les Nègres* and *Les Paravents* were written.

The reasons for Genet refusing to allow this play to appear during his lifetime remain mysterious, although Edmund White, in his introduction to the English text, has some plausible suggestions. He quotes Genet as saying that his early works, written in prison, were conceived with a solitary reader in mind, one who would feel furtive or shameful about acquiring a book by Genet, and who would enjoy it in secret, but 'when I set about creating my plays I had to write for spectators in a group. I had to change my mental technique and to know that I was writing for a public which each time would be visible and numerous.' White concludes that 'the personal, homosexual content of the novels had to be translated into the public, heterosexual terms of the major plays'.[3]

White sees *Splendid's* as a transitional piece, halfway between Genet's extremely personal, autobiographical writings of the late 1940s and the broader canvas of the three great plays of the late 1950s. Albert Dichy, who edited the French text, also sees it this way, although he distinguishes between *Les Bonnes*, in which theatrical artifice is the mainspring of the action, and *Haute surveillance*, a play which clearly uses the same material as Genet's prison novels. He considers *Splendid's* to be closer to the latter than to the former, and holds that since theatrical artifice was to become the central preoccupation of Genet's next play, *Le Balcon*, it was natural that he should reject *Splendid's*. Neither White nor Dichy expands on these suggestions, or develops a reflection on the nature of the transition marked by *Splendid's*. How helpful is the distinction drawn by Dichy, and what light does the play shed on the evolution of Genet's dramatic work?

In the first place, *Splendid's* is clearly linked to Genet's early work through its themes and its characters. Like *Haute surveillance*, it deals with a group that is exclusively male, and its dynamic emerges from the struggles for domination and dreams of escape which are played out within the group. It also shares with that play the theme of the homoerotic attraction exerted by people who are willing to commit themselves to acts which go beyond the limits of reasonable behaviour, or are self-destructive. By deploying a cast of eight, Genet made the interplay of these struggles more varied and more complex than in *Haute surveillance*, since the permutations possible with eight characters are far greater than with three.[4] He also introduced an additional element in that the group contains representatives of both sides of the law: seven of the men are part of a criminal gang, and the eighth is a policeman who has decided to betray his comrades and join the criminals.

But the play goes beyond the exploration, however powerful, of the dynamics governing a group of gay men; its richness lies in the way it draws on a number of quite different, but overlapping sources. These can be understood by considering first the setting, then the language, and finally the dramatic action.

Setting

The setting is described by Genet in the following terms:

> Un hall, au 7ᵉ étage d'un grand palace. À droite et à gauche les portes des chambres. Au fond des fenêtres reliées par un balcon. Lustres. Luxe. Tapis.[5]

Bartlett translates this:

> A hallway, on the seventh floor of a palatial hotel. To the left and to the right, the
> bedroom doors. At the back, windows connected by a balcony. Chandeliers.
> Carpets. Luxury.[6]

As Bartlett astutely points out in the preface to his introduction, this is a perfect
twentieth-century version of the Racinian antechamber. The mere fact that
Genet chooses to write 'palace', rather than 'hôtel', strengthens the sense of an
allusion to neo-classical settings, suggesting both the grandeur of the royal
court, and also an indeterminate, anonymous space between private
apartments, yet not identified with a particular person. He writes, 'as in Racine,
the "world" is elsewhere, heard only in the speeches of messengers (or on the
radio) or in the murmurings of an excited, distant crowd. To leave the room, as
in Racine, is instant death.'[7]

Certain aspects of this setting tie in closely with Genet's preoccupations in the
1940s, others point us forward to his later plays. The classical qualities alluded
to by Bartlett are among the former. As Edmund White has shown, Genet was
very preoccupied with proving his ability to write French that matched the best
literary models,[8] and his careful choice of a setting with classical associations
underlines this.

The setting may also be seen as transitional in its differences from the settings
of *Les Bonnes* and *Haute surveillance*. Both of these plays are set in places that
have a clear social location: 'la chambre de Madame' for the first and 'une cellule
de forteresse' for the second. The fact that these settings are identified (as a rich
middle-class bedroom and a convict cell) makes it possible to perform both of
these plays within the realist-naturalist tradition, and this is how they are most
frequently played. The stage direction for *Splendid's*, on the other hand, makes
it quite clear that the location is not intended to indicate the social class of its
inhabitants, but rather to function as a dream space, an 'in-between' space of the
imagination, in which all kinds of transitions, treasons and transformations are
facilitated. This points forward to the settings of Genet's three plays of the
1950s, all located in indeterminate spaces that self-consciously question their
own status and reality.

The setting, seen in this light, is the most succesful of Genet's three early plays.
It achieves effortlessly the quality that he pleads for in the stage direction to
Haute surveillance: 'The whole play must unfold as if in a dream.'[9] When he
wrote this, Genet was stressing, as he so often did, that his plays should not be
seen as realistic depictions of everyday life. Despite his repeated warnings,
directors of *Les Bonnes* and *Haute surveillance* have too often presented them
as realistic pieces of mimetic action. Only occasionally has a director proved
equal to the imaginative challenge of presenting the action as if it were a dream.

A notable success was the 1969 production of *Les Bonnes* by the Nuria Espert company, directed by Victor Garcia.[10]

Directors who have mounted productions of *Splendid's* have found it easier to establish this oneiric style or tone: examples are the production at the Théâtre des Amandiers by Stanislas Nordey and that of Neil Bartlett at the Lyric, Hammersmith. Nordey's production, designed by Emmanuel Clolus, used the vast dimensions of the Nanterre stage to stress the theatricality of the performance. The action took place on a raised stage, with empty space visible all around. The window onto the balcony was quite clearly false, and when it was opened a slide of Nanterre was projected into the space. A heavy, theatrical drape was used to close off the space in which the heiress has been killed. Bartlett's production, on the other hand, focused attention on the large windows and balcony beyond. These were centrally placed on the back wall, with the stage on a fairly steep rake. A broad strip of carpet broke the stage space up into the shape of a hotel corridor, suggesting rooms to left and right and a long corridor extending out into the auditorium, with another leading off at right angles, parallel to the windows, leading to the stairs. On this minimal set the actors slipped effortlessly in and out of direct address to the audience, alternating between this and passionate interpersonal conflicts.

The indeterminate quality of a setting that does not relate to a particular social condition, but is in some sense a neutral space, points forward to the setting for *Le Balcon*. Both the *palace* of *Splendid's* and the house of illusions of *Le Balcon* share the associations with luxury and with a mood in which people go to shake off their ordinary, limited lives, in order to indulge in imaginative escapism. Both settings share the chandelier (*lustre*) that was the symbol of theatre for Baudelaire and that carries associations of play-acting and travesty as well as of luxury. The central role of the balcony in both plays further emphasises the way in which *Splendid's* may be seen as a forerunner of Genet's later work (its dramatic significance will be discussed under the heading of dramatic action).

The costumes and properties also call for brief comment in so far as they point in the same direction: the gangsters of *Splendid's* are not dressed in their own clothes, but in upper-class evening wear (tailcoats and white ties) that they have appropriated in order to infiltrate the hotel. White ties and tails will again make their appearance in *Les Nègres*, which opens on a minuet danced by four couples in tails and evening gowns.[11] During the course of the play two of the gangsters dress as women, a disguise that has particular significance when Jean is persuaded to put on the dead heiress's evening gown and appear on the balcony (see the discussion of the balcony scene below, under the heading of dramatic action). The principal properties are the sub-machine-guns carried by every character in the play. Sub-machine-guns reappear also, in each of the last three plays, but never with the same insistent threat as in *Splendid's*, where the stage direction specifies that 'they never put down their tommy-guns, not even to dance'. In the later plays, the accent is placed more emphatically on the power of the imagination and the limitations of the application of armed force.

Language

A consideration of Genet's use of language in this play is illuminated by Bartlett's introduction to his translation. Bartlett lays emphasis on the sound of the original text, pointing out how Genet glories in the wealth of puns that is one of the chief characteristics of French: 'Only in French can the word *rafale* be both a name and a burst of gunfire, can the words for sub-machine-gun, sequin and labour share an internally rhyming open vowel' (he is referring to the *ai* sound at the centre of *mitraillette, paillette, travail*).[12] His working assumption was that if the translator changes the pattern of rhyme and assonance, he also changes the meaning. It is certainly the case that his text seems much closer to the original than the translations of Bernard Frechtman, which often appear accurate but lifeless. He goes on to point out that the richness of the play derives from the way it draws on several different linguistic idioms, some having their origin in dramatic and cinematic genres, some in closed social groups. He lists these as:

a) The French *policier* of the 1940s, itself heavily influenced by American pulp fiction, especially Jim Thompson, who was published in Gallimard's *série noire*: '*Splendid's* is not set in America, but it is haunted by a deranged America, a fictional America, an America of the movies, with a few cruelly misplaced details (the knighting of the girl's father, the guillotine) which remind us that this too is a charade.'[13]

b) The gay slang of the all-male reformatory to which Genet was sent as a teenager and the prisons to which he was subsequently condemned. Bartlett quite rightly points out that it is not the argot of contemporary gay culture, but a restricted code specifically rooted in the 1930s and 1940s. Genet made it absolutely clear that he did not see himself as part of the gay liberation movement that emerged in the 1980s in his interview for BBC2 with Nigel Williams. When Williams asked him, 'Avez-vous fait une politique de l'homosexualité?', he replied, 'Mais est-ce qu'il y a une politique homosexuelle?' and when Williams insisted, 'Mais maintenant, à notre époque, c'est une question politique. Parce que vous étiez l'un des premiers qui aient parlé de cette chose en … ', Genet interrupted him fairly brutally: 'Qu'est-ce que vous racontez! Qu'est-ce que vous racontez! Ecoutez, vous avez eu Oscar Wilde … Si on pense uniquement à l'Angleterre, vous avez eu Oscar Wilde, Shakespeare, Byron et combien d'autres … Qu'est-ce que vous racontez!' [14]

c) The language of Racine. Bartlett is no doubt right to stress the Racinian connection, as it is clearer in this play than in any other by Genet. He comments, 'Sometimes the gangsters even speak, spontaneously, remarkably, in perfect unrhymed alexandrines – twelve-syllable lines with a dramatically placed caesura.'[15] The effect of the occasional alexandrine is further enhanced by the number of lines that are imperfect alexandrines (e.g. they have one syllable too many) but are also balanced around a strategically placed caesura. However, Bartlett's 'spontaneously' is perhaps a little misleading. Like everything else in this play, their language strikes the listener as being self-conscious and calculated. It is no accident that, precisely when Bob wishes to draw attention to his own eloquence, he comes out with a perfect alexandrine: 'Mais cette fois-ci je me permets l'éloquence.'[16] There is often a rather arch, knowing quality about the terms in which the members of the gang address one another, and relatively few passages where the rhetoric is also fuelled by the passionate commitment of *Les Nègres* or *Les Paravents*. (Perhaps this provides part of the explanation for Genet's loss of interest in the play.)

The alexandrine lines prove a good test of Bartlett's translation and of the extent to which he has been able to put his stated principles into practice. An early example occurs in the opening dialogue between Jean and the policeman, when they are discussing their tommy-guns. Jean says, 'Ma gâchette est sensible et mon poignet plus lourd.' Bartlett's translation of this shows how he attempted to retain rhythm and assonance as well as meaning: 'I'm light on the trigger and real heavy-handed.' Not only is Bartlett's line an alexandrine, like Genet's, but it also maintains the differentiated assonances of the two halves of the line. In French, of course, there is an additional effect in the contrast between masculine and feminine: the first hemistich, where the meaning is all to do with lightness and delicacy, is feminine, while the second half, speaking of toughness and heaviness, is masculine. Bartlett makes up for this by his more emphasised assonance and his allusiveness to the world of the fictional American gangster, where the combination of the fastidiously delicate and the brutally heavy-handed is a well-established mix. He is less successful with the line of Bob's quoted above: 'Mais cette fois-ci je me permets l'éloquence', which becomes: 'But just this once I'm going to permit myself a little speech.' Although he succeeds in preserving the uneven balance of Genet's line, with the caesura placed (in the original) after the fifth syllable, his second half loses the fastidious precision of Bob's statement.

Taken as a whole, Bartlett's translation is remarkably successful in capturing the linguistic playfulness of Genet's text, and in keeping the flavour of the different kinds of utterance. In his production he was able to enhance this further by giving each of the actors a different 'voice' and often a different accent: some spoke American English, some exaggeratedly correct English, some with a regional accent. The timbre and pitch of their voices, too, varied very considerably, so that the overall effect achieved something of an operatic quality, with an interweaving of high, low and intermediate voices.

Dramatic action

As Bartlett again points out, the action (as in *Les Bonnes* and *Haute surveillance*) observes the classical unities of time, place and action. The nature of that action, too, conforms to the classical model in that it consists largely of a struggle for power amongst the members of the gang. During the course of this struggle, they discover that the power of the game of transformation is as great as the power that comes out of the barrel of a gun. They are conscious of being in a liminal state, faced with the great defining moment: 'We have already stopped living,' says Scott, and Bob agrees with him.[17] As the play unfolds, the main dramatic conflict lies between those who accept this and those who don't; between those who try to lay realistic plans for escape, and those who want no part in such compromises, but who instead accept and welcome the chance of transformation that is provided by the certainty of death.

In the course of these debates and struggles, the joys and the powers of 'le travestissement' are discovered. This word, clearly a key one for Genet, has a wide range of associations in French, covering drag, cross-dressing, dressing-up, parody and misrepresentation. Each of these associations finds enactment in the play, so much so that it might be seen as a set of variations on the theme of 'le travestissement'. Parody is at the heart of the play in the allusions to the models of *film noir* and classical theatre already mentioned. Misrepresentation is also a constant theme in the form of the radio announcer and his regular intrusions upon the action, with a commentary misrepresenting the actions of the gangsters. They are all centrally concerned with how their actions are being represented or misrepresented in the outside world and their actions are largely guided by their perception of the changes in the way they are represented.

This comes to the fore at the end of the play, when most of the gang decide to give themselves up rather than fight to the death or commit suicide, in order to indulge in the pleasures of cowardice. Their motives are very clearly articulated, first by Bravo, who explains that it will be an action carried out in order to disturb and alter the image of a gang of desperadoes that the radio commentator has been building up: 'so as to play one last dirty trick on the police, on Justice, on the Rich, on the Nice, one last filthy trick: to take some shit, to take all of their bullshit and smear it right over the all too pretty image they have of us.'[18] A few lines later, Bob reiterates: 'I for one have had it with being what they've made of me.'[19]

There is a strong Sartrean existentialist tinge to this: the idea of people choosing to respond to the image others have of them is explored again and again in Sartre's fiction and theatre of the 1940s. It is often associated with a concern for the distinctions between behaviour that can be judged as cowardly on the one hand or courageous on the other. It is not surprising that such concerns were a major preoccupation in a society that had just lived through five years of Nazi occupation. But in *Splendid's* Genet was careful to avoid contemporary debates, setting the action in a mythical society, quite unconnected to the real world of post-war France. Because of this, he may have felt that the strong Sartrean overtones in some of the gangsters' discussions about cowardly behaviour made his play seem both derivative and too topical. He often claimed that the effect of Sartre's monumental *Saint Genet, comédien et martyr* was to give him writer's block, and the point at which he tore up the copy of *Splendid's* was just after the publication of Sartre's tome.[20]

Nevertheless, the final 'travestissement', or parody of themselves on the part of the gang in *Splendid's*, was highly original: there is nothing else to compare with it in the theatre of the time. It shows Genet's imagination already working on the theme of identity, self-definition and its betrayals, a pattern that was to find its ultimate embodiment in Saïd of *Les Paravents*. Similarly, the climax of the first part of the play, when Jean dresses up as the heiress, shows Genet playing with the same theme, as it looks forward to the eighth tableau of *Le Balcon*. This scene has exactly the same function within the dramatic action of *Splendid's* as Scene 8 of *Le Balcon*, that is to say it enacts a moment when travesty takes on greater power than reality for the watching crowd in the streets below.

In both plays this leads to a key development in the dramatic action. In *Le Balcon* it results in Roger's admission that his armed revolutionaries have been defeated by the power of the dressed-up figures on the balcony, and his subsequent entry into the repertoire of images enshrined in Madame Irma's house of illusions. In *Splendid's* it provokes a similar clash between guns and images: the policeman-turned-gangster kills the travestied Jean and then prepares to take over the role of gang leader in a last, desperate shoot-out with the forces of law and order. His action fails, after all, to confer on him the desired glamour that will enable him to rule the gang since another transition is simultaneously taking place: the gangsters are succumbing to the temptation to refute their 'tough-guy' image, and giving in instead to the temptation of cowardice. The policeman refuses to join in this new 'travestissement'. Like Roger in *Le Balcon*, he is left in frustrated isolation; he alone does not throw down his tommy-gun, but the weapon he holds has been drained of its potency. He decides to save his skin by rejoining the forces of order.

There is a third example of a transformation or 'travestissement' that points forward to Genet's later work. The gangster Pierrot is obsessed with bringing his dead brother back to life and, in the course of the play, succeeds in doing so by taking on all the characteristics and mannerisms of his brother. This he achieves by practising in the mirror; his actions here are remarkably similar to those of the central character of a ballet which Genet also wrote in 1947. Entitled *'Adame Miroir*, the ballet presents a character whose mirror image comes to life and dances with him in the few moments before his death.[21] The sequences in *Splendid's* which feature Pierrot seem rather disconnected from the rest of the play, but they are evidence that Genet is once again trying out ideas that were to be much more fully explored in, for example, *Les Paravents*, where the membrane separating life from death is no longer a mirror but a paper screen. The characters who burst through it are able to comment on those left alive and on the closure that death provides to the lifelong struggle for self-definition.

Conclusion

In respect of its setting, use of language and dramatic action, *Splendid's* is every bit as powerful as the early dramatic works that Genet allowed to be performed. Edmund White, in his biography, commented that 'all of Genet's novels and plays are at once funerals and *fêtes* and *Splendid's* is no exception'.[22] The handling of the themes of travesty, treachery and death is as successful here as it is in the later plays. Perhaps the reason for Genet's rejection of it was simply that, in 1953, he was beginning to see how he might use drama for an investigation of identity in far more complex terms, terms that would make the Manichean opposition of cop and gangster seem simplistic. It is in his handling of the construction of identity that this play points most clearly towards the later work, both among individuals and on the part of the group. Edward Said has written interestingly about this aspect of Genet's work, calling him a 'traveller across identities':

> Identity is what we impose upon ourselves through our lives as social, historical, political and even spiritual beings. The logic of culture and of families doubles the strength of identity, which for someone like Genet, who was a victim of the identity forced on him by his delinquency, his isolation, his transgressive talents and delights, is something to be resolutely opposed.[23]

Splendid's presents a group of people all of whom are struggling to make sense of their identities in the terms articulated here by Said. In this respect, all of them could stand for a different aspect of Genet himself: each of the characters, in his own way, struggles against the identity imposed upon him by outside forces, and thus the gangsters are forerunners of the blacks in *Les Nègres* and the Algerians in *Les Paravents*. What is lacking in *Splendid's* is the political dimension so evident in the last three plays. Edward Said's explanation of the power of Genet's later work (in which he included *Les Paravents* alongside *Un Captif amoureux*) is precisely that his already original perception of how identity is constructed was further enhanced by the addition of the political dimension, and that political dimension involved espousing the cause of the despised and oppressed:

> But crossing to Algeria and Palestine was ... the expression of a dangerous and subversive politics involving borders to be negotiated, expectations to be fulfilled, dangers to be confronted. And, to speak here as a Palestinian, I believe that Genet's choice of Palestine in the 1970s and 1980s was the most dangerous political choice, the scariest journey of all.[24]

In *Splendid's* we can see Genet beginning to explore the paradoxes of an affirmation of identity outside the accepted social norms that would lead him to be able to challenge the way the West viewed Algeria or Palestine in later works such as *Les Paravents* and *Un Captif amoureux*. Moreover, it is clear that the action, setting and language of *Splendid's* are all of a piece with his last three plays, even if the play's characters are still drawn from the imaginary world of cops and criminals. The mobilisation of the themes of travesty, death and transformation goes much further than the theatrical artifice of *Les Bonnes*, noted by Dichy, and contains the germ of much that was to come later. Despite its transitional status, then, the play is a major addition to the canon of works by Genet.

NOTES

1   Quoted by Albert Dichy in his introduction to *Splendid's* (Décines, 1993), p. 7. Dichy was quoting a letter originally written in English by Frechtman; the translation given here is mine of Dichy's French: 'C'en est fini de *Splendid's*, à moins que quelqu'un ne la ressorte après la mort de Genet. C'est certainement ce qui arrivera un jour ou l'autre. Ce sera alors une de ces trouvailles littéraires sensationnelles comme il s'en produit parfois.'

2   For details of the survival and publication of the text, see Edmund White, *Genet* (London, 1993), pp. 405–6 and 568.

3   Edmund White's introduction in Jean Genet, *Splendid's*, translated by Neil Bartlett (London, 1995), pp. *vii–xii*. Page references throughout this chapter refer to this edition and to the French edition cited in Note 1 above.

4   *Haute surveillance* actually contains a fourth character, Le Surveillant, but he has only a very marginal role to play.

5   Jean Genet, *Splendid's*, edited by Albert Dichy (Décines, 1993), p. 13.

6   Jean Genet, *Splendid's*, translated by Neil Bartlett (London, 1995), p. 3.

7   Jean Genet, *Splendid's*, translated by Neil Bartlett (London, 1995), p. *xv*.

8   See Edmund White, *Genet* (London, 1993) Chapters 6 and 7, e.g. his comment on *Le Condamné à Mort*: 'Equally original is Genet's introduction of prison and pornographic

argot into a traditional blend of alexandrines and otherwise elevated poetic diction'
(p. 206).

9 Jean Genet, *Œuvres Complètes IV* (Paris, 1968), p. 181.

10 This production is the object of a detailed study in *Les Voies de la création théâtrale*,
Vol. 4 (Paris, 1975), pp. 103-315.

11 Genet's stage direction reads as follows: 'Quand le rideau est tiré, quatre Nègres en frac –
non, l'un de ces Nègres, Ville de Saint-Nazaire, sera pieds nus et en chandail de laine – et
quatre Négresses en robe du soir dansent autour du catafalque une sorte de menuet sur un
air de Mozart.'
'When the curtain is drawn, four Blacks in tails – no, one of the Blacks will be barefoot
and wearing a woollen sweater – and four Black women in evening gowns are dancing a
sort of minuet to a tune by Mozart around the catafalque.'

12 Jean Genet, *Splendid's*, translated by Neil Bartlett (London, 1995), p. *xiv*.

13 Jean Genet, *Splendid's*, translated by Neil Bartlett (London, 1995), p. *xv*.

14 A transcription of the interview was published as 'Entretien avec Nigel Williams' in Albert
Dichy (ed.), *L'Ennemi déclaré: textes et entretiens* in Jean Genet, *Œuvres Complètes VI*
(Paris, 1991), pp. 297–306; the English text is published for the first time in Chapter 6 of
this book.

15 Jean Genet, *Splendid's*, translated by Neil Bartlett (London, 1995), p. *xvi*.

16 Jean Genet, *Splendid's*, edited by Albert Dichy (Décines, 1993), p. 38.

17 Jean Genet, *Splendid's*, translated by Neil Bartlett (London, 1995), p. 16.

18 Jean Genet, *Splendid's*, translated by Neil Bartlett (London, 1995), p. 41.

19 Jean Genet, *Splendid's*, translated by Neil Bartlett (London, 1995), p. 42.

20 See Edmund White's comment that Genet liked to claim that Sartre's *Saint Genet, comédien
et martyr* (published in 1952) had given him writer's block, whereas in fact Genet's period
of sterility lasted roughly from 1947 to 1955 (Jean Genet, *Fragments ... et autres textes*
(Paris, 1990), Préface, p. 13). No doubt Genet had already begun to feel the stifling
influence of Sartre long before the publication of *Saint Genet*.

21 The text and photographs of this ballet are reprinted in Jean Genet, *Fragments ... et autres
textes* (Paris, 1990).

22 Edmund White, *Genet* (London, 1993), p. 407.

23 Edward Said, 'On Jean Genet's Late Works' in J Ellen Gainor (ed.) *Imperialism and
Theatre* (London, 1995), p. 238.

24 Edward Said, 'On Jean Genet's Late Works' in J Ellen Gainor (ed.) *Imperialism and
Theatre* (London, 1995), p. 238.

CHAPTER 15

Genet, the Theatre and the Algerian War

David Bradby

IN SHARP CONTRAST to the Americans' involvement in Vietnam, which has been endlessly dramatised in different forms, the realities of the Algerian War, which lasted from 1954 until 1962 and cost 100,000 dead or wounded, have been dealt with by very few French playwrights or *cinéastes*. In fact Genet is the only one to have written a substantial work based on this subject matter while the war was taking place. The one other dramatist with whom he can be compared in this respect is the Algerian playwright Kateb Yacine, whose trilogy *Le Cercle des représailles* offers some intriguing similarities with Genet's three great plays written during the course of the war: *Le Balcon, Les Nègres, Les Paravents*.

There were other attempts to confront the political problems posed by events in Algeria. Michel Vinaver wrote two plays dealing with the troubles, *Les Huissiers* (1958) and *Iphigénie Hotel* (1960),[1] but neither was set in Algeria. They were more concerned with French responses to the war or, rather, were an attempt to map in all its confused day-to-day reality the disintegration of the Fourth Republic under the pressure of events in North Africa. Both of these plays were published at the time, in the influential review *Théâtre populaire*, but were not performed until the end of the 1970s. Vinaver's previous play, *Les Coréens* (set in the Korean war), had been subjected to censorship, and it seems that both Roger Planchon and Jean Vilar, who were interested in his new plays, were discouraged from producing work that might express an unwelcome perspective on the 'events' in Algeria (which were never officially dignified with the status of a war).

Other examples of censorship at the time were Alain Resnais's film *Muriel*, made in 1959, and Jean-Luc Godard's *Le Petit Soldat*, made the year after; neither was given a visa for public exhibition until 1963. The most celebrated case was that of Gillo Pontecorvo's documentary film about Colonel Bigeard's 1957 offensive in the kasbah of Algiers, *La Bataille d'Alger*, made in the years immediately following the war and completed in 1966 (the year of Roger Blin's production of *Les Paravents* at the Odéon). It won the Golden Lion award at the Venice film festival, but was not permitted to be shown publicly in France until 1970, and did not receive a normal release in a Parisian cinema until 1971, when the plate-glass front of the cinema in question was frequently shattered by angry protesters.[2]

After these initial attempts to deal with the war, all written while it was in progress, there was a surprising gap of some twenty years before playwrights once again attempted to stage the conflicts to which it had given rise. This is all the more surprising when one remembers that in the 1960s the French theatre was highly politicised, and anti-colonial plays were common (e.g. Aime Césaire's *Une Saison au Congo* (1966), Armand Gatti's *V Comme Vietnam* (1967), Gabriel Cousin's *Cycle du crabe* (1969). None of them, however, dealt with the decolonisation of Algeria. Perhaps the subject matter was just too sensitive for French playwrights, especially during the 1960s, when French society was facing the problem of reabsorbing around a million *pieds-noirs* (people of French ethnicity, but born and brought up in North Africa). Moreover, the war offered no easy opportunity for public commemoration: it had produced no heroes, no victories, not even a brave organiser of resistance who, like Jean Moulin under the Nazi occupation, could become the object of civic remembrance through the naming of streets, squares or métro stations, despite the amusing fantasy of the Sergeant in Genet's *Les Paravents*, as he dies in Algeria that 'in Cahors they'll give my name to a cul-de-sac where my uncle manufactures matresses'.[3] The street battles provoked by the production of *Les Paravents* in 1966 showed that the memory of the war was still hopelessly entangled in feelings of shame and frustration.

In fact the decade 1958–1968 is notable for the absence of discussion concerning Algeria in any form at all. Political life was dominated by General de Gaulle's successful attempts to distance the French authorities from the Algerian conflict and to steer the country in an entirely new direction. His declared aim was to move France into a position where it could turn its back on its colonial past and start to play a major role in the new technological revolution that was transforming the industrialised countries of the world. An essential condition for his political sleight of hand (or betrayal, as the right saw it) was to silence all discussion on the legitimacy or illegitimacy of French involvement in Algeria.

For a decade, this policy of repressing the past and going all out for industrial expansion was a success. Then came the revolt of 1968, and much theatre of the next few years was preoccupied with making sense of the events of that momentous year. In the mid-1970s, just when one might have expected French dramatists to be turning their attention back to Algeria, there came a rash of plays dealing with the Second World War. It was as if, before dealing with the loss of their colonies, the French first had to to come to terms with the experience of defeat at home and the occupation of their own homeland.[4]

Only in the 1980s did playwrights once again begin to write about the

Algerian War, and by this time they were dealing with it from the distance of a whole generation.[5] Bernard-Marie Koltès, Daniel Lemahieu, Eugène Durif were all children at the time of the war. François Bourgeat, on the other hand, was old enough to have been called up at the time of the war and sent to Algeria as part of his regular military service. Perhaps his age explains why his play is the one most obviously influenced by Genet; in any case it is a striking fact that in plays by all of these authors we find elements that hark back very clearly to Genet's work for the theatre. Bourgeat, like Genet, presents characters who are self-consciously embarked on a ritual re-enactment; Lemahieu uses the device of characters who have died appearing on stage with those still alive; Durif chooses to explore the reality of the war through the eyes of a prostitute in a military brothel; and Koltès explicitly stated that everything he wrote had been influenced by Genet.

It is important to remember that Genet was most insistent that none of his plays should be treated as political tracts. Looking back at the first production of *Les Paravents* in 1966,[6] Roger Blin remembers how Genet was suspicious of his motives in wanting to do the play; Genet knew that Blin had always had a strong commitment to left-wing political causes, and he was determined that his play should not be directed as if it were by Brecht (although he was delighted when the production became the pretext for political battles, as we shall see). In this, Genet was being entirely consistent with the attitude he had always expressed towards the relationship between his plays and political realities. His most famous statement of this attitude was in *Comment jouer Les Bonnes*, when he declared: 'One thing should be noted: this is not a plea on behalf of housemaids. No doubt there is a trade union for domestic servants – that is not our concern.'[7]

Genet was even more emphatic in his preface to *Le Balcon* that the stage should not be seen as a forum in which the problems of society could be resolved. He insisted that, on the contrary, problems set out on the stage should never be resolved on the imaginary plane, because to do so is to leave the audience with the comforting feeling that the problem has been dealt with, and that they have no further responsibility for it:

> No problem set out in the theatre should be resolved on the imaginary plane, especially where the dramatic resolution urges us towards a perfected social order. On the contrary, let evil explode on stage, let it show us naked, leave us haggard if it can, and with no other recourse than to ourselves. The function of the artist, or poet, is not to find practical solutions to the problems of evil. Let them accept damnation.[8]

The point lying behind such affirmations is, of course, that Genet was not writing plays whose aim was to imitate reality; he went so far as to say, in connection with *Les Paravents*, 'Never have I copied life.'[9] Rather, he was operating at the level of received ideas, images, the prejudices that come ready-made in the commonplace phrases of everyday linguistic usage. The maids in *Les Bonnes*, the figures of state in *Le Balcon*, the blacks in *Les Nègres*, the Arabs and the colonials in *Les Paravents*, none of these represent the reality of servitude, power, slavery, colonialism, but its image. They are reflections of the images of these things in the minds of the audience, figures onto which the audience projects its own image of social roles and power relations. This is why Genet insisted on the need for at least one white person to be present at every performance of *Les Nègres*. In this way he emphasised the fact that blackness is a social construct, something culturally determined, having its origin in the mentalities of colonialism. Biological factors such as ethnic origins and skin colour are quite unimportant by comparison with the power of one social group to impose an identity on another group. The blacks of the play are not 'real' blacks, but figures representing the image of blackness that has been devised by the colonial powers and imposed upon all those defined as subject people.

In representing the way images are projected onto one social group by another, Genet exploits the social situation that is fundamental to any theatre performance: one group (the audience) paying for the pleasure of seeing another group (the actors) evoke images of human behaviour. In his letters to Blin about the staging of *Les Paravents*, he insisted on the need for the audience to be visible and clearly involved in the performance.[10] This was something that Patrice Chéreau took one stage further in his 1983 revival of the play at the Théâtre des Amandiers, Nanterre. For this production Richard Peduzzi's design transformed both auditorium and stage, turning them into a space that recalled a poor provincial cinema of the 1950s, so that the audience found itself culturally 'placed' in a way that led to the natural expectation of particular images of the Algerian War, images that might have been expected by the average French cinema-goer of the time. Chéreau also arranged for certain scenes, in which the colonials protest at the behaviour of the Arabs, to be played in the auditorium, in such a way as to stress the interplay of images in the performance.

So single-minded is Genet's focus on the theatrical image that the critic Bernard Dort considers his plays to be entirely self-reflexive. He argues that the effect of Genet's theatre, taken as a whole, is to set up a movement of theatrical self-destruction.[11] This is achieved by a process of charming, fascinating and entrapping the spectators in an imaginary world of reflections. But once it has caught them, it destroys the ground beneath their feet, leaving them with no refuge, no disguise to fall back on and only one certainty: that of death. Unlike more traditional theatre, in which effects such as disguises or masks are used in order to secrete an ultimate truth, Genet pushes them to the point where they reveal only nothingness; Dort quotes Genet's remark about *Les Paravents* being the celebration of *nothing* to justify this reading.[12] His conclusion is that the one thing rigorously excluded from Genet's theatre is reality and this, in turn, makes it impossible for him to be considered as a political playwright. His thesis is persuasive, and we may well accept it, but even as we do so, we are reminded of Genet's protean unseizability, since he is the first to alert us to the fact that in this theatrical universe nothing can ever be taken at face value. In the interplay of conflicting images, he reminds us to be suspicious *also* of what he tells us about it. If he insists that it has nothing to do with politics, maybe the reverse is true?

There are, of course, many famous examples of Genet's playful love of inverting received opinions or standard assumptions (such as the occasion when he was being interviewed by Nigel Williams for the BBC (1985), and insisted on turning the camera on the interviewer and technicians). A telling instance in the case of *Les Paravents* is his answer to people who tried to press him to declare which side he supported in the Algerian War. 'I'm inclined to favour the Algerians,' he answered, 'because I always side with the strongest.'[13] The remark is doubly ironic since a) Genet was known to favour the oppressed, and b) the Algerians were not considered to be 'the strongest'. The consensus among military historians, even today, is that the French army was largely victorious on the ground, but was betrayed by the politicians back home.[14]

The remarkable thing about Genet's plays of this period is that he was the only European writer with the vision to imagine the world from the point of view of the colonised peoples, instead of seeing the disintegration of colonial empires from the Western perspective. In his last two plays, especially in *Les Paravents*, he developed a highly original interpretation of the Algerian War, an interpretation that sought to show how the powerless were acquiring a power of their own, while the military might of the Western nations was proving ineffective in preserving the colonial system. This perspective has become more familiar to us since the collapse of the Soviet empire in Eastern Europe, and the appearance of plays by Vaclav Havel, but it was difficult to see it clearly in the late 1950s, when French theatre was becoming polarised into two opposing camps: those for and those against Brecht. The famous polemic between Kenneth Tynan and Eugène Ionesco, fought out in the pages of the *Observer* in 1958, crystallised this for an English-speaking readership.[15] For the French this polarisation was evident in the increasingly Brechtian slant of the influential review *Théâtre populaire*, whose editorial board included Bernard Dort and Roland Barthes. Genet was always perceived as a special case, somewhat marginal to such considerations, but there is no doubt that to those who were actively engaged in trying to promote political theatre at the time, Genet was seen as a bit of an embarrassment. Blin recalls the way that Genet's refusal to subscribe to left-wing dogma upset the guardians of socialist political correctness at the time:

Genet would say: 'that's fine, go ahead and construct your ideal republic but above all make sure that you keep a corner with a little pile of filth.' That was Saïd [the central character of *Les Paravents*]. What Genet denounces is the inescapable return to order, the revolution triumphant. There is no solution, no political moral to be drawn from his plays. This is something that Sartre blamed Genet for, as did Adamov as well.[16]

Sartre and Adamov had both put their signatures to the 'Manifesto of the 121' (as had Blin); Genet had not.[17]

And yet, with the advantage of hindsight, we can see that Genet's plays had a more profound impact on the French understanding of the issues in the Algerian War than did those of Sartre or Adamov. Adamov, to be fair, wrote very little of direct relevance to the war. But what he did write serves as a pointed example of the dangers of political theatre alluded to by Genet in the passages quoted above (see Notes 8 and 9 below). His contribution consists of two short sketches, published in 1958 in a volume entitled *Théâtre de société*, which also includes a sketch by Guy Demoy and one by Maurice Regnaut.[18] One of Adamov's sketches, 'Je ne suis pas Français', is a straightforward piece of agit-prop, designed to demystify the claim that the mass of the Algerian population could be considered as full French citizens. This claim was more or less accepted by all political parties in the mid-1950s and was still being promoted by de Gaulle during his first year in office (1958), but of course it rapidly became irrelevant as de Gaulle saw the necessity of granting Algerian independence.

Adamov's second sketch escapes the danger of being overtaken by events, but only at the expense of excessive generalisation. It is a sort of *guignol* in which a grotesque figure named 'la cause incarnée' (satirising de Gaulle) establishes a government whose sole aim (beyond his own glorification) is to safeguard the interests of Capital, while keeping the working class in its place. It could be applied to almost any totalitarian ruler who claims to have been sent by providence to rescue his country from disaster, and while it accurately deflates de Gaulle's belief in his heaven-sent mission, it fails as satire because it assumes de Gaulle's aim to be preservation of the status quo in Algeria. In fact, with historical hindsight, we can see that de Gaulle's political astuteness between 1958 and 1962 lay in his ability to change direction faster than his opponents could follow him – something Genet might well have been expected to admire.

Although Sartre made no such direct intervention into the politics of the Algerian War, he had certainly attempted to use the theatre in order to clarify the purposes and limits of direct political action and had encountered similar frustrations. The clearest case of this was his play *Les Mains sales* (1948), designed to demonstrate the need for a pragmatic, independent style of

Communist leadership similar to that of Tito in Yugoslavia. But in performance the play turned out to have a different effect, and it was interpreted as a condemnation of all Communist Party methods, indicating that they were only too ready even to murder for political advantage. As a consequence, Sartre refused all performance rights for the play, considering that despite his good intentions it was 'objectively' anti-Communist. In his play *Les Séquestrés d'Altona* (1959), he attempted to explore the corrosive effect that the use of torture has on those who resort to it. The choice of this subject was motivated by the revelations of the extent to which the French Army in Algeria was employing torture. But the play he wrote was set in and after the Second World War in Germany, and its relevance to Algeria was only in its general theme of paradoxical inversion – 'loser wins' – and the inference that the more the French involved themselves in a fight to retain Algeria at all costs, the more surely they were doomed to lose it.

If Genet was seen as marginal to the political theatre of the time, this was partly because his domestic situation forced him into exile, and he spent relatively little time in France during the years when the Algerian War was coming to its climax. From 1955 to 1961, as Edmund White establishes in his biography, Genet was living with the *funambule* Abdallah Bentaga, planning his tightrope-walking routines, supervising his training, and composing his essay on the writer as high-wire artist. As a French citizen, Abdallah was liable for military service, which at that time meant fighting with the French army against the guerilla forces of the Front de Libération Nationale (FLN) in Algeria. Abdallah was half Algerian (through his father) and so the prospect of being forced to shoot Algerian freedom fighters must have been intolerable. With Genet's encouragement, Abdallah deserted shortly after his call-up in 1957 and, in White's words, 'as a result of this decision Genet and Abdallah lived outside France after 1957. They wandered ceaselessly around Germany, Austria, Belgium and Holland and in the winters they headed for Greece.'[19] There were also prolonged stays in Italy and North Africa.

But although Genet was not domiciled in France, he was not unconcerned with events there. White emphasises the close attention with which he followed events in Europe and Africa. 'Throughout these years [the period of the Algerian War, 1954–62] Genet read several newspapers a day and discussed politics incessantly. Indeed nothing interested him more than international politics, social oppression and the collapse of the colonial system.'[20]

This should come as no surprise, given the subject matter of the last two plays, *Les Nègres* and *Les Paravents*, but once again those warnings of Genet's about the non-political status of his plays have often stood in the way of an assessment of their political force. This is understandable, for as well as the statements already quoted, in which he claims that theatre should not attempt to resolve problems that belong to politics, he was even more insistent that his dramatic work had no positive or constructive function in the political domain. Of *Les Nègres* he said: 'I am not concerned about whether my plays serve the cause of Blacks. Besides, I doubt it. I believe that action, direct struggle against colonialism, can do more for Blacks than a play in the theatre.'[21]

In such declarations we can distinguish two different ideas. The first is that direct action is the only effective way of dealing with political realities: 'It is better to carry out real acts, whose scale may appear small, than theatrical shows that are vain.'[22] The second is that the subject matter of his plays is not to be sought in the hard realities of the real world, but in our heads: 'When we see Blacks, do we see anything other than the precise and sombre phantoms of our own desire? But what do these phantoms think of us? What game are they playing? [*Quel jeu jouent-ils?*]'[23]

'Quel jeu joue-t-il?' is precisely the question that needs to be asked by anyone attempting to assess Genet's influence or impact on theatre and society in France. The first striking thing about these 'jeux', or 'plays', is that in them storyline is relatively unimportant: they are more enactments of ceremonies than of stories. *Les Nègres* offers almost nothing in the way of a conventional storyline or plot. Drama is traditionally supposed to represent conflict between characters, but if one central conflict is enacted in *Les Nègres*, it is a conflict of languages: by imposing the French language on the Africans, the colonisers have forced them to adopt the hidden judgements and prejudices enshrined in the European language. In the play a group of blacks face a 'white' court, played by blacks wearing white masks. Beneath the horrified gaze of the court, the blacks re-enact the rape and murder of a white woman. The court appeals to Racinian purity, metaphoric whiteness, images of light and spotlessness, the white man's civilising mission. The blacks respond with a 'litany of the livid', exploiting the unpleasant associations of pallor; then they begin to develop a new set of value associations, in which positive values are linked with notions of blackness.

Genet's strategy here is not that of ideologically committed writers such as Senghor or Césaire, who, in developing their concept of '*négritude*', exploited those metaphors of blackness to which positive values attach themselves, even in European languages: mystery, fertility, power. Instead Genet picked on all those things that have traditionally been used as insults by whites: smells, savagery, cannibalism. This is the language through which the white colonisers oblige the Africans to represent themselves. It is the only self-image available to them once they have adopted the French language. And so they develop and extend it, they celebrate it to a point of extremism, revel in it grotesquely. Genet's text prescribes the precise details of this ritual: the movements, the music, the use of masks, costumes and props. For example, he specifies a raised gallery running round the back of the stage, from which the court looks down on the action, so that the ceremony of the blacks is caught between the facing ranks of white audience and white court, the gaze of one reflected in the other.

The events that take place on stage are thus presented as trapped within the limited circle of the white man's imagination; as Genet's comment puts it, we are seeing nothing other than the sombre phantoms born of our own desire. What the phantoms speak of is, of course, spoken on behalf of the *others*, those excluded from this circle. But powerful and challenging as they may be, the words spoken remain, at the end of the ceremony, just that: words. The catafalque supposedly containing the corpse of the murdered white is shown to be empty. This point is clarified by the mention, at various points, and especially towards the end of the play, of the *real* crime that is taking place offstage. A traitor to the cause is being tried and executed and the ceremony offered to the white audience was just a diversion. As Genet said, real action is impossible on stage.

In *Les Paravents* the element of ceremonial is equally important but more dispersed. As has frequently been pointed out, this play is different from all of Genet's other dramas in its very broad, Shakespearian scope. No single ceremony is at the centre of the play, but in the course of its sixteen scenes it presents a number of different ceremonies that summon up a wide range of different phantoms.

Like *Les Nègres*, *Les Paravents* openly proclaims its status as a self-reflexive architecture of words and images. From the first word, 'Rose', to the last, 'une chanson', the play exhibits a self-conscious awareness of its own artistic means that frequently goes over into self-parody. The fragility of this verbal architecture is underlined by the tendency of language to disintegrate completely, as in the untranslatable encounter between Le Gendarme, Leila and La Mère at the end of Scene 9, discussing the relative merits of saying 'tu' or 'vous':

> **Gendarme:** ... Entre nous le tu est tu de copain, entre nous et vous le tu qui vient de nous est tu plus mou.
> **La Mère:** Juste. Le vous pour vous ça vous éloigne de nous. Le tu nous plaît, le s'il vous plaît n'est pas pour nous.
> **Leila:** Le mou non plus ... Le tout non plou ... Le vu non plus.
> *Elle rit. La Mère rit.*
> **La Mère,** *enchaînant*: Le fou c'est vous ... le plus c'est mou ... c'est tout au plus ...
> *Elle rit. Leila rit. Le Gendarme rit.*
> **Gendarme:** Le mon c'est plou ... c'est plus mon cul ... Le cul mon coup ... (*Ils rient tous, aux éclats, mais soudain le Gendarme s'aperçoit qu'il partage ce rire. Il éclate.*) Silence![24]

The Gendarme has been drawn despite himself into an attack on the language that guarantees his superiority. To station gendarmes in the colonies is part of the 'civilising mission' of the empire builders, but as he realises bitterly a couple of pages later, it is all a waste of effort: 'We brought you civilisation and you continue to live like vagabonds. Not even beneath the bridges! at the foot of the ruins. Everything. We give you everything: schools, hospitals, the gendarmerie, and for you it all adds up to nothing. Wind. Sand.'[25]

As a counterpart to such playful sequences, in which words are made to question accepted truths, are speeches where they are used (as in all Genet's plays) to build up an image of charismatic power. In *Les Paravents* it is most frequently the women who give vent to such monologues of complex poetic lyricsm, and this reminds us that Genet's first title for the play was *Les Mères*. It is through their wild flights of linguistic fancy that we understand the power of these characters who are, in political terms, powerless. The Mother's great speech to the moon in the middle of Scene 13, for example, or Leila's extraordinary dying monologue as she drowns beneath the layers of her dress.[26] The colonials are aware that their language no longer holds the power it once did; like Sir Harold's gigantic peccary glove in Scene 4, it no longer has the same repressive force to impress and terrify. As Sir Harold's son comments in Scene 13, words themselves are scared, just like the French.[27]

Undoubtedly the aspect of the Algerian conflict that most excited and amused Genet was the way in which each side seemed interested in polishing up its image of itself – certainly more interested in this than in what the enemy was doing. Clearly this can be seen to have a counterpart in the real historical situation: under the Fourth Republic the French were almost obsessively concerned with proving to themselves and to anyone outside who would listen that they had the right to treat Algeria as part of France. All political parties, from the extreme right to the Communists, were agreed on this. On the other side, the Algerians of the FLN were greatly taken up with unifying the rebels under their command within the country and with generating support for their struggle in other Arab countries and in the Communist bloc.

Of course, Genet's treatment of this theme makes no attempt to respect particular historical events; the interplay of reflections is treated with an outrageously poetic almost surrealistic imagination. An example of this is the discussion between the General and his Lieutenant, where the General is worried about the revolutionaries' access to mirrors:

General: … Be careful, lieutenant, of their growing beauty. (*Lyrical.*) Beauty, beauty, that cements armies together, as you say, cement for us but for them as well. (*Pause.*) I wonder, after twenty-eight years in the service, if I hadn't admired my bearing in the mirror, would I have had the courage to defend it? … If that lot, facing us, ever get a mirror between their paws.

Lieutenant: I have given orders for the men to fire instantly at any mirror.[28]

The notion of an army marching into the field with orders to shoot all mirrors on sight may seem like a pure dream-image, but, of course, it may *also* be read as a condensed, poetic way of expressing the refusal of the French to allow self-determination on the part of the Algerians. Furthermore, Genet uses the metaphor as a way of commenting on the inevitable tendency of any revolutionary army to begin to ape the behaviour of the repressive power it overthrows. In the brothel sequence of Scene 14, Ommou fiercely criticises the Arab soldier for imitating the French:

> **Ommou:** Ah! Ah! ... That was predictable! So you lot have already reached the stage of uniform, discipline, pretty march-pasts in shirt-sleeves, parades and heroic deaths as you sing 'Madelon' and the 'Marseillaise', all that warlike beauty ...
> **Soldier:** There are other things than shit and filth ...
> **Ommou:** ... is copied from them, to be their reflection is to turn into them: forehead to forehead, nose to nose, chin–chin, belly–belly, and why not, good God, why not make love to them, mouth to mouth, breath to breath, tongue to tongue, cry to cry, gasp to gasp ... [29]

The scandalous suggestion of the proximity of sexual attraction and armed struggle is reinforced by the brothel setting; another example of a similar juxtaposition is Genet's recommendation that the French soldiers should, in their movements, imitate the Bluebell Girls.[30] The dramatic conflict that is fought out in the play between the French and the Algerians takes place entirely at the level of the image. Gradually, it becomes clear that the image of the soldier as glamorous adventurer, in the style of Beau Geste, has lost its potency, and that the rebels are acquiring a glamour of their own. The missionary, who understands such things, since he, too, deals in symbols of power, is the first to point out that the rebels are acquiring their own beauty. He also points out that the rebellion is caused, initially, by the Europeans rather than the Arabs, since it is they who have provided the examples of cruelty and images of force.[31]

In the face of this interplay of self-consciously reflecting images, Saïd and Leila stand out as the couple who successfully resist this tendency and White sees this, rightly I think, as the main thrust of the play. He recalls Genet saying, 'Listen: the day the Palestinians become institutionalised, I will no longer be on their side.' He goes on to comment that the Nettle family (Saïd, Leila and the Mother) and Ommou resist assimilation. 'They refuse to lead symbolic lives, to take on the status of a banner or flag.'[32]

François Regnault, writing at the time of Chéreau's revival of *Les Paravents*, insisted on 'the poetry of the work [*la poésie de l'œuvre*]'.[33] The poetic point of view, he argued, allowed Genet to understand what nobody else understood at the time, that the question of whether Algeria should remain French or not was completely irrelevant, since the movement towards decolonisation all over Africa was entirely unstoppable. What his play offered to his compatriots was a meditation on how politics is experienced and understood, how our picture of the world we live in alters (or fails to) in response to shifting political realities. For this reason, Regnault saw the play as being about France; he expressed this by calling it a play *on* France: 'Neither for nor against, *on*. [*Ni pour, ni contre: sur.*] As one talks of an engraving on wood. A play that France had to endure, as Athens had to endure the plays of Aristophanes.'[34]

The nature of the battles that broke out during the performances in 1966 would certainly seem to support this view. The fighting that took place both outside the theatre and in the auditiorium was not provoked by particular incidents in the play, though on some evenings the hostile elements waited for the famous farting scene to launch their attacks on the stage. It was more a general protest that, in the words of Jean-Jacques Gautier, a subsidised national theatre should be allowed to dishonour the national flag. Roger Blin's memoirs make it clear that Genet found the scandal highly amusing, especially since Blin's production satisfied him by not trying to falsify the nature of the play by turning it into a political tract. There can be nothing more satisfactory, for a writer who wishes to proclaim his hostility to French society, than the spectacle of one of his plays provoking angry exchanges in the French Chamber of Deputies. Perhaps it was in the light of the public reception of his play that he was prepared to state, in 1970, 'my last play, *Les Paravents*, was nothing more or less than a long meditation on the Algerian War.'[35]

How then can we 'place' Genet's contribution to the dramatic literature of the Algerian War and assess its importance in other than theatrical terms? In the first place, the performances of *Les Paravents* in 1966 took on a political meaning, one that Genet was delighted by (where some dramatists might have been infuriated) precisely because that meaning was extraneous to the work. It amounted to the dying spasms of the old Algérie Française school of thought and showed once more how the forces of the far right were (at that time) locked in a private fantasy which had no contact whatever with the political realities of the real world.

In the second place, it is clear that Regnault's comment about the poet's point of view does not exclude a political dimension. The force of both *Les Nègres* and *Les Paravents* derived from the fact that Genet was the *only* French playwright of the period who, at a time when Empire or Commonwealth were viewed in naïvely paternalistic terms, was moved to picture the world from the point of view of the colonised, not the colonisers. The special difficulty of formulating and expressing this point of view in relation to Algeria can be seen in the history of censorship alluded to at the start of this chapter.

Genet laid considerable stress on death in *Les Paravents*, and was at great pains to underline the congruence between death and his theatre. In one of his letters to Blin, for example, he wrote that 'everything must contribute to breaking through what separates us from the dead'.[36] This is something that is fulfilled, of course, in his simple but original stage image of the characters bursting through the screens of the play's title. The role of death in Genet's theatre is to fix and to finalise, outside the flux of historical time as we normally experience it. Death is the realm where a person finally coincides perfectly with an image, becomes, in fact, nothing other than the image that others have of him or her. In addition, death is, of course, the one constant presence in wars and revolutions, something that becomes, in such situations, a normal rather than an exceptional event, however scandalous. By giving a major place to death in his play, Genet at once liberates himself from the need to take sides in a narrow, propagandistic sense, and at the same time makes it possible for him to represent events from a point of view not otherwise available.

While rejecting the mimetic techniques that we normally associate with theatre that is termed 'political', Genet nevertheless chose dramatic situations that allowed him to conduct a complex meditation on the relationships between political power and imagination, the imagination of social groups as well as of individuals. This is true of every one of his plays, but is pointedly given a Third World colonial setting in his last two plays. He was not writing about how real blacks or Arabs feel – for that we need to go to Césaire or Yacine – he was facing the dark side of the Europeans' attitude: those aspects of their *imagination* that they were not prepared to face. This he achieved by inventing dream-like images (which frequently scandalised his contemporaries) and endowing characters with dream-like language, not limited to how 'real' people speak, while at the same time remaining true to situations that were firmly anchored in reality. This description could equally well describe Koltès and shows what he has taken from Genet.

Jeanette Savona makes the claim that the avant-garde theatre of the last thirty years owes a great deal to *Les Paravents*.[37] Although she does not go on to explain exactly where she detects the play's influence, one can readily see what she must have had in mind. Rejection of a narrowly mimetic theatre that seeks to recreate political realities on the stage is clearly a feature of recent French theatre. This is particularly evident, for example, in the work of the Théâtre du Soleil, perhaps the leading avant-garde political theatre company of the 1970s and 1980s. Ariane Mnouchkine has repeatedly stressed her search for a *theatrical* transposition of the subject matter, even when dealing with the most overtly political topics, such as the French Revolution in the company's memorable productions *1789* and *1793*. But it is intriguing to see that the Théâtre du Soleil, too, failed to confront the Algerian War in their work, preferring to deal with the failures of the British in India (*L'Indiade, ou l'Inde de leurs rêves*, 1987) or of the Americans in Cambodia (*L'Histoire terrible mais inachevée de Norodom Sihanouk, roi du Cambodge*, 1985). Both of these plays were written by Hélène Cixous, herself a *pied-noir* from Oran.

In conclusion, let us consider briefly the influence that Genet's work may have exerted on those young French playwrights who, in the last few years, *have* begun to turn to the Algerian War as the subject matter for their plays. In the first place, it is worth noting that interest in the subject seems to have been sparked off by Chéreau's revival of *Les Paravents* in 1983. Secondly, it is clear that every one of these dramatists felt the need to develop an original structure, as if the very act of confronting this material was problematic. *Djebels* is described by its author as 'not so much a dramatic poem as a dramatic song in which arias and recitatives intermingle'.[38] *Le Retour au Désert* offers a similar intermingling of the chronological and the ritual. All Koltès's previous plays had respected the dramatic unities, especially that of time; but although this play tells a story that unfolds in the course of a certain length of time, maybe around one year, the temporal links between scenes are often unclear, or strictly relative, and Koltès has introduced a ritual division based on four of the five daily Islamic prayers prescribed for the five stages of the day: dawn, midday, afternoon, evening, night. *Djurdjura* is a dream-play, structured almost like a Strindbergian *Stationendrama*, and *B M C* adopts the minimalist structure of simply juxta-posing its two monologues, with no introduction or commentary.

These structures, all self-consciously theatrical in their own way, are eloquent in suggesting the sheer difficulty involved in speaking of the war without a name. The censorship imposed at the time, the uncertainty of what the war was for, the need to face a history of violence, torture and betrayal on all sides, all of these things appear to be unfinished business in the France of today. The dramaturgical solutions adopted by the above playwrights all owe something to Genet in their use of dream form, their preoccupation with the problems of treachery and failure, and their breaking down of the barriers between the living and the dead. Perhaps the most strikingly Genetian figure to make an appearance in all the plays so far mentioned occurs in Koltès's *Le Retour au Désert*, set in a provincial town in Eastern France at the beginning of the 1960s. He is a mysterious character named simply Le grand parachutiste noir, who appears without warning on the balcony of Adrien, a frightened representative of the town's property-owning bourgeoisie. In fact he is a figure from Adrien's imagination whose function is to express both Adrien's sense of insecurity and his nostalgia for the good old days of Empire. 'How did you get in?' asks Adrien, and the Parachutist answers him, 'I dropped in from the sky of course ... I floated down like a little snowflake in summer time, so that you could sleep safe and sound.'[39] As the dialogue develops, Adrien becomes scared that the

Parachutist may be there to plunder rather than to protect and tries to appeal to his patriotism, to which the Parachutist replies:

> I love this land, bourgeois, but I don't love the people in it. Who is the enemy? Are you friend or foe? Who should I defend? Who should I attack? Since I don't know who is the enemy, I shoot everything that moves. I love this land, sure, but I long for the good old days. I'm nostalgic for the soft light of oil lamps, for the glory of a navy under sail. I look back to the colonial era with its cool verandas and its croak of bull-frogs, when evenings were long and when everyone in the country knew his place, stretched out in a hammock, swinging on the rocking-chair or crouching beneath the mangrove, each in his own place, calm and settled, and that place was his. I'm nostalgic for the little nigger boys running about behind their cows, that you could send flying like mosquitoes. Yes, I love this land, let no one doubt it, I love my France all the way from Dunkirk to Brazzaville because I have mounted guard on its borders, I have marched for night after night, gun in hand, ears cocked and eyes towards the foe. And now I'm told I must forget nostalgia, that the times have changed ... My only function is to fight, and my only rest will be in death.'[40]

In the words of Le grand parachutiste noir, Koltès has deliberately included echoes of a famous speech made by de Gaulle at the time, in which he insisted that the French must turn their backs on the nostalgia for colonial myths. This speech by Le grand parachutiste noir shows that things could not be so simple. As an example of an imaginary figure who catches up many of the strands governing the French imagination at the time, he is a worthy successor to the colourful phantoms that people Genet's plays. Like them, he is clearly 'born from the sombre phantoms of our own desire'.[41] But there are not many like him on the French stage; maybe one result of Genet's brilliant success in *Les Paravents* was the long time-gap before other playwrights felt able to follow his lead.

[This is the text of a paper presented at the 'Flowers and Revolution' conference held at Middlesex University, 21 May 1994. A version of this paper appeared in *Theatre Research International*, Vol. 19, No. 3, 1994, pp. 226–37.]

NOTES

1 Both reprinted in *Théâtre Complet*, Vol. 1 (Arles, 1986).

2 See Benjamin Stora, *La Gangrène et l'oubli* (Paris, 1991), especially Chapter 3 and Chapter 17.

3 Jean Genet, *Œuvres Complètes V* (Paris, 1979), p. 344; see also p. 374.

4 In the 1970s, Daniel Besnehard wrote plays set in Nazi-occupied Normandy, Michel

Deutsch and Bernard Chartreux wrote two linked plays about collaboration and betrayal under the title *Violences à Vichy*, Jean-Claude Grumberg wrote *L'Atelier* about a group of women living through the immediate aftermath of the occupation of Paris, and a number of plays dealt with the rise of Nazism leading up to the war, of which the most notable was Ariane Mnouchkine's *Mephisto*. This was also the decade in which Marcel Ophuls' great documentary film of life under the occupation, *Le Chagrin et la Pitié*, was shocking audiences all over France with its revelations of the extent to which ordinary French men and women had accepted collaboration as a way of life.

5 Four particularly successful examples are: Bernard-Marie Koltès, *Le Retour au Désert* (Paris, 1988), Daniel Lemahieu, *Djebels* (Paris, 1988), Eugène Durif, *B M C* (Paris, 1992), François Bourgeat, *Djurdjura* (Paris, 1991). For a further discussion of these playwrights, see my 'Images of the Algerian War on the French stage 1988–92' in *French Cultural Studies* Vol. 5, June 1994, pp. 179–89, reprinted in French as 'Images de la guerre d'Algérie sur la scène française' in *Théâtre/Public*, No. 123, mai–juin 1995, pp. 14–22.

6 Roger Blin, *Souvenirs et propos*, edited by Lynda Bellity Peskine (Paris, 1986), pp. 174–230.

7 Jean Genet, *Œuvres Complètes IV* (Paris, 1968), p. 269.

8 Jean Genet, *Œuvres Complètes IV* (Paris, 1968), p. 35.

9 Jean Genet, *Œuvres Complètes IV* (Paris, 1968), p. 259.

10 Jean Genet, *Œuvres Complètes IV* (Paris, 1968), p. 233. Both *Les Nègres* and *Les Paravents* were directed by Roger Blin and designed by André Acquart, the first in 1959 (Théâtre Lutèce) and the second in 1966 (Odéon – Théâtre de France).

11 Bernard Dort, 'Genet ou le combat avec le théâtre' in *Théâtres* (Paris, 1986), pp. 122–39.

12 'Plays, normally, so they say, are supposed to have a meaning: but not this one. It is a festivity whose elements are disparate, it is the celebration of nothing.' Jean Genet, *Œuvres Complètes IV* (Paris, 1968), p. 223.

13 See Edmund White, *Genet* (London, 1993), p. 564.

14 See for example Georges Fleury, *La Guerre en Algérie* (Paris, 1993).

15 Republished as 'Controverse Londonienne' in *Notes et Contre-Notes* (Paris, 1962), pp. 69–90.

16 Roger Blin, *Souvenirs et propos*, edited by Lynda Bellity Peskine (Paris, 1986), p. 201.

17 The Manifeste des cent-vingt-et-un was a petition circulated and signed by more than 121 well-known people demanding the withdrawal of the French army and self-determination for the people of Algeria. Those who signed were debarred from work on the state radio or television for several years.

18 Arthur Adamov, *Théâtre de Société; Scènes d'Actualité* (Paris, 1958).

19 Edmund White, *Genet* (London, 1993), p. 511.

20 Edmund White, *Genet* (London, 1993), p. 489.

21 Albert Dichy (ed.), *L'Ennemi déclaré: textes et entretiens* in Jean Genet, *Œuvres Complètes VI* (Paris, 1991), p. 23.

22 Albert Dichy (ed.), *L'Ennemi déclaré: textes et entretiens* in Jean Genet, *Œuvres Complètes VI* (Paris, 1991), p. 50.

23 Jean Genet, *Les Nègres au port de la lune* (Bordeaux, 1988), p. 101, cited in Edmund White, *Genet* (London, 1993), p. 494.

24 Jean Genet, *Œuvres Complètes V* (Paris, 1979), p. 233. In English the word-play involving *tu* and *vous* is lost since there is no distinction between a formal and informal usage of 'you' in the English language. Bernard Frechtman in the official English translation (Jean Genet, *The Screens* (London, 1987 edition), pp. 64–5) turns this passage into an exchange of playful banter as follows:

> The Gendarme: ... Between me and you, 'you there' is kind of palsy.
> The Mother: Right. 'Madame''s too-too. 'You there' is woo-woo.
> Leila: 'You there''s taboo ... 'You there' pooh-pooh ... Pooh-pooh on you ...
> (*She laughs. The Mother laughs.*)
> The Mother (*carrying on the game*): But who is who? ... 'You there' coo-coo ... So toodle-oo.
> (*She laughs. Leila laughs. The Gendarme laughs.*)
> The Gendarme: So what's to do? ... to do, to do, but pooh on ... Who? ... On who? ... On 'you there'!
> (*They all roar with laughter, but suddenly* The Gendarme *realises that he is sharing in the laughter. He explodes.*) Silence!

25 Jean Genet, *Œuvres Complètes V* (Paris, 1979), p. 235.

26 Jean Genet, *Œuvres Complètes V* (Paris, 1979), pp. 292–3 and pp. 330–1 respectively.

27 Jean Genet, *Œuvres Complètes V* (Paris, 1979), p. 291.

28 Jean Genet, *Œuvres Complètes V* (Paris, 1979), p. 304.

29 Jean Genet, *Œuvres Complètes V* (Paris, 1979), p. 315.

30 Jean Genet, *Œuvres Complètes V* (Paris, 1979), p. 264.

31 Jean Genet, *Œuvres Complètes V* (Paris, 1979), p. 354.

32 Although, curiously, he then goes on to misquote Warda's wonderful poetic line: 'Non! Non! Pas moi! Je ne flotterai jamais, jamais je ne serai battue des vents' ('No! No! Not me! I will never let myself be unfurled, never be beaten by the winds!'), attributing it to Ommou instead (Edmund White, *Genet*, pp. 558–9). Warda's line appears on p. 319 of Jean Genet, *Œuvres Complètes V* (Paris, 1979).

33 Bernard-Marie Koltès and François Regnault, *La Famille des orties; esquisses et croquis autour des Paravents de Jean Genet* (Paris, 1983), p. 23.

34 Bernard-Marie Koltès and François Regnault, *La Famille des orties; esquisses et croquis autour des Paravents de Jean Genet* (Paris, 1983), p. 23.

35 Cited in Lynda Bellity Peskine and Albert Dichy, *La Bataille des Paravents* (Paris, 1991), p. 59. This book provides an invaluable history of the conflicts to which Blin's production gave rise, and reprints all the reviews that appeared at the time; Jean-Jacques Gautier's review for *Le Figaro* is on pp. 65–6.

36 Jean Genet, *Œuvres Complètes IV* (Paris, 1968), p. 221.

37 Jeanette L Savona, *Jean Genet* (London, 1983), p. 148.

38 Daniel Lemahieu, *Djebels* (Paris, 1988), p. 6.

39 Bernard-Marie Koltès, *Le Retour au Désert* (Paris, 1988), p. 55.

40 Bernard-Marie Koltès, *Le Retour au Désert* (Paris, 1988), pp. 56–7.

41 See Note 23 above. For further discussion of the playwrights mentioned in the last part of this chapter, see Note 5 above.

CHAPTER 16

Jean Genet's May Day Speech

Allen Ginsberg

Editor's note: His May Day speech was the most significant speech Genet ever made during his visits to the United States. On 1 May 1970, at the culmination of a two-month US tour to foster the cause of the Black Panthers, he spoke before a gathering of 25,000 as part of a three-day rally on the Yale campus at New Haven in support of Bobby Seale, who had been indicted for murder. Genet was one of a line-up that included Jerry Rubin, Abbie Hoffman, Dave Dellinger, Ralph Abernathy and David Hilliard. His appearance had not been announced in the press because of his illegal status in the US; the day after this speech, having been summoned to present his papers and entry visa by the immigration authorities in Connecticut, Genet beat a hasty retreat from the US and crossed the border to Canada. He never returned to the US.

The English translation of Genet's speech was done by the poet and critic Richard Howard, who didn't want to be credited in the published edition, brought out by City Lights Books in the summer of 1970. Priced at $1, the profits of *May Day Speech* went to the Black Panthers, who helped distribute the brochure. The text of the speech was prefaced by an introduction by Allen Ginsberg, which is reproduced here. In the original edition, Ginsberg's introduction ended with a call for readers to send donations to the Black Panther Legal Defense Fund.

MAY DAY 1970 at Yale satisfied the most ancient traditions of Academy when school strike shut down Establishment social classes and 20,000–30,000 youths assembled with black men, church men, bohemian and professor elders to sit under grassy sky before a wooden platform raised under the portentous stone columns of New Haven's imitation-classic Courthouse – What Blake would have made of that priestly facade! – to hear Jean Genet, most eminent prosateur of Europe and saintly thinker of France, most shy poet of XX Century slipped criminally into forbidden America through Canada border, standing flanked by clownish tragic reality of Revolution of Consciousness and Body in America – Yippie Saints Rubin, Hoffman, peaceful Saint Dellinger,

many musical and professorial politic thinkers, black philosopher street theorists
and actionaries, and great Big Man leader of New Haven Panthers that day –
deliver his historic psychopolitical *Commencement* Discourse to the Academy
and Polis of America, to youthful lovers of all lands' races, and especially to the
tender terrified whites assembled under the Eye of metal-Armed Masked Robot
National Armies and Gas-weaponed Police – all of us black and white now
Scholars in Hell! on New Haven's Green – pronouncing the very terms of the
desired Merciful Survival Armistice and Union between black and white races
in America that might bring peace to the entire world.

M Genet appeared short, round headed, white skull'd, pink faced with
energetic cigar, drest in Amerindian style brown leather-thonged Jacket, he
spoke first into the microphone in French, explaining (as I remember, myself
sitting far left of the iron-pole joint-footed platform accepting burning grass
reefer stubs from varicolor-shirted youths thick bearded seated round, long
haired and short naked-minded newborn scholars of police-state reality,
Apocalyptic Biblical Revolution for Millenium our mortal lot–) his presence in
American and introducing his text, which he explained would be read for him
in English by Mr Big Man (whose Name Genet pronounced happily Beeg Man)
– And so after a page, Mr Big Man bent to the Microphone, and straining over
the fresh English/American translation read Genet's sentences in gentle and firm
voice. Genet had not been advertised for that first day's convocation; many
Newsmen had not yet arrived to the giant crowd nor were aware that Genet's
person and prose were fortunately and intelligently the first offering of the
afternoon, and many inattentive folk on the green didn't know that Big Man's
speech was Genet's composition.

The exquisite common sense of Genet's document on racism was immediately
apparent – to those of us whose consciousness attended his classic language
while we eyed the bannered mass multitude seated on ground, batteries of
cameras TV'd in front circle, FBI-Window-telescopes in high floors of Bank
Department Edifices walled over New Haven Green – black flag and red, scroll'd
cannabis leaf insignia and 50-starred stripes, helicopter passed roaring overhead
– and the Panthers and their righteous cause and the grievous, mean, bitter
murderous injustice dealt them by our Government was explained again clearly
once for all and established irrevocably in conscience and consciousness in *white
terms* unmistakable, and in language that commanded a new 'delicacy of heart'
as the next political dimension of White Reality, confronted with age old
bestiality and desensitization of heart that had shrouded white mind for 400
years of contemptible histrionics.

Genet's prayer for himself, for ourselves, remarkably included this tender odd
affirmation for all: 'Personally, I place a certain trust in man's nature, even the
nature of the most limited man.'

Here follows the compete text of this classic discourse, a true commencement exercise marking the historic Graduation of white mentality to a 'delicacy of heart' hitherto forbidden in fear and greed by Universities and Press, Church, Foundations, Unions and Advertising Freakdoms, and fumbling, conspiring, dangerous, trembling criminal Police Agents. The Appendix – analysis of Establishment centers of hypnosis and repression was not read aloud on the Green at New Haven May Day 1970, but was added by M Genet as a nine-paragraph'd thoughtful index of our civilization's mortal ills, a communicable diagnosis.

Allen Ginsberg
June 1970

CHAPTER 17

Letter to Allen Ginsberg

Jean Genet

Editor's note: On leaving the United States after the 1968 Republican National Convention, Genet wrote the following letter to Allen Ginsberg.

I DO NOT want to leave this country, Allen, without telling you that even at night, you were my only sunshine, my only light in America.

There is no question of my forgetting who you nor your flower boys are. May you be happy. And may you never lose your poetic eloquence. And may we meet again anywhere in the world: these are my three wishes, in the shape of a Buddhist fish.

I embrace you.

[Translated by Mary Beach in Bill Morgan and Rob Rosenthal (eds), *Best Minds: A Tribute to Allen Ginsberg* (New York, 1986), p. 116.]

CHAPTER 18

The Politics of Saint Genet

Ian Birchall

JEAN-PAUL SARTRE'S famous essay *Saint Genet* played a crucial role in establishing Genet's reputation. But not only did it analyse Genet's past; it prefigured his future. Sartre, at a crucial turning-point in his life, reflected on the political implications of Genet's work, and identified tendencies that came to fruition in the last decades of Genet's life.

In the late 1940s Sartre was invited to write a preface for the collected works of Genet. He had known Genet since 1944, and, with Jean Cocteau, he had approached the President of the Republic in 1948 on Genet's behalf to reprieve a substantial prison term. However, among Sartre's many talents that of writing to a required length was conspicuously absent. When the preface was finally delivered for publication in 1952 it was somewhat longer than originally envisaged. It ran to 692 pages, and constituted the entire (very thick) first volume of the series of Genet's collected works.

Saint Genet is a complex and extraordinarily rich work. Jean-Bernard Moraly and Edmund White have shown that some of the biographical information is inaccurate, but, as Sartre explained in his last interview, the work was based on extensive discussions in which he submitted various hypotheses for Genet to judge (though he concedes that he did not always accept Genet's verdict). Hence a good part of the responsibility for any inaccuracy must be Genet's rather than Sartre's.[1]

Genet himself gave varying reactions to the book, from resentment to the claim that he never read it all.[2] Nonetheless, it remains an important attempt to grasp Genet's life and work as a totality. As well as presenting detailed analyses of Genet's writings, it contains extensive reflections on Marxism, psycho-analysis, language, morality and French society. Susan Sontag in her essay on *Saint Genet*[3] locates Sartre's book in the trajectory of his thought, arguing that in 1952 Sartre was poised to move on from philosophy and psychology, either towards ethics or towards politics, group action and history. He chose the latter and Sontag describes *Saint Genet* as 'his complex gesture in the direction he did not go'.

The exact opposite is true. *Saint Genet* is a crucial link in the chain of development that took Sartre towards the specific brand of Marxism he espoused. Sartre used Genet to work out his own political positions, prefiguring in a remarkable manner Genet's own political evolution.

To understand the political significance of *Saint Genet* it is necessary to give a brief outline of Sartre's own political biography. From the Resistance onwards he aligned himself with the left, but did not yet regard himself as a Marxist. He wished to maintain a political dialogue with the French Communist Party (PCF), but it saw him as a threat to its influence, and in the late 1940s launched a series of blistering attacks on him. In 1948 Sartre helped to launch the Rassemblement Démocratique Révolutionnaire, an attempt to provide an alternative to both Stalinism and Social Democracy, which soon collapsed under the pressures of the Cold War. Increasingly Sartre found himself pushed into political co-operation with the PCF, though he never ceased to distrust it in philosophical as well as organisational terms. 1952 marked the crucial turning-point; on Sartre's own account the crunch came with the demonstration in May of that year against General Ridgway, Eisenhower's successor as Supreme Allied Commander. Jacques Duclos, the acting leader of the PCF, was arrested for having two pigeons in his car, allegedly part of his line of communication with Moscow! Sartre wrote *Les Communistes et la paix*, a public offer to co-operate with the PCF, 'arguing on the basis of *my* principles not of *theirs*'.[4] The offer was accepted, rather hesitantly at first, by the PCF and for the next four years (until the Hungarian uprising of 1956) he co-operated closely, visiting the Soviet Union and participating in Communist-sponsored peace conferences. At the same time he broke dramatically with his former friend Albert Camus, in a dispute that hinged on attitudes to Marxism and Communism. The short-term events that precipitated the change of stance of 1952 took place after the publication of *Saint Genet*, but this change was the product of an evolutionary process over time – in fact precisely the period that Sartre spent writing *Saint Genet*.

The initial response to *Saint Genet* was a mixed one. The 692-page tome did not lend itself to instant reviewing, and few of the immediate comments gave evidence of adequate consideration of the intricacies of the argument. Genet was perceived as a profoundly troubling figure. His criminal past helped to make him such, but it is also clear that his homosexuality was one of the aspects that made Sartre's advocacy seem so outrageous. For those who did not have the energy to work their way through Sartre's disquisition on saintliness, the very title was a provocation – the 'pervert' had been canonised. Thus Robert Kemp denounced the 'obscenity' of *Saint Genet* in an article that was overtly homophobic.[5]

This hostility to Sartre's study derived from a prevailing climate of homophobia. The legal obstacles to homosexuality in France had been tightened in the preceding years. The Vichy regime had introduced in 1942 a new law criminalising homosexual relations involving men under the age of twenty-one and in 1945 de Gaulle's government maintained these same laws. Daniel Guérin, who contributed articles on sexual matters to the left press, lamented the change of atmosphere between the 1930s and the 1950s; in the former period, he claimed, gays were able to meet and socialise freely in a way that had become impossible by the 1950s: 'It would require a whole book to paint a full picture of the different kinds of suffering, the interior struggles, humiliations, wrongs, rebuffs, advances, persecution, blackmail, threats, which make up the everyday life of the homosexual.' (It is, however, interesting to note that the French laws were never as restrictive as the British; in France the legal barriers were mainly concerned with relations with minors, that is, with the 'age of consent'.) In 1954 a deputy asked the then Minister of the Interior – François Mitterrand – to keep checks on civil servants known to be homosexual.[6]

This homophobia was just as widespread in PCF circles as in any other part of French society. The PCF was in general very conservative on sexual matters. It opposed birth control and abortion as vigorously as the Catholic Church, basing itself on out-of-context quotations from Marx on Malthus; motherhood was extolled as an exalted state. The pioneer feminism of de Beauvoir's *Le Deuxième Sexe* received a hostile response in PCF quarters; its youth section preserved 'family values' by having separate sections for males and females.[7]

In the 1930s Communists, notably Ilya Erenburg, had accused the Surrealists of homosexuality as a means of insulting them.[8] In a pamphlet published in 1947 the Communist Jean Kanapa took up the theme, accusing Sartre of corrupting youth and putting homosexual characters in his novels.[9] As Moraly points out, the PCF did not admit those homosexuals who were 'too ostentatious' (*trop voyants*) to membership.[10] Even in the 1970s the PCF lagged behind other Communist Parties in its response to gay oppression.[11] Perhaps such sexually conservative ideas on the part of the self-proclaimed party of the working class explain the lines in *Le Balcon* where Irma says 'If the rebels win ... I'm lost. They're workers. No imagination. Prudes and maybe chaste.'[12]

In a speech in June 1947 – at the start of the Cold War – Andrei Zhdanov (the specialist on cultural questions on the Central Committee of the Communist Party of the Soviet Union) denounced *Les Temps modernes*:

> The journal *Les Temps modernes*, edited by the existentialist Sartre, recommends its new discovery – the book by the writer Jean Genet, *Journal du Voleur*, which begins with the words 'Treachery, theft and homosexuality, these will be my fundamental themes' ... The plays of this Jean Genet are staged with great prominence in the Paris theatres, and Jean Genet himself is begged to visit America. Such is the 'last word' in bourgeois philosophy.[13]

The PCF were adept at taking a hint: no party member was likely to disagree with someone as close to Stalin as Zhdanov. The PCF daily paper *L'Humanité* charged *Haute surveillance* with being an exemplar of Western society, which had produced a writer who was a common criminal.[14] Among the few writers who refused to sign a petition in support of Genet in 1948 were Louis Aragon and Paul Eluard, the two leading PCF poets.[15] As far as I can establish, no publication associated with the PCF published a review of *Saint Genet*.

In any analysis of *Saint Genet* it is important to keep this political context in mind. Sartre was projecting onto Genet his own reasons for seeking a *rapprochement* with the PCF, but also the very deep reservations he continued to have about the PCF's Stalinist politics. The posthumous publication of Sartre's *Cahiers pour une morale*, the sequel on morality promised on the final page of *L'Être et le néant*, greatly aids our understanding of his preoccupations in *Saint Genet*. In attempting to base a set of moral principles on existentialist premises, Sartre's central concern is with oppression. In the *Cahiers* he attempts a definition of oppression, founded on his view of freedom: oppression involves a human agent and a human victim. We cannot be oppressed by a rock, only by a free human will. (A rock becomes an obstacle only in terms of a human project, so a rock can destroy a human body but not human freedom.)[16] Only a free human will can be oppressed, precisely by the project of another to deny the victim's freedom and turn her/him into an object. The project of oppression is always contradictory; the rapist turns his victim into an animal, yet seeks to possess a free woman, so his attempt is doomed to failure.[17] The victim of oppression, as a free human being, is always in some sense complicit in her/his own oppression. (There is an echo of this in *Le Balcon*, when the Judge tells the thief that he, she and the torturer are all bound together.)[18] For only if I am in some sense complicit in my own oppression do I retain the power to emancipate myself from that oppression.

Sartre had shown his preoccupation with oppression in a number of earlier works; in his study of anti-Semitism[19] he examined the question of oppression from the point of view of both the oppressor and the oppressed. He had also encouraged de Beauvoir to write *Le Deuxième Sexe*, a work which parallels *Réflexions sur la question juive*, and to which Sartre makes many cross-references in *Saint Genet*. *Réflexions, Le Deuxième Sexe* and *Saint Genet* form a triptych devoted to oppression by race, gender and sexual orientation.

Sartre had long been interested in the problem of gay oppression, as can be seen from the depiction of Daniel in *Les Chemins de la liberté*. That he retained this concern to the end of his life is shown by the last interview he gave before his death, to the gay magazine *Le Gai Pied*.[20]

Sartre shows Genet as a victim of homophobia, but he also faces the fact that there are anti-Semitic elements in Genet's work. As Edmund White shows, these are not to be found in Genet's published writing;[21] Moraly's claims that Genet was anti-Semitic derive in part from a failure to distinguish anti-Semitism from the anti-Zionism manifested in his support for the Palestinian cause in the last two decades of his life.[22] But Sartre reports remarks that Genet had made to him in private conversation, notably that he could not sleep with a Jew. Sartre comments that this is precisely because Genet recognises the Jew as victim and martyr: 'What is repugnant to Genet in the Jew is that he rediscovers in the Jew his own situation.'[23] Hence Genet perceives the Jew as oppressed, like himself; but Genet is attracted not by the suffering of the oppressed but by active revolt – he is reported as saying that he supported the Algerians against France because he always supported the strongest.[24]

In pointing to the centrality and ambiguity of the theme of oppression in Genet's work, Sartre anticipates Genet's development, for it was clearly through a recognition of his own oppression that Genet moved in his later years to a recognition of affinity and hence solidarity with other categories of the oppressed. His later identification with Black Panthers and Palestinians was rooted in an understanding of his own oppression both as a criminal and as a homosexual. As he said in his 1964 *Playboy* interview, 'it is perhaps homosexuality which made me understand that Algerians were men like any others'.[25] Genet's complex evolution helps us to see that the unity of the oppressed is possible, though it is not easy or automatic.

It is not only the development of Genet that Sartre prefigures; he is also in some sense prefiguring the development of the entire left. The PCF's conservatism on questions of female and gay oppression derived from a theory which saw all questions of oppression in terms of a mechanical model of class; at the same time in practice it often capitulated to the worst prejudices of its proletarian base. Sartre does not deny the centrality of class, but he does believe that class must be integrated into a complex enough model to explain questions of oppression as well as exploitation. Only thus can Marxism regain after Stalinist distortion its role as a philosophy of human self-emancipation. Since *Saint Genet* much good and much bad has been written on the question of the relation of oppression to exploitation, but Sartre must be recognised as one of the pioneers who first posed the problem in opposition to the dominant Stalinist orthodoxy. His friendship with Genet was obviously one of the motive forces that impelled him to do so.

Sartre's theory of oppression depends essentially on his notion of freedom: only free human beings can oppress or be oppressed. Hence Sartre's insistence on the fact that Genet chose his homosexuality. In his *Playboy* interview Genet rejects this and claims that his homosexuality was in no sense the result of choice; it was imposed on him like the colour of his eyes.[26] But Genet's opinion on the matter is not a knock-down argument. He can be countered by a simple inversion of the traditional Freudian Catch 22. For a Freudian my claim that I dislike my mother is merely confirmation of my subconscious desire to sleep with her. For Sartre, Genet's denial that he chose homosexuality is proof that he is in 'bad faith', that he is refusing to take responsibility for his own choice.

It would be easy to get stuck in an irresoluble debate about free will. It is unlikely that either Sartre or Genet would have had any truck with the shoddy science and rigged data that has led to the recent alleged discovery of a 'gay' gene, but the question of how far we choose our own sexuality is a complex and still open one. However, it is not the heart of the argument. As Sartre puts it: 'The important thing is not what is made of us, but what we ourselves make of what has been made of us.'[27] The issue is not whether Genet chose to be a homosexual, but how he chose himself *as* a homosexual. One does not choose to be female, black or Jewish, but one chooses how one assumes such an identity. Hence Sartre's insistence that Genet's talent is not a mysterious given ('mildew of the brain, a supernumerary bone'),[28] but rather invented by Genet in response to his agonising situation.

In the concluding summary of *Saint Genet* Sartre states his aim in writing the book: 'to show the limits of psychoanalytic interpretation and Marxist explanation and to show that only freedom can give an account of the totality of a person'.[29] In this sense *Saint Genet* stands in the middle of Sartre's series of existential biographies from Baudelaire to Flaubert. Not every petty-bourgeois is Valéry, and not every gay thief is Genet. Sartre's constant preoccupation is with inserting the question of freedom into Marxism. Such was the dominance of Stalinism over French intellectual life before 1968 that Sartre was not always aware that what he was trying to achieve was not introducing freedom to Marxism, but rather restoring it to the rightful place it had at the heart of Marxism from the 1844 manuscripts onwards. Marxism is a theory of the self-activity and self-emancipation of the working class; human freedom and human praxis were always at its heart until it was transformed into a deterministic ideology by Stalinism. The fact that Sartre made his *rapprochement* with the PCF carrying *Saint Genet* in his intellectual baggage is an indication that he had by no means subscribed fully to the Stalinist distortion of Marxism.

Another of Sartre's preoccupations in the *Cahiers* was the question of ends and means. Sartre rejected the proposition that 'the end justifies the means'; that, he points out, would imply a view of history in which ends are already given and means are simply the quickest route to attaining them.[30] For Sartre, history involves the invention of ends as well as means. Socialism is not something already clearly defined which may be reached a little quicker if we adopt brutal means. On the contrary, the quality of socialism we achieve will depend on the means we have used to get it. As Sartre and Merleau-Ponty wrote in 1949, a socialism that bases itself on labour camps does not deserve the name of socialism.[31]

So for Sartre what matters is the dialectical interaction of means and ends (his formulations in the *Cahiers* are greatly indebted to Trotsky's essay *Their Morals and Ours*). This same problematic underlies the structure of *Saint Genet*, with the account of the three metamorphoses that went to make up the writer Genet. Genet begins by simply inverting the categories of good and evil presented by bourgeois society; he pursues evil for evil's sake, which, like art for art's sake, attacks accepted values but fails to go beyond them; and only when he transcends this dichotomy instead of merely reproducing it, by becoming an aesthete and then a writer, does he become 'Genet' as we know him, inventing himself as a unique individual.

In *Le Diable et le bon dieu* (1951) Sartre produces a variation of Genet's evolution. Goetz, the hero of this drama set in sixteenth-century Germany, begins as a pursuer of 'evil for evil's sake', in the same mould as Genet, except that he is powerful, and hence much more efficacious in his evil-doing. Goetz's first metamorphosis is to reject evil in favour of good, to pursue love; Sartre shows the vacuity of this Utopian project which ends in ruins. In the last moments of the play Goetz undergoes his second metamorphosis and becomes a political militant, ready to use violence that good may come out of it, rejecting morality in the name of praxis; the curtain falls as he leads his troops into a battle whose outcome we never know.

By studying the process of self-invention in Genet's biography, Sartre asserts the importance of seeing human history itself as a process of self-invention. Socialism is not exhausted by a simple definition (planned economy, etc.), but will be the product of human self-emancipation, just as Genet's *œuvre* is the product of a tortuous self-invention.

That Sartre did not have a thoroughly articulated critique of Stalinism when he wrote *Saint Genet* is shown by the bizarre parallel that he draws between Genet and Bukharin in the concluding pages. Sartre sees Bukharin, a member of the Bolshevik leadership in 1917, tried and murdered by Stalin in 1938, as a 'traitor' to Communism, just as Genet is a traitor to bourgeois society, evoking the same repulsion from Communists as Genet does from the respectable bourgeoisie.[32] Sartre seems here to be following Merleau-Ponty's defence of Stalinism in *Humanisme et terreur*,[33] using the example of Genet to justify the Stalinist purges. It is evidence of Sartre's recognition of the need to have 'dirty hands', but shows a complete failure to study concretely what means were employed by Stalinism and how those means conditioned, and were conditioned by, the ends. It is not one of the most creditable passages in *Saint Genet*; the best one can say is that the Stalinists were probably not happy to be defended in these terms.

But if *Saint Genet* embodies some of Sartre's reservations about the Stalinist Marxism he was on the point of embracing, it is also a Marxist work. The concepts of class and property are central to the account of Genet's childhood.

Sartre was later to lament that most Marxists see human beings as coming into existence the day they draw their first wage packet.[34] In *Saint Genet* he shows how a Marxist account of childhood must draw on concepts of ideology and hence of class. The whole ideology of private property helped to form the young Genet, and in particular enabled him to construct his experience of theft. 'Work, family, homeland, honesty, property: this is his conception of the Good, it is engraved for ever in his heart.'[35] (The first three terms were the Vichy slogan that replaced 'Liberty, equality and fraternity'.) Sartre argues that the fact that Genet was adopted by a peasant rather than a proletarian family was crucial to determining the set of values he rebelled against:

> If he had been placed in a working-class family, if he had lived in the suburbs of a city, if he had become used from his earliest years to hearing the very right of property challenged, or if his adoptive father had worked in a socialised sector of production, he would perhaps have learnt that one *is* also what one *does*.[36]

To this he contrasts what he sees as the essentially conservative consciousness of the peasantry, for whom 'one is formed by what one *has*; the peasant acquires the silent immobility of his field'.[37] (While Genet's adoptive father was in fact an artisan rather than a peasant, though he did own a cow and a meadow, Sartre's account is not seriously misleading, as the man was certainly not a proletarian and as Dichy and Fouché have pointed out, the rhythms of agricultural life were profoundly felt by the whole village.)[38]

In many ways this was a remarkable analysis for a French Marxist. Over twenty per cent of the French population were still engaged in agriculture, and a far greater proportion were only one generation off the land. For the PCF, as for every section of the French left, the peasantry were viewed as the solid allies of the proletariat; indeed, some of the PCF's strongest electoral bases were in peasant areas. French left intellectuals, from the historiographers of the French Revolution with their admiration of Robespierre's defence of small property ownership up to the Third-Worldists of 1968, have romanticised the peasantry. Sartre's blunt identification of the reactionary nature of peasant consciousness is one more reason why *Saint Genet* was such a cause of scandal.

Saint Genet's central concern is with Genet as a writer. Sartre had already set out his view of 'committed literature' in *Qu'est-ce que la littérature?* (1947). *Saint Genet* offers an opportunity to assess Sartre's concept of commitment in literature applied to the case of a particular writer, and indeed undermines some of the stereotypes that have been ascribed to *Qu'est-ce que la littérature?*

Sartre is often accused of taking a narrowly instrumental attitude towards literature, and of rejecting poetry in favour of prose. But if we take the definition he offers in *Qu'est-ce que la littérature?* – that the prose writer uses language but the poet refuses to *use* it[39] (in other words, for the poet language is not a means to an end but an end in itself) – it is clear that in many ways Genet is more of a prose poet than a prose writer in the normal sense. In *Orphée noir* (1948) Sartre had already argued enthusiastically that 'the only great revolutionary poetry' of that time was that of the black francophone writers of Africa and the West Indies.[40] In *Saint Genet* he develops an account of literary language far more complex than anything to be found in his earlier writings.

Douglas Collins argues that 'Genet's writings ... are far removed from every essential feature of engaged literature as described by Sartre in *What is Literature?* Genet in fact stands the old Sartrean ideal on its head and is praised for so doing.'[41] But Collins is operating with too narrow a concept of politics; if 'politics' is about the whole question of how human beings can liberate themselves from oppression, then Sartre is right to see Genet as a highly political writer.

Certainly Genet saw himself as being in some sense a committed writer. Edmund White claims that 'he did not see his plays as political', citing in his support the passage from the *Playboy* interview where Genet asserts that 'a direct struggle against colonialism does much more for Blacks than a play.'[42] But he omits the immediately following passage in which Genet states: 'I tried to get a hearing for a profound voice which the Blacks and all alienated beings could not get to be heard'[43] – a much more 'committed' statement.

'No-one could imagine for a moment that it is possible to write a good novel in praise of anti-Semitism', claimed Sartre in *Qu'est-ce que la littérature?*,[44] a proposition that has persistently aroused wrathful fulminations, mainly from those who have not troubled to enquire what he actually meant by it. Sartre is arguing that a work of literature which dehumanises its Jewish (or black, or female, or gay) characters is betraying itself as literature. Shakespeare may have been an anti-Semite – but *The Merchant of Venice* is not an anti-Semitic work, because Shylock is given some of the best lines in the play to defend himself. Likewise Sartre claims, quite explicitly and perhaps exaggeratedly, that Genet was an anti-Semite; but he also stresses that this 'anti-Semitism' derives from Genet's recognition of Jews as oppressed. He is not writing 'in defence' of anti-Semitism; rather, the impetus for his writing is a hatred of oppression, which would lead him to *Les Nègres*.

Sartre thus made use of Genet in planning out his own political path; equally Sartre may have influenced Genet in his subsequent evolution. Moraly has written of what he calls the 'fourth metamorphosis' of Genet's career, his transformation into a political activist and writer. In his last interview Genet declared that he was 'on Lenin's side'.[45] There is at least a possibility that Sartre assisted in this metamorphosis. In *Saint Genet* he declares, in an almost taunting tone:

A wicked person who claims to be such succeeds only in propping up social morality since he admits that evil is abominable. He would be much more feared if he consented to call himself a revolutionary. As a Communist, Genet would be worthy of the hatred of the bourgeoisie; but he is only wicked.[46]

Moraly quotes an article from *Paris-Presse L'intransigeant* (30 December 1952) to the effect that Genet had applied to join the PCF but had been turned down.[47] If this is true it is interesting to note that the date comes just after the publication of *Saint Genet*; Genet may well have been rising to Sartre's challenge to make himself more dangerous, for there seems little else to instigate such a move in Genet's thought and work at the time.

It is ironic that in the end Genet came far closer to the PCF than Sartre; in the 1970s it was Genet, and not Sartre, who was a welcome contributor to *L'Humanité*, while Sartre was reviled for his Maoist links. In 1974 Genet publicly attacked Sartre in the columns of *L'Humanité*,[48] allegedly for failing to support the struggles of immigrant workers, but in fact for not campaigning for François Mitterrand in the presidential election. (Genet's pro-Soviet stance in his later years may have derived from a hope that the USSR would assist the Palestinian cause as well as from a desire to outrage.)

At the time of the writing of *Saint Genet*, Genet had not produced his best works of revolutionary theatre, namely *Le Balcon*, *Les Nègres* and *Les Paravents*. Sartre himself is on record as saying that he did not find Genet's later theatre as impressive as his earlier writings and that he did not see *Le Balcon* as a political play.[49] Whether Sartre influenced their production or merely predicted it is impossible to disentangle; what is certain is that *Saint Genet* is both the recognition of a revolutionary writer and a revolutionary text in its own right.

NOTES

1 'Jean-Paul Sartre et les homosexuels' in *Le Gai Pied*, 13 April 1980, pp. 1, 11–14 (Sartre interviewed by Jean Le Bitoux and Gilles Barbedette).
2 Edmund White, *Genet* (London, 1993), pp. 437–9.
3 Susan Sontag, *Against interpretation* (London, 1967), p. 97.
4 Jean-Paul Sartre, *Situations VI* (Paris, 1964), p. 168.
5 Robert Kemp, 'Répugnances' in *Les Nouvelles littéraires*, 14 August 1952, p. 3.
6 Antony Copley, *Sexual Moralities in France 1780–1980* (London, 1989), pp. 193, 215; Daniel Guérin, *Son Testament* (Paris, 1979), p. 104.
7 Ian Birchall, *Workers Against the Monolith* (London, 1974), pp. 134–5.
8 André Breton, *Position politique du surréalisme* (Paris, 1972), p. 99.
9 Jean Kanapa, *L'Existentialisme n'est pas un humanisme* (Paris, 1947), p. 97.
10 Jean-Bernard Moraly, *Jean Genet – La vie écrite* (Paris, 1988), p. 230.
11 Cf Jean-Pierre Januel in *Masques*, No 2, Autumn 1979, pp. 111–12.
12 Jean Genet, *Œuvres Complètes IV* (Paris, 1968), p. 76.
13 Andrei Zhdanov [Jdanov], *Sur la littérature, la philosophie et la musique* (Paris, 1972), pp. 63–4.

14 *L'Humanité*, 12 March 1949; cited in Philip Thody, *Jean Genet* (London, 1968), p. 161.

15 Edmund White, *Genet* (London, 1993), p. 353.

16 Jean-Paul Sartre, *Cahiers pour une morale* (Paris, 1983), p. 338.

17 Jean-Paul Sartre, *Cahiers pour une morale* (Paris, 1983), p. 190.

18 Jean Genet, *Œuvres Complètes IV* (Paris, 1968), p. 49.

19 Jean-Paul Sartre, *Réflexions sur la question juive* (Paris, 1946).

20 See Note 1 above.

21 Edmund White, *Genet* (London, 1993), p. 643.

22 Jean-Bernard Moraly, *Jean Genet – La vie écrite* (Paris, 1988), pp. 147–8.

23 Jean-Paul Sartre, *Saint Genet, comédien et martyr* (Paris, 1952), p. 230.

24 Edmund White, *Genet* (London, 1993), p. 564.

25 Albert Dichy (ed.), *L'Ennemi déclaré: textes et entretiens* in Jean Genet, *Œuvres Complètes VI* (Paris, 1991), p. 24.

26 Albert Dichy (ed.), *L'Ennemi déclaré: textes et entretiens* in Jean Genet, *Œuvres Complètes VI* (Paris, 1991), p. 12.

27 Jean-Paul Sartre, *Saint Genet, comédien et martyr* (Paris, 1952), p. 63.

28 Jean-Paul Sartre, *Saint Genet, comédien et martyr* (Paris, 1952), p. 629.

29 Jean-Paul Sartre, *Saint Genet, comédien et martyr* (Paris, 1952), p. 645.

30 Jean-Paul Sartre, *Cahiers pour une morale* (Paris, 1983), p. 191.

31 'Les Jours de notre vie' in *Les Temps modernes*, 51, January 1950, pp. 1153–68; the article was written by Merleau-Ponty, but carried Sartre's name.

32 Jean-Paul Sartre, *Saint Genet, comédien et martyr* (Paris, 1952), pp. 655–8.

33 Maurice Merleau-Ponty, *Humanisme et terreur* (Paris, 1947).

34 Jean-Paul Sartre, *Critique de la raison dialectique* (Paris, 1960), p. 47.

35 Jean-Paul Sartre, *Saint Genet, comédien et martyr* (Paris, 1952), p. 14.

36 Jean-Paul Sartre, *Saint Genet, comédien et martyr* (Paris, 1952), p. 18.

37 Jean-Paul Sartre, *Saint Genet, comédien et martyr* (Paris, 1952), p. 19.

38 Albert Dichy and Pascal Fouché (eds), *Jean Genet: essai de chronolgie* (Paris, 1988), pp. 30–1.

39 Jean-Paul Sartre, *Qu'est-ce que la littérature?* (Paris, 1964), p. 17.

40 Jean-Paul Sartre, *Situations III* (Paris, 1952), p. 233.

41 Douglas Collins, *Sartre as Biographer* (Cambridge, Mass, 1980), p. 101.

42 Edmund White, *Genet* (London, 1993), p. 488.

43 Albert Dichy (ed.), *L'Ennemi déclaré: textes et entretiens* in Jean Genet, *Œuvres Complètes VI* (Paris, 1991), p. 23.

44 Jean-Paul Sartre, *Qu'est-ce que la littérature?* (Paris, 1964), p. 80.

45 Albert Dichy (ed.), *L'Ennemi déclaré: textes et entretiens* in Jean Genet, *Œuvres Complètes VI* (Paris, 1991), p. 304. (See also Chapter 6 of this book.)

46 Jean-Paul Sartre, *Saint Genet, comédien et martyr* (Paris, 1952), p. 194.

47 Jean-Bernard Moraly, *Jean Genet – La vie écrite* (Paris, 1948), p. 230; see also *Aux Écoutes du monde*, 6 January 1956, p. 27, which reports that both Genet and Sartre have joined the PCF!

48 'Jean Genet et la condition des immigrés' in *L'Humanité*, 3 May 1974, p. 12.

49 Jean-Paul Sartre, 'La police frappe les trois coups …' in *Situations VII* (Paris, 1965), p. 316.

CHAPTER 19

Genet and Artaud: The crematorium and the slaughterhouse

Stephen Barber

WHAT CONNECTS JEAN Genet and Antonin Artaud most tangibly is the extraordinary figure of Paule Thévenin, and the role she played as friend, editor and dominant negotiator in the lives and work of these two writers. When Paule Thévenin died in September of 1993, I wrote in an obituary of how she had been involved in the work of the two most 'extreme' figures of twentieth century French writing, Artaud and Genet. But in dealing simultaneously with Artaud and Genet, it is vital to emphasise that these are extremities at a tangent, extremities in two parallel creative worlds. These extremes are those of initiating and sustaining an exploration into the raw matter of human existence and sexuality, into the active disintegration of the links between identity and society. They are also extremes of language, carried by work which examines how the linguistic may be transformed or fragmented into new configurations that project with intensity the sensations of the physical, the compulsion for reinvention, and the moral duty to renounce and execrate national identity and its imageries. Those are the tangents at which the work of Genet and Artaud mesh with as great a degree of tension and resistance as of coincidence.

The period of time in which the work of Artaud and Genet intersected in Paris was in the immediate postwar years. After Artaud had undertaken his notorious and influential 'Theatre of Cruelty' project in the mid-1930s, he left Paris and embarked on journeys to Mexico and to Ireland, from where he was deported in September 1937, and spent the next nine years in a number of French lunatic asylums. He emerged from the last asylum, Rodez, in May 1946 and returned to Paris, where he had been notorious as a leading member of the Surrealist movement in the mid-1920s. Jean Genet's penal incarceration had ended much earlier, on 15 March 1944, several months before the liberation of Paris from the German occupying forces. Within days of his return to Paris, Artaud came into contact with Paule Thévenin, who at that time was in her early twenties. She first visited Artaud to ask him to record his new work for a radio programme with which she was involved, and Artaud consented. In his solitude at the asylum of Rodez, Artaud had elaborated an imaginary family of erotic warrior-children which he named his 'daughters of the heart to be born' – daughters who would fight battles to liberate him from the asylums, and would also bring him the large quantities of heroin which were being denied him there. Artaud immediately incorporated Paule Thévenin into this bizarre and transformational family of daughters, the first living woman to receive such a distinction.

Artaud's first radio recording was not a success, but in the following year, 1947, he was invited to record a long broadcast by the head of literary programmes at Radiodiffusion Française, Fernand Pouey. Artaud made his recording, which he titled *Pour en finir avec le jugement de dieu*, with three collaborators: Paule Thévenin, the theatre director Roger Blin and the actress Maria Casarès. All three of these collaborators would also be crucial in Jean Genet's theatrical work. *Pour en finir avec le jugement de dieu* was the first stage in Artaud's project to resuscitate the Theatre of Cruelty, but this time with the determination that it would not be assimilated into the Parisian literary milieu in the way that his performances of the 1930s had been. His texts written for the recording delineate a ferociously surreal post-war world of autopsied bodies, schoolboys' semen and deliriously dancing figures engaged in a terminal battle against the reviled figure of 'god'. Artaud interposed his spoken texts with passages of screaming and with improvised glossolaliac duets which he recorded with Roger Blin. Artaud's recording was banned by the head of the radio station on the day before it was due to be transmitted in February 1948. The grounds given were that it was inflammatory, obscene and blasphemous. Fernand Pouey, who had commissioned the work, then threatened to resign as a matter of principle. Although it is usually claimed that Pouey lost his job, this was apparently not the case – his widow told me in 1987 that the scandal blew over – and in the same year, 1948, Pouey also commissioned a broadcast from Jean Genet.

This was *L'Enfant criminel*, in which Genet wrote of the necessary cruelty of the Mettray reformatory for boys, where he had spent the years from 1926 to 1929: 'These cruelties had to be born and to develop necessarily out of the desire of these children for evil'.[1] Like Artaud's conception of cruelty, Genet depicts a force of cruelty which is integral and self-willed, intentional rather than imposed by exterior forces. With an irrational and discursive precision which approaches that of Artaud's own broadcast, Genet writes of the bogus society which comprises his intended audience of radio listeners. And where Artaud had depicted a calamitous post-war world in which visions of genocide and suppression had sustained themselves and remained dominant, Genet likewise emphasises the survival of these imageries into the contemporary world, while also paralleling them with his world of Mettray. He wrote: 'The newspapers still show these photographs of corpses caught on the barbed wire fencing, in the crematorium ovens; they show nails torn off, tattooed skin ... A rose is growing to become a plant of incredible beauty, whose twisted and tortured petals show up red – a rose under the sun of hell, naming terrible names: Maïdenek, Belsen, Auschwitz, Mauthausen, Dora ... But nobody knows that for as long as the children's prisons have existed in France, the children and men there have also been tortured.'[2] For Genet the immediate imageries transmitted by the international media connected intimately with the world of his own identity and existence, in which the reformatory of Mettray had been a source of torture, but also, overwhelmingly, an enduring origin of elation, desire and joy. Similarly, for Artaud the first intimations of the Cold War nuclear confrontations between Stalinist Russia and the corrupt Western world were channelled insistently into his own exhilarated creative imageries, in which an apocalyptic nuclear attack would pale into insignificance when balanced against Artaud's own project for a reconstituted human body of delirious gestural violence.

Genet's planned broadcast of *L'Enfant criminel* met with the same fate as Artaud's *Pour en finir avec le jugement de dieu*: it was censored by the radio station and was not recorded or transmitted; Genet published it as a text in 1949, while *Pour en finir avec le jugement de dieu* also appeared only in an inadequate textual version. Artaud died from a self-administered overdose of chloral hydrate in March 1948, at the age of fifty-one, shortly after the banning of this recorded work. Throughout the last two years of Artaud's life, Paule Thévenin had worked with him, preparing his manuscripts and supporting him through his many quarrels with old ambivalent enemies such as the Surrealist leader André Breton. Her husband Yves Thévenin, regularly supplied Artaud with morphine (just as he was to provide Genet with Nembutal in future years) and so incurred the wrath of Artaud's family, who claimed that young friends of Artaud's such as the Thévenins had hastened his death. This led to over four decades of court cases and harassment since soon after Artaud's death Paule Thévenin took on the massive task of editing Artaud's *Œuvres Complètes* for publication, an almost life-long project which remained unfinished at the time of her death in 1993. Artaud had entrusted her with this work on the day before he died by making her his literary executor. Genet, too, was at one time to appoint Paule Thévenin as his literary executor, but his demands on their relationship ensured that such an arrangement could not be sustained. While for Artaud Paule Thévenin was the faithful and silently protective daughter, for Genet she perhaps played two roles of greater intricacy – that of the solicitous collaborator and that of the tenaciously vocal mother.

The imagery of the crematorium oven which Genet developed in *L'Enfant criminel* was also persistent in Artaud's recasting of the Theatre of Cruelty in the months after his release from the asylum of Rodez. In a text written in August 1946 and intended to serve as the introduction to his *Œuvres Complètes*, Artaud wrote: 'The theatre is the scaffold, the gallows, the corpses cut into pieces, the crematorium oven or the lunatic asylum./Cruelty is the massacre of human bodies.'[3] He was preoccupied at this point by memories of two of his closest friends from the 1930s who had died in the wartime concentration camps, the Surrealist poet Robert Desnos and the painter Sonia Mossé. And in Artaud's writings on theatre from the 1930s, he had initiated ideas of a theatrical event which would act with a unique impact of conflagration upon its spectators, making them participants in a feral experience whose imagery was one of a consuming fire and of gesture. Most notoriously, Artaud wrote of the participants of his desired theatre being 'like torture victims who are being burned and who are making signs from the stake'.[4]

But, despite this related obsession in the work of Artaud and Genet, it seems certain that they never met in these post-war years, despite the fact that they both inhabited the St Germain-des-Prés cafés such as the Café Flore and had mutual friends. This may have been because Genet was associated in Artaud's mind with literary figures such as Jean Cocteau or Jean-Paul Sartre, a figure whom Artaud would claim to 'abominate', as his friend Jacques Prevel recalled.[5] It should be noted in this context that Sartre had willingly donated a manuscript to an auction designed to raise funds to guarantee Artaud's release from the asylum. It may also have been that Artaud, who was notably unreceptive to the literary milieu that surrounded him, would have viewed Genet with hostility as just another young writer. As Artaud remarked to Prevel in 1946: 'When I hear people talking about a new poet, I want to shoot him at point-blank range.'[6] This fury was reserved especially for upstarts such as the young 'Lettrist' poets Isidore Isou and François Dufrêne, but Genet's status in these years may have evoked for Artaud the sudden and shameless notoriety which he associated with the Lettrists. Both Artaud and Genet had a considerable number of publishers in these years, notably Marc Barbezat of the publishing house l'Arbalète, who was engaged in publishing work by both writers; they had also shared a publisher in Robert Denoël, murdered in a Paris street in December 1945, shortly before Artaud's release from the asylum of Rodez. Denoël had also published books by Louis-Ferdinand Céline which had been denounced as anti-Semitic, and though he appeared to have been the victim of a random shooting as he was changing the wheel of his car, in retrospect it seems likely that he was assassinated because of his alleged former role as a collaborator with the German occupying forces.

Of course, it may well have been that Genet himself would have been reluctant to meet Artaud, rather than the other way round. Artaud was a forbidding presence, but also an unrecognisable one, since the nine years of his asylum internment and his fifty electroshock treatments there had transformed him from the handsome Surrealist poet and film actor of the 1920s and 1930s, into a toothless, invective old man who expectorated insults and poems simultaneously. We could assume that they would have had at least some elements of common experience, both having spent time at the Sainte-Anne psychiatric hospital in Paris – Genet had been there under psychiatric observation as a fifteen-year-old youth in 1925, while Artaud had spent several periods of drug disintoxication there in the mid-1930s before being compulsorily interned under Jacques Lacan from 1938 to 1939, as a prelude to being transferred to the asylum of Ville-Évrard and then on to Rodez. Moreover Genet and Artaud had a common interest in the figure of the third-century Roman Emperor Heliogabalus, whose four-year reign had been characterised by murder, incest, debauchery and a nihilistic disdain for the powers of government, before he was himself murdered by his own bodyguards and thrown into a sewer. Artaud had written a biography of Heliogabalus for Robert Denoël in 1933 and Genet had written a play around Heliogabalus's life in the early 1940s for the young actor Jean Marais.

Another, less coincidental, bond between Genet and Artaud was their openly enthusiastic response to the fall of France to the invading German army in 1940. From his asylum, Artaud regarded the events of the Second World War as being vaguely apocalyptic, but his indifference to the fate of the French nation was immovable. His view of the corruption of France ranged with adept flexibility from the sexual to the criminal to the linguistic. For Artaud the humiliation of France presented the opportunity for a curative searing of both its infected and exhausted language and its complicitous and passive population. Artaud, along with Genet, desired a France so perverted, execrated and debased that it would finally produce a maximal, extraordinary purity that would saturate every level of human existence. And for both Artaud and Genet, the ultimate desire was that the France that had maliciously incarcerated and refused them both would be annihilated.

The meeting between Paule Thévenin and Genet came in the mid-1960s, nearly twenty years after Artaud's death. In the intervening years, Paule Thévenin had worked incessantly on the editing of Artaud's *Œuvres Complètes*, although due to the opposition of Artaud's family only two volumes had so far appeared and Paule Thévenin was compelled to perform the task anonymously. Certainly by this time her attitude and thinking were saturated with Artaud's writings, which demanded absolute rigour and lack of compromise; however, she was also preoccupied with left-wing politics, having from childhood been a close friend and supporter of Roland Dumas, who would become President Mitterrand's foreign minister in the 1980s. Politics of any kind had always been anathema to Artaud, especially since the Surrealists' affiliation with the French Communist Party in 1926 had proved to be one of the many reasons for his expulsion from the Surrealist group in that year. According to different accounts, Paule Thévenin was introduced to Genet either by the publisher Marc Barbezat or, more probably, by Roger Blin, who in the time since his collaboration with Artaud had become one of the most innovative and provocative theatre directors in Paris, celebrated most notably for his 1953 production of Samuel Beckett's *Waiting for Godot*. At this time Genet was working on his final and most ambitious play, *Les Paravents*, and he needed someone who could help him prepare the vast manuscript of the play, which Roger Blin was to direct at the Odéon theatre in Paris in the spring of 1966, with a cast which included Artaud's former collaborators Maria Casarès and Jean-Louis Barrault. Roger Blin had previously directed the first production of Genet's play *Les Nègres* in 1959. Genet had been working on *Les Paravents* since 1956, and its evolution was marked by the depth of his formulations about the dynamics of his theatre, which became articulated in the numerous notes and letters which he wrote to Roger Blin during preparations for the production. Paule Thévenin collected and edited these notes for publication, and also edited a text which Genet wrote at the same time, *L'Étrange mot d'* ... It is in this work, through the intermediation of Paule Thévenin, that the intersection of Artaud's and Genet's ideas about the necessities and the nature of performance is most clearly marked.

In his notes from the time of *Les Paravents*, Genet writes again of the crematorium, this time as the authentic site of a theatrical act which he believes should take place in extreme proximity to both fire and death, and also close to the heart of the city. In Genet's conception of the performance space, the act takes precedence over the demands both of death and of life. The ideal performance would take place in a cemetery from which all but a few fragments of tombs would be cleared, so that the intimation, dignity and gravity of death are transmitted to that performance. Similarly, in Artaud's theatre, life itself is subordinated to this vital gravity of the event, which imprints the existence of its spectators with the gesture of performance. Genet argues that theatre is dispensable in the face of an act of revolution; however crucial the experience of theatre may be, it is superseded by the force of revolution. He writes: 'If, one day, human actions were to become more and more revolutionary, the theatre would no longer have any place in life.'[7] But for Artaud revolution and theatre are so seamlessly and violently welded together, in an imagery of the insurgent human body and its recreated languages, that such a detachment between theatre and revolution is inconceivable. What attracts Genet to the crematorium is the stiff phallus of the chimney, spurting smoke and ashes, while for Artaud the essential element of the performance space is its capacity to roar cacophonically with human and mechanical noise, so his idealised space is the factory.

More crucially, both Artaud and Genet envisage the desired performance as unique, disintegrating the nature of representation and repetition itself. While he was preparing his recording *Pour en finir avec le jugement de dieu*, Artaud

wrote: 'I abject all signs./I create only machines of instant utility.'[8] His projected
unique event of gestural cruelty would fracture the constraints placed on human
consciousness and resuscitate existence, which for Artaud had become
incapacitated and duplicated. In his writings from the time of *Les Paravents*,
Genet too projected an incendiary event which would be unrepeatably urgent
and immediate, and would, he said, 'illuminate the world of the dead'.[9] He
aimed for what he called 'a unique performance, possessing such an immense
and radiating intensity that it will act to inflame its spectators, thereby also
illuminating and disturbing all those who were not present'.[10] The extravagant
conception and sheer length of *Les Paravents* ensured that although it was
staged for a number of performances it retained this sense of a distinctive and
powerful unrepeatability. Genet was also concerned to isolate his own theatre
from theatre in general, to create a barrier between his work and that of theatre
as a literary and social definition and movement. He placed his valorisation on
the essential dirt, outrage and invective of his theatre, which he said would leave
his spectators with the physical taste of ashes and corruption in their mouths.
Just as Artaud always demanded that the existing moribund theatre should be
destroyed in order for his own theatre of plague and cruelty to be brought into
existence, so Genet conceived of an origin for his own theatre in its separation
from the reprehensible cleanliness of the existing theatre. He wrote: 'If my
theatre stinks, it's because the other smells good.'[11] Artaud, in his work of the
late 1940s, would assert that all vital creative work was undertaken by
exploration into the dirt of existence; writing in 1946 of his journey to Mexico
undertaken ten years earlier, he noted: 'I have come to Mexico to make contact
with the Red Earth/and it stinks in its fragrance;/and it smells good in its stink.'[12]
He also reversed what he viewed as the social definitions of health and illness,
declaring that his own state of lifelong sickness was more authentic and urgent
than that of health, which he considered an abject surrender to human and
social complacency.

The role of the performer in Genet's theatre is conceived with a rigour that
parallels Artaud's own view of the absolute subjugation of the Theatre of
Cruelty's actor to the director. But Artaud and Genet both allowed for a
resurgence of the will of the performer in exceptional conditions. Genet wrote
to Roger Blin: 'Never allow the actor to forget himself, unless this self-
forgetfulness were to be pushed to the point where he would piss in front of the
audience.'[13] For Artaud this state of unleashed oblivion in the performer would
be potentially more dangerous – at the time of the 1930's Theatre of Cruelty, he
wrote that fury generated in the actor would lead to unstoppable acts of
justifiable criminality such as murder; later, in a letter to André Breton about his
own performance of furious screams and denunciations at the Vieux-Colombier
theatre in 1947, he concluded that his ideal performer would now be one who,

he wrote, 'would bring bombs out of his pockets and throw them in the audience's face with a blatant gesture of aggression'.[14] Certainly, Artaud's ideal and ultimately only performer was himself, exposed and furious on the stage of the Vieux-Colombier, whereas Genet's theatre remained exterior to this volatile arena of the performer subject to chance, oblivion and violence.

As Genet wrote to Roger Blin: 'The theatre is a place close to death, where all liberties are possible.'[15] When Genet travelled to Japan in the second half of the 1960s, he would have witnessed something of the huge impact which Artaud's work was exerting in all areas of performance and art there, most notably in the Japanese Butoh dance form, initiated by Tatsumi Hijikata, a close collaborator of the novelist Yukio Mishima. It might well be argued that in the entire field of theatre and performance, Artaud's theories have only ever inspired one experiment of real value, Butoh. Hijikata developed performances of contorted gesture and insurgent sexuality whose primary inspiration in their imageries of death and resuscitation was Artaud's recorded scream; Hijikata would claim at the end of his life (he died in the same year as Genet, 1986) that the only one of his possessions to which he accorded any value whatsoever was his cassette of *Pour en finir avec le jugement de dieu*. Like the work of Genet and of Artaud, Hijikata's Butoh performances were unique projections of voids and absences, of violences and exclamations.

On his return from Japan, Genet undertook no further theatrical projects. Instead, from the end of the 1960s to the mid-1980s, the principal years of his friendship with Paule Thévenin, he engaged himself politically and morally with the Black Panthers in the United States, with the Red Army Faction in Germany and with the Palestinians in their exile. With these ambiguously political involvements Genet certainly moved away from most of Artaud's concerns, but it was in the context of his connection with the Black Panthers that Genet made his only explicit written reference to Artaud. In his introduction to the prison letters of George Jackson, written in July 1970 in Brazil, Genet notes that 'a certain complicity links the works written in prisons or asylums (Sade and Artaud share the same necessity of finding in themselves what must lead them to glory, that is, despite the walls, the moats, the jailers and the magistrates, into the light, into minds not enslaved)'.[16] The evident implication is that we can, with Genet's authority, put Genet himself in the Marquis de Sade's place. We are able to distinguish the alliance of a determinedly self-willed exploration into identity and liberation between Artaud and Genet.

During their friendship Paule Thévenin closely advised Genet on his courses of action, notably in the matter of his film *Un Chant d'Amour*. In 1975, the producer of *Un Chant d'Amour*, Nico Papatakis, arranged for the film to be submitted for a censorship visa to allow its first commercial release. The film, which had been shot in 1950, was presented as having been recently made, and won a prize which Genet angrily rejected in a piece in the newspaper *L'Humanité* (13 August 1975). As Nico Papatakis commented in his interview with Jane Giles for her book on *Un Chant d'Amour*: 'Maybe I was the closest friend he had outside of his boyfriends, but Paule Thévenin took him. He put himself into the political things. He went close to the Communists and the whole thing was – God! – a mess.'[17] It is certainly true that Paule Thévenin conducted her quarrels in the Parisian literary world as a kind of guerrilla warfare, inciting fear and awe in equal measures. Gaston Ferdière, Artaud's psychiatrist at Rodez, told me in 1987: 'I fear that woman more than anything in this world.' Paule Thévenin reassured both Artaud and Genet of their status as poets; her respect and commitment to these two writers was absolute. But while Artaud and Paule Thévenin were still strongly allied at the time of Artaud's death in 1948, Genet deserted her as a friend two or three years before he died in April 1986. Paule Thévenin's version of this break, told both to me and to Genet's biographer Edmund White, was that Genet, who was suffering from throat cancer, was distressed by the death of her husband from the same disease, and consequently shunned her because she was a constant reminder to him of his own mortality. But it may well have been that her intense and extensive literary contacts and entanglements – and her preoccupation with completing her edition of Artaud's *Œuvres Complètes* – ultimately proved alienating to Genet.

Since the AIDS-related deaths of Hervé Guibert in 1991 and Cyril Collard in 1993, the only living French writer who could be compared to Artaud and Genet is Pierre Guyotat, whose most significant work, the novel *Éden, Éden, Éden* was published in an English translation in 1995. Guyotat has acknowledged the debt of inspiration he owes to Genet and Artaud with his performances of 'active homages', appearing at an Artaud event in the early 1970s, and also at the event organized at the Odéon theatre in Paris to mark the twenty-fifth anniversary of the production of Genet's *Les Paravents* in 1991. Guyotat provoked great controversy in France in 1970 when *Éden, Éden, Éden* (his third novel) was published by Gallimard and was immediately subjected to censorship restrictions by the French Ministry of the Interior; these restrictions remained in force until the election of Mitterrand in 1981. A number of French writers, including Genet and Roland Barthes, supported Guyotat through what for him was an atrocious experience, documented in his *Littérature interdite* (1972). Paule Thévenin also took up Guyotat's cause with tenacity, and her friend Roland Dumas became his lawyer. Guyotat's work deals with acts of prostitution which constantly expand in scale, intensity and number. His world, like Genet's, is inhabited by boy prostitutes, the odour of sperm and death, and by a pervasive violence which is transformed into the origins of a new language of human identity. This language in his writing is welded into a headlong, exclamatory rush towards extreme obscenity. And like Artaud, Guyotat views the act of writing as a raw exudation of physical material, creatively expectorating deadly substances which are savage and interrogative in their impact upon the reader and the spectator. Most recently, in 1989 and in 1993 in Paris, and in 1995 in London, Guyotat has undertaken a series of extraordinary semi-improvisational performances.

All three of these utterly independent writers – Genet, Artaud and Guyotat – speak with blunt and sensational desire against the apparition of society. The action of writing becomes a disciplined and committed intervention which cracks censorship wide open in all its horror.

[The translations in this chapter are by the author.]

NOTES

1 Jean Genet, *L'Enfant criminel* in *Œuvres Complètes V* (Paris, 1979), p. 383.

2 Jean Genet, *L'Enfant criminel* in *Œuvres Complètes V* (Paris, 1979), p. 389.

3 Antonin Artaud, *Préambule* in *Œuvres Complètes I* (Paris, 1976), p. 11.

4 Antonin Artaud, *Le Théâtre et Culture* in *Œuvres Complètes IV* (Paris, 1980), p. 14.

5 Jacques Prevel, *En compagnie d'Antonin Artaud* (Paris, 1974), p. 36.

6 Jacques Prevel, *En compagnie d'Antonin Artaud* (Paris, 1974), p. 56.

7 Jean Genet, *L'Étrange mot d'* ... in *Œuvres Complètes IV* (Paris, 1968), p. 16.

8 Antonin Artaud's notes for *Pour en finir avec le jugement de dieu* in *Œuvres Complètes XIII* (Paris, 1974), p. 273.

9 Jean Genet, *Lettres à Roger Blin* in *Œuvres Complètes IV* (Paris, 1968), p. 11.

10 Jean Genet, *L'Étrange mot d'* ... in *Œuvres Complètes IV* (Paris, 1968), p. 15.

11 Jean Genet, *L'Étrange mot d'* ... in *Œuvres Complètes IV* (Paris, 1968), p. 13.

12 Antonin Artaud, *La Culture Indienne* in *Œuvres Complètes XII* (Paris, 1974), p. 71.

13 Jean Genet, *Lettres à Roger Blin* in *Œuvres Complètes IV* (Paris, 1968), p. 13.

14 Antonin Artaud, *Lettres à André Breton* in *L'Éphémère*, 8, 1968, p. 21.

15 Jean Genet, *Lettres à Roger Blin* in *Œuvres Complètes IV* (Paris, 1968), p. 12.

16 Jean Genet, Introduction to *Soledad Brother: the Prison Letters of George Jackson* (London, 1971), p. 18.

17 Jane Giles, *The Cinema of Jean Genet: Un Chant d'Amour* (London, 1991), p. 73.

CHAPTER 20

Publishing Adventures

Albert Dichy

Editor's note: This article was first published in *Le Monde*, 10 September 1993.

THE STORY IS so good it must be true: the brochure with Genet's first poem, *Le Condamné à Mort*, is said to have been run off – one hundred copies at the author's own expense – by a man who printed forged food coupons. So it was under the auspices of falsification that Genet, a dealer in corrosive material – '*My hand smuggled in a burden of grief*' – entered the world of literature in 1942, in the middle of the German Occupation.

It would be an understatement to say he was not expected. Genet remained true to his principles as a thief, and it was through a concealed door, clandestine publishing, that he broke into the 'house'. Of the five novels he published between 1943 and 1948, and which constitute the main portion of his work, only *Miracle de la Rose* bears the name of a publishing house, L'Arbalète. And it will always be to the lasting honour of Marc Barbezat that he was the only publisher who had the courage to put his name on the first edition of a novel by Genet.

The four other books appeared 'under cover' and without a publisher's name. Three of them carry the traditional formulation used on erotic works: 'Published privately by a book-lover'. It was in the context of books said to be 'for private circulation only' that Genet's first works saw the light of day. Today we know the names of the anonymous publishers of these first books: the publication of *Notre-Dame-des-Fleurs* was entrusted by Jean Cocteau to his young secretary Paul Morihien and carried out by Robert Denoël. Terrified by the book he was publishing, and perhaps fearing he might find himself joining the author in prison, this 'very wicked gentleman', as Genet called him, did not think it was enough to remove the name of his publishing house from the book's cover: he demanded that the author's name should be removed as well. Genet was furious and indignant. ('He's risking prison? I've spent my whole life there,' he said to Cocteau, who pleaded with him to accept.) He refused point blank: his name was his only property. Besides, the repeated flourishing of his surname within his work would have rendered the precaution futile. Printed in Paris (and not Monte Carlo, as the original edition states in order to create a false trail) in December 1943, the 350 copies of *Notre-Dame-des-Fleurs* were, for the most part, sold discreetly after the Liberation to people in Cocteau's circle.

We also owe to Paul Morihien, Genet's first publisher, the splendid but anonymous edition of *Querelle de Brest*, printed in November 1947, and illustrated with audacious (but unsigned) drawings by Cocteau. Some of the 524 copies printed were seized by the police the following year during a raid on the bookshop run by Paul Morihien just round the corner from Cocteau's flat in the Palais-Royal district. The original edition of Genet's most outrageous work, *Pompes funèbres*, where the image of a member of [Pétain's] militia and a German soldier is set up as a votive offering to the memory of Jean Decarnin, a young Communist member of the resistance, killed during the battle to liberate Paris, strangely gives 'Bikini' as the place of publication.

In reality it was Gallimard in Paris who clandestinely printed the 495 copies. Having been charmed by Genet, an author who was dear to him in every sense of the term, Gaston Gallimard crept cautiously in December 1947, after two years of hesitation, onto the slippery slope of illegality. But he was so inexperienced in clandestine publishing that he soon decided to entrust others with the task of disposing of the works through alternative channels.

It was in Switzerland that *Journal du Voleur* first appeared. Albert Skira, the unacknowledged father of the original edition, printed 400 copies of the book at Geneva, giving 'no date or place of publication', as the bibliographies put it. Ignored by the numerous catalogues of the publishing house, *Journal du Voleur* was clandestinely despatched to Paris one autumn night in 1948.

It is not of purely historical interest to recall these circumstances. They had a major impact on the works themselves. Being marginalised and excluded – against Genet's own wishes – from the traditional channels of publishing, Genet's major work was consequently developed outside of any sort of regulation, without obstacles of any kind, and even without any concern about its reception (not a single review of his clandestinely published works appeared in the press). It unfolded in the realm of the unpublishable. As a result it is possible to trace how the work increases in violence and in power from *Notre-Dame-des-Fleurs* to *Querelle de Brest*. *Journal du Voleur*, which is dedicated to Sartre and Simone de Beauvoir, appears from this point of view already tainted and perhaps weakened by the beginnings of social acceptance.

The almost unmediated transition from such private publication to the appearance in 1951 of the *Œuvres Complètes* published by Gallimard, has the air of a publishing *coup d'état*. Instigated by Sartre, who wrote the preface, but who also interceded on his behalf with Gallimard, this produced a sudden upheaval in Genet's social and literary status: the small-time crook had been turned into a great writer, when he was scarcely forty years old, when he had only been writing for nine years, and when most of his works were totally unknown. Gaston Gallimard's undertaking, going ahead of public opinion, was thus a real publishing achievement.

This consecration had a perverse effect: since at the time it seemed impossible to publish Genet's books as they stood, his publisher asked him to expurgate his texts to avoid censorship. Genet conformed to this requirement so well that Robert Gallimard, who had partial responsibility for the publication, protested at the extent of the cuts and asked for certain passages to be restored. Thus access to a 'normal' mode of publishing was accompanied by a normalisation of the texts themselves, the expurgated versions of which continue to be propagated in many current editions of the works, notably in all the translations.

The publication of Genet's *Œuvres Complètes* – which was already inherently surprising – also gave rise to one of the most famous aberrations of modern literary history: Sartre's preface. Sartre's commentary fills the whole of the first volume of the series (which is by far the largest). So, if an unsuspecting reader goes into a bookshop and asks for the first volume of Genet's works, he will come out with a book by Sartre. Within his own works, Genet is allowed to speak only when we reach Volume II.

The strangeness of this form of publication thus raises an insidious question about the friendly 'contest' which brought the writer and the philosopher into contact and set them one against the other: which one is swallowing the other?

For a long time the winner seemed to be Sartre: a whole generation, including the major critics of their time (Blanchot, Bataille ...) read Genet through Sartre, thought they were reading Genet when they were reading Sartre. But today Genet seems to have become the definitive winner: most of his new readers have read him in paper-back editions (published since 1976) or became aware of his work through his major plays, written later than Sartre's essay. But things are not so simple: although recent research, notably Edmund White's fine book on Genet's life, has shown that most of the biographical elements on which Sartre built his monument are erroneous, these mistakes have in no way invalidated Sartre's essay, which retains all its persuasive power in face of and against the facts.

Now what sort of book draws its strength, not from references to reality, but from its internal coherence? The novel. So Sartre didn't lose the game, but in the debate between literature and philosophy set in motion by the publication of Genet's *Œuvres Complètes*, it is literature that has the final word.

Bibliography

1. WORKS BY GENET

Jean Genet's *Œuvres Complètes* is published in six volumes by Éditions Gallimard, Paris
I: Jean-Paul Sartre, *Saint Genet, comédien et martyr* (1952)
II: *Notre-Dame-des-Fleurs, Le Condamné à Mort, Miracle de la Rose, Un Chant d'Amour* (1951)
III: *Pompes funèbres, Le Pêcheur du Suquet, Querelle de Brest* (1953)
IV: *L'Étrange mot d' ..., Ce qui et resté d'un Rembrandt déchiré en petits carrés ..., Le Balcon, Les Bonnes, Haute surveillance, Lettres à Roger Blin, Comment jouer 'Les Bonnes', Comment jouer 'Le Balcon'* (1968)
V: *Le Funambule, Le Secret de Rembrandt, L'Atelier d'Alberto Giacometti, Les Nègres, Les Paravents, L'Enfant criminel* (1979)
VI: *L'Ennemi déclaré: textes et entretiens*, edited by Albert Dichy (1991)

'Adame Miroir/L'Enfant criminel (Paul Morihien, Paris, 1949)
L'Atelier d'Alberto Giacometti, Les Bonnes, L'Enfant criminel, Le Funambule (L'Arbalète, Décines, 1958)
Le Balcon, with lithograph by Alberto Giacometti (L'Arbalète, Décines, 1956; revised edition with preface, 1960)
The Balcony, translated by Bernard Frechtman (Faber and Faber, London, 1960)
The Balcony, translated by Bernard Frechtman (Grove Press, New York, 1960)
The Blacks, translated by Bernard Frechtman (Faber and Faber, London, 1960)
The Blacks, translated by Bernard Frechtman (Grove Press, New York, 1960)
Les Bonnes (first version L'Arbalète, Lyons, 1947; both versions J-J Pauvert, Sceaux, 1954)
Un Captif amoureux (Gallimard, Paris, 1986)
Le Condamné à Mort (L'Arbalete, Décines, 1948)
'Four Hours in Shatila' in *Journal of Palestine Studies*, 6, 1 (1983)
Fragments ... et autres textes, with preface by Edmund White (Gallimard, Paris, 1990)
Funeral Rites, translated by Bernard Frechtman (first published by Anthony Blond, London, 1969; Panther Books, London, 1971)
Funeral Rites, translated by Bernard Frechtman (Grove Press, New York, 1987)
Haute surveillance (Gallimard, Paris, 1947, 1949)
Interview with Hubert Fichte in *The New Review*, Vol. 4, No. 37, April 1977, translated by Patrick McCarthy (originally published in *Die Zeit*, 13 February 1976)
Interview with Madeleine Gobeil in *Playboy*, April 1964
Introduction to *Soledad Brother: the Prison Letters of George Jackson* (Cape, London, 1971)
'Jean Genet, Affirmation of Existence Through Rebellion', interview with Jean Genet and Leila Shahid Barrada by Rüdiger Wischenbart in *Journal of Palestine Studies*, Winter 1987, Vol. XVI, No. 2, Issue 62
'Jean Genet et la condition des immigrés' in *L'Humanité*, 3 May 1974
Journal du Voleur (Gallimard, Paris, 1949)
Lettres à Olga et Marc Barbezat: (L'Arbalète, Décines, 1988)
The Maids/Deathwatch, translated by Bernard Frechtman (Grove Press, New York, 1954, 1962)
The Maids/Deathwatch, translated by Bernard Frechtman (Faber and Faber, London, 1961)
May Day Speech (City Lights Books, San Francisco, 1970)

Miracle of the Rose, translated by Bernard Frechtman (first published by Anthony Blond, London, 1965; Penguin, Harmondsworth, 1971)

Miracle of the Rose, translated by Bernard Frechtman (Grove Press, New York, 1966)

Les Nègres (L'Arbalète, Décines, 1958; new edition with 33 photographs from the original production, 1960)

Les Nègres au port de la lune (Éditions de la Différence, Bordeaux, 1988)

Our Lady of the Flowers, translated by Bernard Frechtman (first published by Anthony Blond, London, 1964; Panther Books, London, 1966)

Our Lady of the Flowers, translated by Bernard Frechtman (Grove Press, New York, 1963)

'The Palestinians' in *Journal of Palestine Studies*, 3, 1 (1973)

Les Paravents (L'Arbalète, Décines, 1961)

Poèmes (*Le Condamné à Mort, La Galère, La Parade, Un Chant d'Amour, Le Pêcheur du Suquet*) (L'Arbalète, Décines, 1962)

Pompes funèbres (Gallimard, Paris, 1953)

Prisoner of Love, translated by Barbara Bray with introduction by Edmund White (Picador, London, 1989)

Querelle of Brest (first published by Anthony Blond, London, 1966; translated by Gregory Streatham, Faber and Faber, London, 1973)

Querelle of Brest, translated by Anselm Hollo (Grove Press, New York, 1989)

Reflections on the Theatre and other writings, translated by Richard Seaver (Faber and Faber, London, 1972)

The Screens, translated by Bernard Frechtman (Grove Press, New York, 1962)

The Screens, translated by Bernard Frechtman (Faber and Faber, London, 1963, 1987)

Splendid's (L'Arbalète, Décines, 1993)

Splendid's, translated by Neil Bartlett (Faber and Faber, London, 1995)

The Thief's Journal, translated by Bernard Frechtman (Grove Press, New York, 1964)

The Thief's Journal, translated by Bernard Frechtman (first published by Anthony Blond, London, 1965; Penguin, Harmondsworth, 1967)

'Violence et brutalité' in *Le Monde*, 2 September 1977

2. GENERAL BIBLIOGRAPHY

Arthur Adamov, *Théâtre de Société: Scènes d'Actualité* (Les Éditeurs Français Réunis, Paris, 1958)

Dennis Altman, *Homosexuality: Oppression and Liberation* (Outerbridge and Dienstfrey, New York, 1971)

Antonin Artaud, *La Culture Indienne* in *Œuvres Complètes XII* (Gallimard, Paris, 1974)

—, *Lettres à André Breton* in *L'Éphémère*, 8, 1968

—, Notes for *Pour en finir avec le jugement de dieu* in *Œuvres Complètes XIII* (Gallimard, Paris, 1974)

—, *Préambule* in *Œuvres Complètes I* (Gallimard, Paris, 1976)

—, *Le Théâtre et Culture* in *Œuvres Complètes IV* (Gallimard, Paris, 1980)

—, *The Theatre and its Double*, translated by Mary Caroline Richards (Grove Press Inc., New York, 1958)

Aux Écoutes du monde, 6 January 1956

Stephen Barber, *Weapons of Liberation* (Faber and Faber, London, 1996)

Lynda Bellity Peskine and Albert Dichy, *La Bataille des Paravents* (IMEC, Paris, 1991)

Ian Birchall, *Workers Against the Monolith* (Pluto, London, 1974)

Jean Le Bitoux and Gilles Barbedette, 'Jean-Paul Sartre et les homosexuels', interview with Sartre in *Le Gai Pied*, 13 April 1980

Roger Blin, *Souvenirs et propos*, edited by Lynda Bellity Peskine (Gallimard, Paris, 1986)

François Bourgeat, *Djurdjura* (Théâtrales, Paris, 1991)

David Bradby, 'Images of the Algerian War on the French stage 1988–92' in *French Cultural Studies*, Vol. 5, June 1994

—, 'Images de la guerre d'Algérie sur la scène française' in *Théâtre/Public*, No. 123, May–June 1995

André Breton, *Position politique du surréalisme* (Denoël/Gonthier, Paris, 1972)

Michael Bronski, *Culture Clash: The Making of Gay Sensibility* (South End Press, Boston, 1984)

Peter Brooks and Joseph Halpern (eds), *Genet: A Collection of Critical Essays* (Prentice-Hall Inc., Englewood Cliffs, New Jersey, 1979)

Maurice Chevaly, *Genet I: L'Amour cannibale* (Éditions Le Temps Parallèle, Marseilles, 1989)

—, *Genet II: L'Enfer à Fleur de Peau* (Éditions Le Temps Parallèle, Marseilles, 1989)

Mohammed Choukri, *Jean Genet in Tangier*, translated by Paul Bowles with introduction by William Burroughs (Ecco Press, New York, 1974)

Hélène Cixous, *Three Steps on the Ladder of Writing*, translated by Sarah Cornell and Susan Sellers (Columbia University Press, New York, 1993)

Richard Coe, *The Vision of Jean Genet* (Peter Owen, London, 1968)

Douglas Collins, *Sartre as Biographer* (Harvard University Press, Cambridge (Massachusetts), 1980)

David Cooper, 'Sartre on Genet' in *New Left Review*, 25, May/June 1964

Antony Copley, *Sexual Moralities in France 1780–1980* (Routledge, London and New York, 1989)

Donald Webster Cory, *The Homosexual in America* (Paperback Library, New York, 1963)

Quentin Crisp, *The Naked Civil Servant* (Rinehart and Winston, New York, 1968)

Margaret Cruikshank, *The Gay and Lesbian Movement* (Routledge, New York, 1992)

Albert Dichy (ed.), *L'Ennemi déclaré: textes et entretiens* in Jean Genet, *Œuvres Complètes VI* (Gallimard, Paris, 1991)

Albert Dichy and Pascal Fouché, *Jean Genet: essai de chronologie 1910–1944* (Bibliothèque de Littérature française contemporaine de l'Université Paris 7, Paris, 1988)

Bernard Dort, 'Genet ou le combat avec le théâtre' in *Théâtres* (Seuil, Paris, 1986)

HL Dreyfus and Paul Robinow (eds), *Michel Foucault: Beyond Structuralism and Hermaneutics* (Harvester, London, 1982)

Martin Duberman, *Stonewall* (Dutton, New York, 1993)

Eugène Durif, *B M C* (Comp'Act, Paris, 1992)

Georges Fleury, *La Guerre en Algérie* (Plon, Paris, 1993)

Michel Foucault, *Discipline and Punish*, translated by Alan Sheridan (Penguin, London, 1979)

Hans-Georg Gadamer, *Truth and Method* (Sheed and Ward, London, 1975)

J Ellen Gainor (ed.), *Imperialism and Theatre* (Routledge, London, 1995)

Jane Giles, *The Cinema of Jean Genet: Un Chant d'Amour* (BFI, London, 1991)

Juan Goytisolo, *Makbara*, translated by Helen Lane (Seaver Books, New York, 1981)

—, *Makbara*, translated by Helen Lane (Serpent's Tail, London, 1993)

—, *The Virtues of the Solitary Bird*, translated by Helen Seaver (Serpent's Tail, London, 1991)

Daniel Guérin, *Son Testament* (Encre Éditions, Paris, 1979)

Jérôme Hankins (ed.), *Genet à Chatila* (Solin, Paris, 1992)

Michael Stephen Henderson, 'Discourses of the Self: Confession in the Works of Jean Genet', doctoral thesis (University of California, 1991)

L'Humanité, 12 March 1949

Eugène Ionesco, *Notes et Contre-notes* (Gallimard, Paris, 1962)

—, *Notes et Contre-notes*, translated by Donald Watson (Calder, London, 1965)

Jean-Pierre Januel, article in *Masques*, No. 2, Autumn 1979

Andrei Jdanov [Zhdanov], *Sur la littérature, la philosophie et la musique* (Éditions Norman Béthune, Paris, 1972)

Carl Gustav Jung, *Memories, Dreams, Reflections*, recorded and edited by Aniela Jaffé (Collins, London, 1983)

Jean Kanapa, *L'Existentialisme n'est pas un humanisme* (Éditions Sociales, Paris, 1947)

Michael Kaufman (ed.), *Beyond Patriarchy: Essays by Men on Pleasure, Power and Change* (Oxford University Press, Toronto, 1987)

Robert Kemp, 'Répugnances' in *Les Nouvelles littéraires*, 14 August 1952

Seymour Kleinberg, *Alienated Affections* (St Martin's Press, New York, 1980)

Bernard-Marie Koltès, *Le Retour au Désert* (Minuit, Paris, 1988)

Bernard-Marie Koltès and François Regnault, *La Famille des orties; esquisses et croquis autour des Paravents de Jean Genet* (Éditions Nanterre/Amandiers, Paris, 1983)

Milan Kundera, *Life is Elsewhere* (Faber and Faber, London, 1986)

Jacques Lacan, 'Motifs du crime paranoïaque; le crime des sœurs Papin' in *Le Minotaur*, No. 3, December 1933

Daniel Lemahieu, *Djebels* (Actes Sud-Papiers, Paris, 1988)

Jean Marais, *Histoires de ma vie* (Albin Michel, Paris, 1975)

Tony Marotta, *The Politics of Homosexuality* (Houghton, Boston, 1981)

Maurice Merleau-Ponty, *Humanisme et terreur* (Paris, 1947)

—, 'Les Jours de notre vie' in *Les Temps modernes*, 51, January 1950

Kate Millett, *Sexual Politics* (Garden City, New York, 1969)

Kate Millett, *Sexual Politics* (Virago, London, 1977)

Jean-Bernard Moraly, *Jean Genet – La vie écrite* (Éditions de la Différence, Paris, 1988)

M Morris and P Patton (eds), *Michel Foucault: Power, Truth, Strategy* (Sydney, 1979)

Camille Naish, *A Genetic Approach to Structures in the Work of Jean Genet* (Harvard University Press, Cambridge (Massachusetts), 1978)

Friedrich Nietzsche, *Thus Spoke Zarathustra: A Book for Everyone and No One*, translated by RJ Hollingdale (London, 1990)

—, *Twilight of the Idols* or *How to Philosophise with a Hammer* and *The Anti-Christ*, translated by RJ Hollingdale (London, 1990)

Tony Parker, *The Unknown Citizen* (Penguin, Harmondsworth, 1966)

Kenneth Patchen, *An Astonished Eye Looks Out of the Air* (Untide Press, Waldport, 1945)

Gene A Plunka, *The Rites of Passage of Jean Genet, The Art and Aesthetics of Risk Taking* (Fairleigh Dickinson University Press, London and Toronto, 1992)

Jacques Prevel, *En compagnie d'Antonin Artaud* (Flammarion, Paris, 1974)

Simon Raven, *Boys will be Boys* (Anthony Blond, London, 1963)

CJ Rawson, 'Cannibalism and Fiction: Part II: Love and Eating in Fielding, Mailer, Genet and Wittig' in *Genre*, Vol. 2, No. 2, 1978

Edward Said, 'Cry Palestine' in *New Statesman and Society*, 10 November 1995

Jean-Paul Sartre, *Cahiers pour une morale* (Gallimard, Paris, 1983)

—, *Critique de la raison dialectique* (Gallimard, Paris, 1960)

—, *Les Mots* (Gallimard, Paris, 1964)

—, *Qu'est-ce que la littérature?* (Gallimard, Paris, 1964)

—, *Réflexions sur la question juive* (Gallimard, Paris, 1946)

—, *Saint Genet, comédien et martyr* in Jean Genet, *Œuvres Complètes I* (Gallimard, Paris, 1952)

—, *Saint Genet, Actor and Martyr*, translated by Bernard Frechtman (George Braziller, New York, 1963)

—, *Situations III* (Gallimard, Paris, 1949)

—, *Situations VI* (Gallimard, Paris, 1964)

—, *Situations VII* (Gallimard, Paris, 1965)

—, *What is Literature?*, translated by Bernard Frechtman (Methuen and Co. Ltd, London, 1987)

—, *Words*, translated by Irene Clephane (Penguin, Harmondsworth, 1985)

Jeanette L Savona, *Jean Genet* (Macmillan, London and New York, 1983)

Michael Silverstein, 'God Save the Queen' in *Gay Sunshine*, November 1970

Patti Smith, *The Coral Sea* (WW Norton and Co., New York and London, 1996)

—, *Early Work, 1970–1979* (WW Norton and Co., New York and London, 1994)

—, *Woolgathering* (Hanuman Books, New York and Madras, 1992)

Charles Socarides, 'The Growth of Overt Homosexuality in the City Provokes Wide Concern' in *The New York Times*, 17 December 1963

Susan Sontag, *Against interpretation and other essays* (Farrar, Straus and Giroux Inc., New York, 1966)

—, *Against interpretation and other essays* (Eyre and Spottiswoode, London, 1967)

—, *Under the Sign of Saturn* (Vintage Books, New York, 1980)

Benjamin Stora, *La Gangrène et l'oubli* (La Découverte, Paris, 1991)

Philip Thody, *Jean Genet: A Study of his Novels and Plays* (Hamish Hamilton, London, 1968)

Michel Vinaver, *Les Huissiers* (1958), reprinted in *Théâtre Complet*, Vol. 1 (Actes Sud, Arles, 1986)

—, *Iphigénie Hotel* (1960), reprinted in *Théâtre Complet*, Vol. 1 (Actes Sud, Arles, 1986)

—, *Les Voies de la création théâtrale*, Vol. 4, (CNRS, Paris, 1975)

Edmund White, *Genet: A Biography* (Chatto and Windus, London, 1993)

—, *Genet: A Biography* (Alfred Knopf, New York, 1993)

—, *Nocturnes for the King of Naples* (St Martin's Press, New York, 1978)

—, *Nocturnes for the King of Naples* (Deutsch, London, 1980)

—, *The Selected Writings of Jean Genet* (The Ecco Press, New Jersey, 1993)

Oscar Wilde, *The Picture of Dorian Gray* (Dover Publications, New York, 1993)

—, *The Picture of Dorian Gray* (Penguin, London, 1994)

Anno Wilms, *Lindsay Kemp and his Company*, with preface by Derek Jarman (GM Press, London, 1987)

Index